GREAT BRITAIN AND

The Confederate Navy,

1861–1865

JOHN BULL'S NEUTRALITY

"Look here, boys, I don't care twopence for your noise; but if you throw stones at my windows I must *thrash you both*. (*Punch*—October 3, 1863)

GREAT BRITAIN AND

The Confederate Navy,

1861–1865

Frank J. Merli

With a foreword by Howard Jones

INDIANA UNIVERSITY PRESS
BLOOMINGTON • INDIANAPOLIS

This book is a publication of

Indiana University Press
601 North Morton Street
Bloomington, Indiana 47404-3797 USA

http://iupress.indiana.edu

Telephone orders   800-842-6796
Fax orders   812-855-7931
Orders by e-mail   iuporder@indiana.edu

First published 1970 as part of the Indiana University Social Science Series
(No. 27) and copyrighted 1965, 1970 by Frank J. Merli. Reprinted 2004
with a new foreword.

The paper used in this publication meets the minimum requirements of
American National Standard for Information Sciences — Permanence of
Paper for Printed Library Materials, ANSI Z39.48-1984.

Manufactured in the United States of America

Cataloging information is available from the Library of Congress.
ISBN 0-253-21735-0 (pbk. : alk. paper)

1 2 3 4 5 09 08 07 06 05 04

TO THE MEMORY OF
Thomas W. Green
SOUTHAMPTON
ENGLAND

Contents

Illustrations

Foreword

It is my distinct pleasure to write the foreword to Frank J. Merli's 1970 classic study, *Great Britain and the Confederate Navy, 1861–1865*. If ever a historian has succeeded in bringing attention to the international dimension of the American Civil War, Frank has done so in this masterful work. Richly researched, elegantly written, and soundly reasoned, his model monograph stands at the top of the list of those surprisingly few studies that examine the role of foreign issues in shaping the outcome of America's most cataclysmic event. For too long, writers have focused almost exclusively on leaders and land battles at the expense of acknowledging the importance of diplomatic and naval affairs in the Civil War. Frank, however, chose to address the latter, much to the betterment of our field.

For nearly four decades, from the time I met Frank until his untimely death in late December 2000, our friendship was personally close and professionally integral to my own writings on Civil War diplomacy. How readily did he share his revelations from the "Merli Archives" that derived from a vast array of depositories both in the United States and in England. How willingly did he take time from his own research and writing to read and reread my first foray into the labyrinth of Anglo-American relations during the Civil War. How much better my manuscript after he had waded through it, offering generous, gracious, and always gentlemanly suggestions that I eagerly incorporated into the final work. Indeed, *Union in Peril: The Crisis over British Intervention in the Civil War* bears Frank's imprint as silent collaborator.

Frank and I were extremely fortunate to have studied with
Professor Robert H. Ferrell at Indiana University and to have
had our writings benefit from the "Ferrell Treatment." Not
only did Professor Ferrell provide expert guidance in research, but he taught the twin pillar of writing. What is the
value of research if the writer fails to convey the meaning and
importance of events in an interesting manner? The bane of
historians is a turgidly written and highly detailed manuscript
aimed only at specialists in some obscure niche in the field.
There, on the campus in Bloomington, Professor Ferrell
warned against the dangers of the adjective, of passive voice,
of baggage words, and of incorporating every note into the
manuscript. Frank certainly carried away these lessons, as
shown in both his teaching and his writing while at Queens
College in New York for more than thirty years.

*   *   *   *   *

Both perception and mythology played vital roles in Civil War
diplomacy. The South mistakenly believed that its rich stores
of cotton would pressure the British into sympathizing with
its drive for independence; the North just as erroneously suspected the British of conspiring with southerners to destroy
the Union. As Frank convincingly demonstrates, Prime Minister Lord Palmerston and his foreign secretary, Lord John
Russell, pursued a policy of "indifferent neutrality" (p. 255)
toward the American war. In summarizing Palmerston's thinking, Frank asserts that Britain "had neither eternal friendships nor eternal enmities. She had only eternal interests" (p.
259). Those interests, the South ultimately realized, did not
dictate intervention in the American war. From the British
perspective, southern separation appeared to be the only
practical solution to preventing a prolonged war that would
devastate North *and* South while hurting other nations' commerce as well.

To stop the war, the Palmerston ministry, Frank argues,
came "perilously close" (p. 257) to offering a mediation in
the autumn of 1862, only to shy away when it feared that
intervention could lead to war with the Union. British interest in mediation had risen after the South's victory at Second

Bull Run in late August, but the lethal stalemate at Antietam the following month, according to Frank, convinced the Palmerston ministry that the South had not yet proved itself on the battlefield. Moreover, neither Palmerston nor Russell could ignore the South's ties with slavery, despite early assertions by both North and South that their conflict related exclusively to Union and independence. Even though Palmerston considered mediation the most feasible approach to ending the war, he came to realize that the Union considered *any* interventionist proposal a hostile act.

Especially intriguing is Frank's analysis of French involvement in these events. Emperor Louis Napoleon III seemingly toyed with the Confederacy, repeatedly suggesting that he favored the South but refusing to intervene until the British took the initiative. At one point he told British shipping magnate, parliamentary member, and Confederate sympathizer William S. Lindsay in Paris that he might even act unilaterally in supporting a European call for opening southern ports by a "proper demonstration of force" (p. 188). "It was a vague promise," Frank insists, "the kind at which the wily emperor was a master" (p. 188). As heir to a once powerful and sprawling French empire, Napoleon III exploited the American conflict in an attempt to re-establish his nation's glory in Europe and to build a puppet regime in Mexico. "Nothing," Frank asserts, "illustrates the Southern capacity for self-delusion so well as their naïve insistence that Napoleon III was an active partisan of their cause" (p. 223). By the autumn of 1864 Confederate leaders had recognized the perfidy of the emperor. As their minister in Paris, John Slidell, bitterly remarked after so many dashed hopes, "The weak have no rights; the strong no obligations" (p. 225).

Small consolation perhaps, but the truth about French motives had eluded the Union as much as it had the Confederacy. From Washington's viewpoint, a French intervention, either with or without England's participation, posed a serious threat that President Abraham Lincoln and his secretary of state, William H. Seward, had to combat along with an early string of lost battles and weak military leaders at home.

Frank's enduring contribution is to remind us of the international scope of history by, in this instance, weaving the South's attempt to build a navy in England (as well as in France) into the diplomatic and maritime fabric of the Civil War. He shows how this "modern" war rested heavily on naval technology while also demonstrating how both Lincoln and his counterpart in the South, President Jefferson Davis, struggled over maritime affairs along with the fighting on land. The Union navy, however, was stodgy and out of date both in its organization and in its ships, whereas the founders of the Confederate navy, Stephen Mallory as secretary and James Bulloch as his talented contractor overseas, were forward looking and innovative. In this regard, Frank tells an intricate story of the subterfuge waged by Bulloch against the Union consul in Liverpool, Thomas Dudley, as they grappled over the clandestine Confederate shipbuilding enterprise. Unfortunately for the South, Davis failed to grasp the importance of sea power to the war, and his followers lacked the necessary industrial resources and knowledgeable workforce to build an effective navy. In the meantime, the South's inept fiscal arrangements eroded the naval effort from within, resulting in conflicting policies and chaotic financial dealings. The South *might* have won recognition and the outcome of the war *might* have been different, Frank argues, had the Confederacy succeeded in building a navy based on swift-moving cruisers capable of raiding Union commerce and running the blockade, and on ironclad rams designed to attack Union blockaders and protect the southern coast.

But this was not to be, Frank says, because the Palmerston ministry never found it in the British national interest to intervene in the war. First, a tenuous balance in the House of Commons repeatedly stymied the London government, seldom giving it the political freedom to act without decisions laden with compromises. Second, Palmerston was the arch pragmatist who, although not supportive of either the French or the Americans, refused to take any action that freed Napoleon to pursue his adventurous pursuits or that dragged the crown into the American war. "Those who in quarrels interpose will often get a bloody nose," Palmerston warned Russell; "if you would keep out of strife, step not in twixt man and wife" (p. 39). Third, even though the prime minister and his foreign secretary opposed slavery, they saw no overriding motive to become involved in the conflict. This proved especially difficult for Russell, who as a Whig viewed it as a struggle for southern independence against northern empire and yet as an Englishman favored emancipation over secession. Strict neutrality offered the wisest solution. Only the "fortune of arms," he asserted, could justify recognizing the South as a nation (p. 40).

Frank heavily criticizes Confederate diplomacy while praising that of the Union, but he admits that even if the South had had capable diplomatists, it could *not* have altered the war's verdict. The South's chief diplomat in London, James Mason, was "arrogant" and "a little dense," while "heavy-handed in negotiation and too sure of his own opinions." Indeed, Frank concludes, Mason "probably did the South more harm than good" (p. 31). The Union minister to England, however, was Charles Francis Adams, the highly respected descendant of the august Massachusetts family that had produced two presidents. Only when it appeared that the South had acquired ironclad rams did he lose his characteristic diplomatic demeanor and rashly proclaim to Russell in a note of September 5, 1863, "It would be superfluous in me to point out to your Lordship that this is war" (p. 201). Russell, however, had already decided against allowing the Laird rams to fall into southern hands — thus ignoring his legal advisers and choosing instead to purchase them for the Royal Navy. "September at Birkenhead, no less than July at Gettysburg, doomed the Confederacy," Frank concludes (p. 194). And yet, he asserts, had the rams made it to the Confederacy, it remains problematical whether they would have made any difference in the war.

In the end, Frank insists, the Palmerston ministry recognized the danger of intervention and, although not always on solid legal ground, devised ways to stay out of the conflict. The British Foreign Enlistment Act of 1819 was the real culprit, for it permitted the building of warships in British yards as long as the builders did not equip or arm them and they did not go to a nation at war with Britain. As Bulloch saw matters, all he had to do was equip a contracted vessel outside England. Adams found it impossible to prove to the British courts' satisfaction that the equipping had taken place inside England, that the ship had been built for the Confederacy, and that its purpose was to war against the United States. But Russell had to take some remedial action in view of the rising number of claims against British insurance companies combined with angry calls from shipping firms to exert greater control over maritime affairs. How much easier it would have been, Frank ponders, if Parliament had been politically free to authorize the government to seize suspected war vessels departing England to countries not licensed to receive them. But once the outcome of the war became clear, he wryly observes, "Britain did what was necessary rather than what was legal" (p. 256).

One of the many tragedies associated with Frank's early death is his unfinished work on the *Alabama* crisis during the Civil War. No one could be more familiar with the primary sources than was Frank. His story threatened to remain untold until the editors at Indiana University Press recently made two wise decisions. One was to reissue this path-breaking work on the Confederacy's attempt to build a navy; the other was to invite David Fahey, a specialist in Anglo-American social history and close friend of Frank's, to complete his career-long study of the *Alabama*. So together, and fittingly so, have appeared Frank's two signature works, *Great Britain and the Confederate Navy* and *The Alabama, British Neutrality, and the American Civil War.*

Frank is sorely missed by his wife Margaret and family, his friends, his students and colleagues at Queens College, the profession, and all others fortunate to have known him. But his words remain alive here, providing a rich testimonial of his devotion to his craft. This book on the Confederate navy along with his posthumous study of the *Alabama* illustrate how seriously Frank regarded the responsibility of writing history and how closely he adhered to that sacred task.

Howard Jones
University of Alabama
June 2004

Preface

This book, which is part of a larger study of Anglo-American relations in the nineteenth century, has a double purpose. First, an attempt has been made to examine the responses of Her Majesty's government to Confederate efforts to build naval craft in British yards. Although the highlights of that story are well known, many of its details have never been spelled out. It is of particular interest that Southern shipbuilding provided Crown officials with a number of widely spaced opportunities to evaluate the consequences of such activity and to relate their conclusions to the constantly evolving definitions of British national interests. Because Confederate naval construction impinged on many other facets of policy making over a long period of time, a study of the program provides the investigator with a perspective and continuity that are lacking in other approaches for measuring the British attitude toward the war. The second—more difficult—task was that of relating the findings of this study to that growing body of recent books on the international dimension of the American Civil War. The past decade or so has seen publication of a number of major works on this subject—one thinks immediately of those by Warren Spencer and Lynn Case, Martin Duberman, Joseph Hernon, Jr., Glyndon Van Deusen, Philip Van Doren Stern, and Stuart Bernath.

In the present study, which can be considered an extended essay in Anglo-American history, I have tried to focus on the leading problems as they must have appeared to the statesmen at Whitehall and Windsor. Like all such studies, this one owes a heavy intellectual debt to the classic account by E. D. Adams,

Great Britain and the American Civil War—a work for which I have a high professional regard. Wherever it has seemed necessary to take issue with earlier views on the subject of the British response to the war, I have offered my "revisions" with much trepidation and a keen awareness that at many crucial points the evidence is incomplete, ambiguous, or open to alternative interpretation. In the main, however, I have been less concerned "to startle with new material" than "to persuade with old."

A consideration of the following chapters should make it evident that I have had to stray into areas—for example, naval technology and legal theory—that I am imperfectly familiar with; I therefore hope that readers more expert than I am in such fields will tolerate these excursions into their professional domains.

MECKLENBURGH SQUARE, LONDON

Summer, 1970

F. J. M.

Acknowledgments

In preparing this book for publication, I have incurred many personal and professional debts, and though it is impossible to mention all the persons or institutions that have assisted me, a few of them merit special mention and public thanks.

Material from the Royal Archives at Windsor Castle is used by gracious permission of Her Majesty Queen Elizabeth II. Mr Robert Mackworth-Young and Miss Jane Langton (with their assistants) made my work at Windsor a most enjoyable experience. Material from the Public Record Office, London, is used by permission of the Controller of Her Majesty's Stationery Office. Mr K. Timings first introduced me to the resources of the PRO, and over the years he has been generous in his assistance to me. The Trustees of the Broadlands Estate kindly permitted me to use the papers of Lord Palmerston, and Miss Frances Ranger made my work in that valuable collection easy and pleasant. Material from the British Museum is used by permission of the Keeper of Manuscripts, Mr T. C. Skeat. Mr Rupert Jarvis, former librarian of H. M. Customs and Excise Library, shared with me his vast knowledge of the records of that institution. Mr E. W. Paget-Tomlinson of Liverpool and Mr A. S. E. Browning of Glasgow answered a large number of technical questions and furnished useful information about shipbuilding in the 1860s. Professor Peter Payne allowed me access to two important collections of material and helped me search through them. Officials of Alexander Stephen and Sons, Ltd., of Glasgow opened their records of Civil War shipbuilding and allowed me free use of them.

Mr John Bailey of London and Mr Vernon Simms of St Albans

provided hospitality and good cheer on many occasions, as did a number of others during my visits to England and Scotland.

Professor Gerald Graham of King's College, University of London, gave me expert guidance during my year at that institution and allowed me to test some of my ideas in his seminar. Professor John Hawgood of Birmingham University invited me to address some of his students, initiating thereby a long friendship. The director and staff of the United States Educational Commission in the United Kingdom offered generous assistance to me, while fellow Fulbright scholars C. S. Williams, B. J. Rahn, and M. Uehling took time from their own research to help with mine.

In Great Britain the directors and staffs of the following institutions helped in many ways: Public Record Office, British Museum, City of Liverpool Museum, Kelvin Grove Museum, Mitchell Library, Southampton Public Library, Historical Manuscripts Commission, National Register of Archives, Bodleian Library, Scottish Record Office, H. M. Customs and Excise Library, and the Institute of Historical Research.

In America the directors and staffs of many archives and libraries provided expert assistance: Indiana University, Harvard University, Princeton University, University of Chicago, University of North Carolina, University of Rochester, Norfolk Public Library, New York Public Library, New York State Historical Society, Franklin D. Roosevelt Library, Huntington Library, Library of Congress, and the National Archives.

The U.S. State Department gave me a Fulbright award for a year of study in Great Britain; the Graduate School of Indiana University has provided generous financial support over many years—including a subsidy to defray the cost of manufacturing this book. Mrs Rose Temple of Terre Haute, Indiana, generously endowed a "summer fellowship for Frank" to allow me to return to England for a few months of intensive research.

The editors of *Civil War Times Illustrated, American Neptune, Maryland Historical Magazine, Civil War History,* and *History Today* have granted permission to reproduce material that originally appeared in their journals. Rear Admiral E. M. Eller, Director of Naval History, U.S. Navy Department, and his staff have provided valuable assistance. Mr Philip Van Doren

Stern helped in the early stages of the work, providing encouragement, good advice, and many hours of conversation on the subject of the Confederate navy; his warm response to my initial request for aid was much appreciated. Professor Gerald Strauss of Indiana University read an early draft of the work and offered many useful suggestions for improvement—in fact, his dissatisfaction with that version spurred a major revision. Professor T. A. Wilson of the University of Kansas assisted in a number of important ways, as did William E. Geoghegan of the Smithsonian Institution, Capt. R. Steen Steensen of the Royal Danish Navy, and Mr J. A. Yocum of Evansville, Indiana. Professors Lynn Case and Warren Spencer provided a useful exchange of views on the French side of the story.

During a period of little progress, my former colleague, David Fahey (now at Miami University, Oxford, Ohio) read the entire manuscript with a sharp eye, offered suggestions for improvement, and encouraged me to push on with the job. Mrs. Joan Jander of Dyer, Indiana, provided competent and cheerful help in a number of ways, checking references, reading proof, typing and retyping the manuscript, and compiling the index. The readers for the press suggested a number of changes; the line-by-line critique of the anonymous outside reader did much to determine the final form of the work. If these pages should again come to his attention, he will recognize how valuable his comments were and how much they were appreciated.

The careful attention of Walter Albee and Sandy Mathai at the I. U. Press improved the style of the book and saved me from many embarrassing errors.

Two men bear a special relationship to this work. Those who know of my association with them will perhaps understand something of my sense of deep appreciation for what they have done for me and for the large part each has played in making this book possible. On my first visit to England, in 1961, it was my good fortune to meet Mr Tom Green, of Southampton, who was a constant source of information and support. He put his vast knowledge of Southern naval affairs at my disposal, shared with me his deep understanding of Civil War history, offered constant hospitality and good cheer. His untimely death was a great loss. Dedication of this book to his memory can repay only a small portion of my debt to him. I like to think he would have enjoyed it; certainly no one was better qualified than he to measure its merit or weigh its defects.

At this point, it is a pleasure to add my name to that growing list of students who have benefited from the advice and example of Robert H. Ferrell of Indiana University. Over the years he has been a patient critic of my work, and whatever qualities of clarity and precision this book may possess are traceable to his incisive criticism of its earlier versions. For me, as for many others, Professor Ferrell has come to personify an ideal participant in the student-teacher relationship.

Of course, any errors of omission or commission are my responsibility.

GREAT BRITAIN AND

The Confederate Navy,

1861–1865

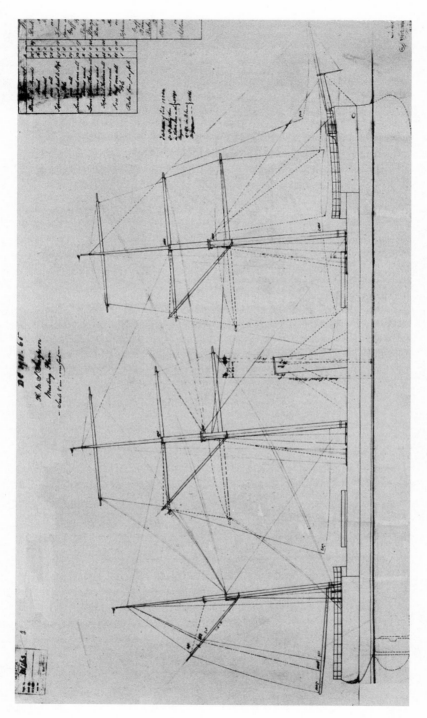

MASTING PLAN FOR H. M. S. *SCORPION*

This was one of the Laird rams (see also illustration on p. 181).

ONE | PROBLEMS AND PLANS

ONSEQUENCES of great moment for both the Union and Confederacy turned on Great Britain's response to the American Civil War. If there was one single factor that could have assured Southern independence, it was that the government of Queen Victoria, acting out of malice or self-interest, or perhaps sheer bureaucratic inefficiency, might have permitted the Confederate States of America to build warships in British yards and get them to sea where they could prey on Northern commerce, break President Abraham Lincoln's blockade, and give the Southern army access to almost unlimited war material.

Anxious statesmen of the North, especially the president and secretary of state, saw British construction of a Confederate navy as a sinister danger for the Union. From the outset of hostilities in April, 1861, the overburdened imaginations of Northern leaders suspected a plot by which the ministers of the Crown were scheming to aid the South in dismembering the Union. The steps in such a plan might not be altogether obvious, but their implications would stand clear to men of judgment. First, Queen Victoria's government would proclaim the belligerent status of the South (and many "I told you so's" and knowing nods were exchanged when the Queen did just that) ; then the British would recognize the new nation and send diplomatic representatives to Richmond, its capital. Accompanying such moves would be closer economic relations and pressure for loosening the blockade, the use of British vessels to transport supplies to the South and cotton to England, and perhaps even a willingness to construct—and arm—a Confederate navy in the Queen's dominions, converting British territory thereby into a network of naval outposts and supply depots for the South. From such action, so the Northern prognosis went, Her Majesty's government might then move to open hostilities, a war against the Union. And in the event of Anglo-American conflict, would not the Queen's admittedly bellicose prime minister, Lord Palmerston, seek to enlist the aid of Emperor Louis Napoleon III of France, who, with his dream of empire in Mexico, would need little urging to engage in North American adventures?

Because possession of a foreign-built fleet might enhance Southern powers of resistance, might disrupt the Northern navy's proposed war of attrition, might even tip the scales against the Union, President Lincoln slowly came to see that all moves which threatened to widen the war by giving it an international dimension had to be countered effectively. In this view he was soon joined by the two men in his cabinet who would be most directly concerned in devising countermeasures to the grand design of the South, Secretary of State William H. Seward and Secretary of the Navy Gideon Welles. These men recognized that they would have to prevent European involvement in the war at all costs, that even limited intervention by Britain and France might guarantee Southern independence. They began to see, if not always clearly and consistently, that war with the two most powerful maritime nations of the world would be national suicide; they understood, too, that European interest in an uninterrupted supply of cotton might generate friction as the blockade began to cut off supplies of that staple. Soon after the outbreak of hostilities, in early July, when the Confederates sent out the proto-cruiser *Sumter*, it became painfully clear that the ap-

plication of steam power to the ancient techniques of commerce raiding had added an entirely new dimension to naval
war and that the guerillas of the sea could do an impressive
amount of damage to Northern shipping—and do it with
virtual impunity. In addition, Union officials quickly sensed
that the activity of Southern ships stirred up a lively press
and public interest in the administration's proposals to cope
with this novel threat to national security. There was always,
they realized, a distinct possibility that an aroused public
opinion might demand stronger policy and more aggressive
personnel. From every point of view the threat of Southern
seapower presented Lincoln's government with problems of
the first magnitude.[1]

*　*　*　*　*

For his part, President Davis would have to make the sea
an important element in his strategy, for it soon appeared
that the influence of sea power was destined to have a considerable effect on the course of the war. By a fortuitous
combination of circumstances, the Confederates had been
presented with a marvelous opportunity to cancel out some
of the North's naval supremacy—if the proper ships could
be obtained in Europe.

The American Civil War, sometimes called history's first
"modern" war, coincided with a major transition in naval
technology. It has been well said that a sixteenth-century naval
contemporary of Sir Francis Drake would have been perfectly at home on a warship of the 1840s, but that he would
have been lost on those developed in the 1860s. For during
some two decades in the mid-nineteenth century, naval
science advanced more than it had in a cycle of centuries. In
that period, introduction of the steam-powered warship—
propeller-driven, armor-plated, and equipped with rifled
shell guns set in revolving turrets—had ushered in a new
era of sea war and in the process had doomed most of the
fleets of the world to obsolescence. In the 1850s the Euro-

pean powers, particularly France, led the way toward the
new age of steam and iron. During the Crimean War a floating battery—a sort of slow-moving ironclad barge—had reduced the Russian fortifications at Fort Constantine and
that feat had deeply impressed contemporary observers. In
the years that followed, French naval engineers—primarily
Dupuy de Lôme, designer of *La Gloire,* the pride of the
emperor's fleet—had pioneered many ideas for ocean-going
armor-plated warships. When launched in 1859, de Lôme's
ship was beyond doubt the most formidable war machine
afloat, able, some said, to destroy without assistance half the
navies of the world. Napoleon III had seen the need for
innovation in naval architecture and had become an ardent
advocate of experiments to perfect them. He had selected the
right man to execute his plans, had given him ample financial
support, and had backed him completely and consistently.
The naval revolution of the nineteenth century, according
to its leading student, James Phinney Baxter, resulted primarily from the determination of Napoleon and the genius
of de Lôme. With that talented combination in charge, it
was easy for the French to believe that in naval technology
they were "en avance sur les autres nations," as one of their
admirals told the French Academy of Sciences.[2]

The British, always sensitive to any challenge to their
naval supremacy, and willing, as Richard Cobden remarked,
to bear any expense to maintain superiority at sea, moved
to counter the cross-Channel threat. Suspicious of Napoleonic
ambitions and egged on by a vociferous press and Parliament,
the Admiralty set in motion an aggressive program of ironclad construction designed to redress the naval balance and
go their rival one better. Her Majesty's government launched
the revolutionary *Warrior* in 1860, a vessel that, in the words
of one recent commentator on British naval history, was "a
match for all her existing line-of-battle consorts put together." That expert, Admiral G. A. Ballard, also pointed
out that this vessel introduced four "great departures" from

the traditions and customs of royal naval construction by incorporating these features: a network of internal watertight compartments, armor plate, an iron frame and hull (which differentiated it from *La Gloire,* a wooden-framed vessel sheathed in iron plates) , and a vastly increased beam. (The *Warrior* was about 120 feet longer between perpendiculars than the largest ship-of-the-line; in the preceding 300 years that particular dimension had increased only 100 feet.) In addition to improvements in naval architecture, the British were making rapid progress in gun technology, turret construction, metallurgy, metalworking machinery, and weaponry. The quality of workmanship won a worldwide reputation and put Britain in the forefront of the technological revolution: she became "the arsenal, treasury, and dockyard of the greater part of the world."[3]

Prior to the outbreak of hostilities in 1861, however, the implications of such developments went largely unnoticed in the Federal navy. Although a number of Americans had made important contributions to various phases of the emerging technology—Robert Fulton, Matthew C. Perry, John M. Brooke, and John A. Dahlgren, to name only a few—the Union navy had done little to prepare itself for the new direction in sea war. This was so for a number of reasons: for one thing, many naval officers, especially in the higher echelons of command, simply had not understood the nature or importance of the advances in naval technology. Many of the older officers had outlived their usefulness but remained in rank, a bulwark against reform. Their presence prevented the promotion of aggressive younger men to posts of command and responsibility. The stultifying seniority system, with its built-in tendency to "substitute apathy and indolence for zeal and energy," often elevated unimaginative and incompetent men, while suppressing those of individuality and initiative. The lack of opportunity drove bright, ambitious men out of service in distressingly large numbers. (It is worth noting that two of the most imaginative naval innovators of the war, James D. Bulloch and Gustavus V. Fox, one Confederate, one Union, after some fourteen and eighteen years respectively, had resigned naval commissions shortly before the war and returned to civilian life.) Still another defect in the old navy was the absence of what is now called a general staff, a high-level planning body charged with the task of coordinating policy and keeping abreast of new developments in naval science. It was abundantly clear by 1861 that the "system" had permitted, indeed had induced, neglect of that basic tenet of the navy, "to maintain itself, in all its branches, matériel, personnel, and organization, in the most perfect state that is possible of readiness and efficiency for war."[4] In short, the navy had neglected its *raison d'être,* preparedness. When war came, it was far from ready; it was, rather, wholly unfit for the task at hand. One naval historian summarized its plight in this way:

In matériel, it had a few ships suitable for cruising purposes, and it had superior ordnance; but half the fleet was antiquated, and the rest was displaying the flag on distant stations. As to the personnel, it is useless to deny the fact that the list was heavily weighted by the old officers at the head, who had reached their position, not because of merit, but because of the date when they happened to enter the service; that the middle of the list was suffering from long stagnation, and from the absence of any inducement to effort; and finally, that the young men, who were to bear the brunt of the work, were altogether too few for the needs of the service.[5]

The fault was not exclusively with the navy, however, for the support of Congress left much to be desired. Shortly before the war, when a naval appropriation bill came before that group, John Sherman of Ohio proposed a large decrease, and his colleague, Owen Lovejoy, echoed the demand for economy by saying that the army and navy were of no use whatever and that he wanted "to strike a blow at this whole naval expenditure and let the navy go out of existence."[6] Little wonder that when its greatest challenge came, the Federal navy found itself decrepit, disorganized, and demoralized, in a condition that was made very much worse by the lethargic response of James Buchanan's administration to the impending crisis: When Lincoln proclaimed his blockade of nearly four thousand miles of enemy coast, he had about forty ships to implement it.

Perhaps the condition of the Union navy, its virtues as well as its vices, can be demonstrated by a review of one now famous episode. Secretary of the Navy Welles, in a report to the special session of Congress that convened on July 4, 1861, had merely recommended creation of a board of three able naval officers to investigate plans for ironclad vessels; in contrast, his Confederate counterpart had made his proposals for procurement of such ships in early May. Congress did not get around to appropriating funds for Welles's ships until August; six more weeks elapsed before his board made its report in mid-September—the board approached its task gingerly, for as it candidly confessed, it really had "no experience and but scanty knowledge in this branch of naval architecture." Then, another three weeks or so passed before the navy authorized ironclad construction. (The South, meanwhile, despite severe limitations in equipment and personnel, had construction of its history-making ironclad well underway and was moving heaven and earth to prepare it for combat.) The Union's answer to this Southern threat, the *Monitor*, was the only one of three vessels approved by Welles's board that could be completed in time to challenge th Confederates for control of Hampton Roads in March, 1862. At that, the *Monitor* was barely in time to prevent destruction of an entire Federal squadron. Had its arrival been delayed even for a day, the Confederate ironclad *Virginia* would have destroyed every Union vessel in the vicinity. The Union navy and its chief came in for some harsh criticism in the Northern press. The North, however, could take some consolation from the existence of an industrial plant that, once properly geared for the task, could handle rush jobs, such as the *Monitor,* with impressive speed; construction of the vessel took approximately three months from keel laying to launch. This was an impressive performance, although at the time its significance went largely unnoticed.[7]

In the historic encounter at Hampton Roads, as in so many other naval matters, initiative lay with the South. Having no traditions to overcome and forced by the presss of circumstance to improvise, she was free to embrace the unorthodox, to take her advantages where she found them or to create new ones. The Union navy had been in operation for nearly a century, that of the Confederacy for scarcely a year, and yet the new navy had stolen a march on its more experienced rival. In the stalemate of that first ironclad confrontation there was acute embarrassment for Mr. Lincoln's navy because the underrated civilian who served as Confederate naval chief had "completely outthought and outmaneuvered" his professional opponents: Seeing what the experts had not seen and acting on what he saw, he and his associates had beaten their opponents to the punch by performing a small miracle of improvisation.[8] It was a masterly performance.

*   *   *   *   *

The Confederate Navy Department began its official life at Montgomery, Alabama, on February 21, 1861, and soon thereafter Stephen Russell Mallory of Florida assumed control of its operations and continued to direct them for the duration of the war. Born at Trinidad in either 1810 or 1811 (Joseph T. Durkin, his biographer, considers the latter year more probable) and brought to America at about nine years of age, he had grown up in Key West, taking an active part in its maritime business and achieving some distinction in the practice of admiralty law and local politics; in 1850 he hàd moved into the national political arena as senator from his adopted state. During much of his congressional career he served as chairman of the Committee on Naval Affairs, a

position which brought him in contact with domestic and
foreign developments in ship design and armament. Partly
because of his "considerable experience in naval affairs" and
partly because of the "exigencies of political geography"
Davis had selected him for a key cabinet position—"a post
that a statesman of unique and pre-eminent qualities, with a
thorough grasp of naval history and unusual administrative
gifts, would have found a fair field for his powers." His
qualifications for that office were then, and remain now, a
subject of some dispute. John Newland Maffitt, a thoroughly
competent if not entirely unbiased commentator on naval
affairs, regarded the appointment as a serious mistake; two of
the three Florida representatives on the Confederate Committee on Naval Affairs voted against his confirmation; other
critics saw him as weak and willing to knuckle under to pres-
idential meddling in the affairs of his department. At some
points his knowledge of naval matters was surprisingly superficial; at others it was downright naive. At the time of his
appointment, despite wide technical and administrative experience, he had acquired only the status of "a clever amateur" in the realm of naval affairs.

In the conditions of 1861, however, amateur standing was
perhaps more an asset than a liability, especially when, as
in Mallory's case, it complemented a notable ability to grow
into a job. His responses to the challenges of his office displayed a flair for improvisation and experimentation, plus
intellectual acuity and common sense. He possessed in full
measure that long patience which is one of the hallmarks of
talent, and his careful attention to detail marked him as a
capable, conscientious administrator. He had, in addition,
a certain boundless zest (his biographer Joseph Durkin calls
it a passion) for the potential of his post and a willingness to
take a large view of its responsibilities. Soon after Fort Sumter fell, he recommended to the Confederate Congress the
"wisdom and expediency of fighting with iron against wood."
Far more quickly than his Northern counterpart, he had

seen the need for ironclads and set out to get them with a relentless determination that reflects much credit on him: his energetic pursuit of that objective constitutes perhaps "his chief claim to praise." His knowledge of naval affairs, his careful counsel, his zeal, ability and integrity, in the words of Jefferson Davis, provided "a most valuable support" for the Confederate cause.[9]

It was obvious to the new secretary that the Confederacy could not construct a navy in its own territory, at least not immediately. During the prewar decades, when industrial expansion was becoming characteristic of America, the agrarian South failed to attract any important share of manufacturing enterprises, primarily, one suspects, because of its heavy economic investment in cotton production and its even heavier social commitment to the peculiar institution which made that production so profitable. A disproportionate amount of wealth frozen in land, cotton, and slaves left little capital free for industrial ventures, while the ideological climate and the cheap labor supply largely precluded the migration of free workers or outside funds to the South for non-agrarian development. At the court of King Cotton very few industrial retainers were needed, so the Confederacy embarked on its bid for independence sadly deficient in the weapons needed to achieve it. It should be noted, however, that in time the South, under the spirited leadership of Josiah Gorgas, achieved a very remarkable success in beating its plowshares into swords.[10]

Having in 1861 few foundries or iron mills able to turn out heavy plate and ordnance, the South could not at once develop factories to produce the three- and five-hundred horsepower engines needed for warships. The South also lacked an adequate rail network, was short of skilled labor, and had only rudimentary mining and lumbering facilities. To add to its difficulties, the Union blockade soon slowed the importation of machinery and equipment. The privately sponsored blockade runners of the early years of the war could not handle cargoes of heavy machinery profitably, so they concentrated on bringing in small, high-priced articles such as cigars, brandy, corsets, and perfumes that did little to aid the war effort. It would be difficult to imagine any maritime country more destitute of means for naval construction than the South shortly after secession: One present-day student of Confederate naval activity summarized those deficiencies as "notorious."[11]

Participants in the effort to give the South its badly needed navy have left vivid recollections of the paucity of resources for that task. One of the most active agents, and a thoroughly reliable witness, later recalled: "It is quite safe for me to state that at the beginning of the year 1861 there was not, within the whole boundary of the Confederacy, a single private yard having the plant necessary to build and equip a cruising ship of the most moderate offensive power."[12] The justly famous Raphael Semmes, who in the first months of the war personally experienced many of the difficulties of fitting out a ship, recorded that "the South had neither shipyards nor workshops, steam mills nor foundries, except on the most limited scale. . . . We had not the means in the entire Confederacy of turning out a complete steam engine of any size." If the witness exaggerated somewhat in describing the ports of the South as "hermetically sealed," he did not miss the mark when he recalled that the Confederacy had "very indifferent means" for creating a navy.[13] An early historian of Southern naval activity—one who, incidentally, had the perspective provided by participation in the activity he described—asserted that all the manpower and material required "to complete and equip a war vessel could not be commanded at any one point of the Confederacy."[14]

Mallory, too, frequently commented on the lack of means to implement his plans. To take but one example, he reported to Davis on August 16, 1862: "The want of expert mechanics and of iron and the absence of tools and workshops for such work as heavy ironclad ships require, greatly curtail the ability of the Confederacy in the construction of this class of vessels." The lack of skilled craftsmen throughout the South caused serious setbacks in production schedules; the scarcity of mechanics was due, said Mallory, to the absence of Southerners in military service and to the exodus of Northerners and foreigners who before the war had constituted an important part of the section's skilled labor force.[15] The editor of one Virginia newspaper summarized conditions when he reminded readers of their utter dependence on outside sources of supply for most of the industrial needs of life. We are, he wrote, "dependent upon Europe and the North for almost every yard of cloth, and every coat and boot and hat that we wear, for our axes, scythes, tubs, and buckets, in short, for everything except our bread and meat . . . [and in the event of a rupture with the North] we should in all the South, not be able to clothe ourselves; we could not fill our firesides, plough our fields, nor mow our meadows; in fact, we would be reduced to a state more abject than we are willing to look at even prospectively."[16] Necessity dictated that the Confederacy turn to Europe for rams, ironclads, and steam cruisers, as well as guns and ammunition for them.

* * * * *

For the post of chief of overseas purchasing, the Navy Department selected James Dunwoody Bulloch. He was in every way an admirable choice. Born near Savannah, Georgia, on June 25, 1823, Bulloch soon felt the call of the sea, became a midshipman in the United States Navy at sixteen, and served for about fourteen years, including a tour of duty on government-sponsored mail steamers to the Gulf of Mexico and California. But, as he said, promotion in the navy "was slow, and the certainty of remaining in a subordinate position until age had sapped the energies and ambition had ceased to inspire was depressing."[17] He gave up his commission in 1853 to exploit the more rewarding opportunities beckoning in commercial steam navigation, and for the remainder of the prewar decade devoted himself to private shipping ventures in New York City. Like many other men in America during the troubled springtime of secession, Bulloch had a decision to make. He had no property or economic interest in the South, yet his "heart and head" went instinctively—though not, as he admitted in a charming passage, imprudently or prematurely— with the region of his birth; after the attack on Sumter, he fell "into line on his own side" and offered his services to the new government. At the outbreak of hostilities, **Bulloch was** in New Orleans commanding a private Northern vessel, the *Bienville,* which he insisted on returning to its New York owners, despite heavy local pressure to confiscate the ship for the South. With that task completed, he journeyed to Montgomery, met Mallory on May 8, and learned that the department wished him to go abroad at once. Somewhat surprised and taken aback by the secretary's laconic proposition, he saw what it portended. Mallory proposed a near-impossible task: to create a navy in foreign shipyards for an unrecognized country that had neither credit to build ships nor open ports to sustain them.

Wide experience in many phases of naval service, maritime business, and commercial shipping had equipped Bulloch with superb qualifications for his new post. "It is doubtful," according to one authority, "whether anyone in the entire Western Hemisphere was as well fitted for his special task as Bulloch was."[18] He brought to his assignment a rare combination of attributes: competence and courage, ingenuity and integrity, discretion and determination—the list could be extended. He was the sort of person who moved smoothly in British business and social circles, creating good will for his cause and country. Intelligent, and handsome in an austere way, with a huge mustache and muttonchop whiskers, he was patient, tactful, honest: a natural negotiator, an ideal agent to find and exploit loopholes in Her Majesty's neutrality laws and to capitalize on sympathy for the South. Mallory armed him with wide powers, which were never misused; nor did his judgment fail in the delicate negotiations that he carried on for the authorities in Richmond. Throughout the war his hand remained sure and true. Bulloch was far more important to the South than the ill-fated, if more famous, envoys to Europe, James Mason and John Slidell. One recent student of Confederate naval affairs has gone so far as to place Bulloch in the august company of Robert E. Lee, as the two greatest Southerners produced by the war. But, partly because of the nature of his task and the techniques needed to carry it out, and partly because too few students of the war have a proper appreciation of the importance of seapower in the South's struggle for nationhood, Bulloch's contribution to the Confederate cause remains unsung. His battle against dedicated Union opponents and suspicious Crown customs officials, his duel of wits with British and French authorities and with agents of the American ministers in London and Paris, are fascinating if little-known chapters of Civil War history that deserve a wider audience. Bulloch himself told much of that story with modesty, accuracy, and good grace in his postwar memoir, *The Secret Service of the Confederate States in Europe.*[19]

The Southern strategy of sea war, as mapped by Mallory and associates at Montgomery in his early weeks of tenure as naval secretary, embraced two cardinal approaches. These the secretary outlined to Bulloch at their May meeting when he explained the reasons for sending an agent to Europe. The first objective of the European business, a matter of prime importance, was "to get cruisers to sea as soon as possible, to harass the enemy's commerce, and to compel him to send his own ships-of-war in pursuit." The agent's number-one task was the purchase or construction of a special class of ship: self-sustaining cruisers for raids on the North's vulnerable and very valuable merchant marine. With such weapons, Mallory hoped to play havoc with Union economic life, unnerve the populace of Northern coastal cities, disrupt enemy trade, and induce war weariness. He also hoped that by striking at ships and shipping the South could scatter the Union fleet over a large part of the seven seas, thereby weakening the Union blockade. The ships that Mallory wanted immediately were those that could do the greatest amount of damage to the enemy's commerce in the shortest possible time. In the selection or design of such ships he gave his agent a considerable freedom of choice, noting only that the necessity for staying at sea for long periods suggested a combination of steam and sail.[20]

The second part of the Southern plan—though not part of Bulloch's original instructions—called for construction of a new kind of ship. It envisioned a small flotilla of specially-constructed ironclad rams, armed with rifled guns, to challenge the Union navy for control of the Southern coast. Such ships, Mallory had explained to the chairman of the Naval Committee in Congress, could create fear along the Northern coast, disrupt blockade stations, and might, with a fair chance of success, engage the entire Federal fleet.[21]

This plan, with its balance of wisdom and audacity, captured Bulloch's imagination, and he enthusiastically accepted Mallory's commission. The next day he began his journey to Britain to put it into operation. In early June he arrived at Liverpool, the city that would be home for the rest of his life, and his final resting place.

When the North learned what the South was plotting, when the implications of Southern strategy began to percolate through the minds of Northern leaders (and they soon had ample opportunity to learn about such things), they were much alarmed. It rapidly became clear that the Confederates had a good prospect of getting not merely a fleet of cord and canvas, but one of steam and speed, of rifled guns and revolving turrets: a hard-hitting, fast-moving ironclad force incorporating every advantage that the technological revolution was then bringing to naval war. Union leaders began to recog-

nize the consequences of such activity and to understand that
if the Crown cooperated with the Confederacy, if the ministers
of the Queen permitted such a fleet to sail, then the Southern
bid for independence might prove successful.

TWO | BRITAIN'S DILEMMA

*W*HEN WAR came in 1861, the Confederate States needed outside sources of supply, expected foreign recognition, and hoped for European intervention. Whether or not they achieved such objectives depended in large measure on the diplomats of Europe, and these men immediately recognized that initiative vis-à-vis transatlantic affairs lay with decisions made by Her Majesty's government: Victoria held the key to Europe's response. How she used it would go far toward determining the war's outcome. Indeed, it would hardly be going too far to say with the historian, Allan Nevins, "that the future of the world as we know it was at stake."[1] As we see now after a century of study, the Confederacy could not have achieved independence without European, that is, British intervention. And if there had been a truncated Union the history of the past hundred years would have taken a much different course. Could a divided, perhaps "balkanized," America have mustered the economic and industrial might needed for defense against German aggression in 1914 and 1941? Could that Anglo-American unanimity so important in the two world wars and the cold war of more recent time have developed if Britain had aided Jefferson Davis in making a nation?

* * * * *

Not aware of future complexities, statesmen often single-mindedly confront the problems of the moment. In the spring

19

of 1861 no one knew how Her Majesty's government might react to the war in America because conditions in Britain were a strange composite of contradictions, of tensions seeking equilibrium. Though enjoying the final years of what one recent writer has called an age of equipoise, the country was watching as dimly-seen and little-understood forces gathered for an assault on the old order.[2]

Of the myriad pressures prompting or preventing government action, a few merit mention here.[3] While the English ruling class despised slavery, it also distrusted democracy, and saw that failure of the large overseas experiment in self-rule might check agitation for extension in Britain of the electoral reforms of 1832. The aristocracy wasted few tears over the apparently imminent disruption of the American nation, believing, as they told one another in print and conversation, that "the great Republican bubble has burst." Much of the anti-American tone of the British press reflected this domestic political concern: many Englishmen, especially in the upper classes, rejoiced at Union setbacks, not because of innate hostility toward the North but because they feared more democratic rule at home.[4]

Other reasons helped create good will for the South in British aristocratic circles. The David-Goliath aspect of the struggle appealed to sympathy for the underdog, while the genius of Lee and "Stonewall" Jackson was much esteemed. There was a widespread, though not very accurate, view of the "cavalier" element in the South as the true heir of British traditions. Then, too, much animosity was aroused by longstanding resentment over a Yankee predilection for brag and bluster, by a Northern penchant for twisting the lion's tail, and by the belief that Americans harbored deep antagonisms against Britain.

Another obstacle to amicable Anglo-American relations was misunderstanding about the nature of the Civil War: to many, even to some who were sympathetic to the Union, the struggle between the sections seemed devoid of principle or

moral purpose. Lord John Russell spoke for a sizeable segment of opinion when he told an audience at Newcastle-on-
Tyne that they saw two parties fighting, not about slavery,
"but contending, as so many States of the Old World have contended, the one for empire and the other for power."[5] If
Britons failed to see the connection between slavery and the
war, it was partly the fault of the North. Lincoln's early reluctance to clarify the slavery issue caused many foreigners to
question Union motives. To Americans it was obvious that
the British did not understand politics on the other side of the
Atlantic. "They think this is a hasty quarrel," the American
minister, Charles Francis Adams, explained privately to his
son, "the mere result of passion, which will be arranged as
soon as the cause of it shall pass off. They do not comprehend
the connections which slavery has with it, because we do not
at once preach emancipation. Hence they go to the other
extreme and argue that it is not an element in the struggle."[6]
In the seeming absence of moral purpose, Englishmen discussed the war as if it were the usual old world conflict about
"boundaries, successions, territorial partitions, dynastic preponderance."[7] To this uncertainty about war aims was soon
added skepticism about Northern ability to restore the Union:
after the first battle of Bull Run, humanitarian sentiment for
an end to hostilities began to grow in Britain.

The desire for an end to fighting had economic roots, too.
British maritime interests insisted that the blockade was
neither legal nor binding—that it was really a blockade in
name only, a "paper blockade" without sufficient force to
prevent entrance to Southern ports. Moreover, American tariff policy caused considerable uneasiness and much ill will in
British commercial circles. The "ominously protective Morrill tariff which had become law two days before Lincoln's
inauguration" stirred "deep resentment" in British trade
centers, as did the threat of curtailed cotton shipments for the
mills of the Midlands. The self-appointed parliamentary
spokesman of the skilled working class and staunch supporter

of the Union cause in Britain, John Bright, warned Northern friends of danger. In a letter to the chairman of the Senate Foreign Relations Committee, Charles Sumner, Bright sketched British opinion: "With our upper-class hostility to your country and government, with the wonderful folly of your tariff telling against you here, and with the damage arising from the blockade of the Southern ports, you will easily understand that the feeling here is not so thorough and cordial with you as I could wish it to be." Russell once remarked that Northern tariff policy was rather an odd way to placate animosity abroad, and privately Palmerston was saying, "We do not like slavery, but we want cotton, and we dislike very much your Morrill tariff."[8] Like many of his countrymen, the prime minister realized that Britain's reaction to the war depended in large measure on cotton.

The South naturally placed high hopes in that commodity's ability to bring about European involvement in the war; Confederates assumed that cotton was king and that his domain was worldwide. "At the beginning of the war," Clement Eaton has written in his *History of the Southern Confederacy,* "the Southern people had an illusion that cotton was king, very much like the belief of the French people prior to World War II in the impregnability of the Maginot line."[9] Because over three-fourths of the cotton used in Europe came from America, it was widely thought in the South that cotton would have power to coerce the textile manufacturing nations of Britain and France to come to the aid of the Confederacy. A cotton shortage would silence the spindles of Lancashire and Lyons, an event that would force Victoria and Napoleon to press Lincoln for a relaxation of the blockade. Union refusal to open the ports must bring on an Anglo-American confrontation, war, and Southern victory: such was the Confederate calculus. Britain needed cotton, to be sure, but it would "not do" for Her Majesty's government to break a blockade to get it because national interests might later demand a rigid interpretation of the definition of blockade, as they had in Napoleon's time. Unfortunately for the South, European supplies of cotton were larger than usual in 1861, and before long alternate sources of supply began to supplement the cotton brought out past the blockaders, so the expected pressure for a loosening of the blockade did not materialize. There was still another aspect to cotton diplomacy that the South had miscalculated: the attitude of the British workers. As Henry Hotze reported to Secretary of State Judah P. Benjamin:

There is only one class which as a class continues actively inimical to us, the Lancashire operatives. With them the unreasoning—it would perhaps be more accurate to say instinctive—aversion to our institutions is as firmly rooted as in any part of New England. . . . They look upon us, and by a strange confusion of ideas, upon slavery as the author and source of their present miseries and I am convinced that the astonishing fortitude and patience with which they endure these miseries is mainly due to a consciousness that by any other course they would promote our interests, a feeling which certain supposed emissaries of the Federal Government have worked zealously to confirm.[10]

Control of Canada and of the Atlantic sea lines also gave Britain a peculiar interest in American affairs, but no one could tell how she might indulge that interest.

Part of Britain's difficulty in responding to the war stemmed from a precarious political balance which existed in the House of Commons, where an unstable alignment of forces held power. The Palmerston ministry, which represented a wide divergence of views and had made compromises in every direction, was devoting much attention to the mundane task of remaining in office. Party fragmentation and social compromise, as Asa Briggs has noted, "maintained politics in a state of truce, of arrested development."[11] The middle years of the century lacked a "powerful directing force" at Westminster; there was a "lull, a centre of indifference" at Whitehall. Drift and lack of direction marked mid-century politics and diplomacy.[12] According to one distinguished commentator, the domestic history of Great Britain in the twilight years of the age of Palmerston was "depressingly barren"; it was a period of "political doldrums"; another sees it as a time of drifting purpose.[13] Lord Derby, leader of the opposition—if that is not too strong a word—once remarked that he could not remember any other period "when party spirit was so completely dead . . . when there was so little to fight about."[14] Knowing that domestic and foreign foes lay in wait to exploit any weakness and fully conscious of his narrow majority in the Commons, the prime minister felt "well satisfied" with things as they were—as a prudent politician he would do nothing to disturb the parliamentary status quo.[15] The ministry included too many shades of opinion to permit clear policy anent America; one might better say its diversity almost prevented policy.

Still, the seventy-seven-year-old prime minister knew how to harness diverse talent. A politician of infinite resource and guile, a master of diplomatic invective, a great parliamentarian, Palmerston was a pragmatist completely devoted to British interests.[16] With exactly the right touch of swashbuckler about him to give credence to the German rhyme which called him a devil's son, he had a perfect talent for serving up that mixture of "careful foresight and carefree swagger" so dear to British hearts.[17] He represented "a certain gross manliness, both personally and nationally; he was an aristocrat and a landowner with an appeal to the class below his own; he was at once insular and cosmopolitan, breezy and adroit."[18] One of the most perceptive writers of the age, Walter Bagehot, pinpointed an important facet of Pam's popularity when he noted that "though he was not a common man, a common man might have been cut out of him," for he had "all that a common man has and something more."[19] Another Englishman explained his appeal by saying that what the nation liked in him was a certain "You-be-damnedness!"[20] For whatever reason, he was popular, and he profited politically from that popularity, from his ability to interpret, to personify, as it were, the prejudices of his countrymen. He did not have to act the part of John Bull because, as Donald Southgate reminds us, "he lived it."[21] He knew instinctively that the British "like seeing in their statesmen a reflection of themselves," that the public "loves to hear the tunes it knows well, especially when played with skill and dexterity."[22] *Punch* captured something of Pam's jaunty air, pictured him with a straw in his mouth, casual, debonair but determined, truly "the most English minister."

In the mid-nineteenth century many Englishmen were anti-French and anti-American. So was Palmerston. He would have lost no sleep over America's loss of power, but he would do nothing to hasten that result. His view of the nation's welfare dictated neutrality, not involvement. A major reason for prudence in transatlantic affairs was, of course, the restive state of Continental politics. It seems certain that European affairs, especially French machinations, claimed far more of his attention than did the domestic troubles of the Americans. One Confederate noted this facet of Palmerstonian diplomacy when he told Judah Benjamin that the prime minister was "far more deeply engrossed" with rivalries in Europe than he was "with the fate of constitutional government in America." It was far more important to Pam to thwart Napoleonic designs in Greece or Italy and to check his ascendancy in Europe than it was to map any policy toward America, for both sides of the Potomac were essentially alien to Europe's affairs. It suited Pam's purposes to give few hints about his policy, except to say that prudence dictated keeping "quite clear of the conflict between North and South."[23]

British indifference to the war coincided with Union wishes. When the American minister left Washington for his London post, the State Department had few specific instructions for him, though Seward had sketched in the bare essentials of administration policy and set limits within which Adams might maneuver. There were a number of assumptions about policy that Adams had to keep in mind. Seward argued that the secession crisis was really of no concern to European statesmen: he wanted them to regard the separation as temporary. Because any hint of recognition or prospect of foreign aid might increase Southern resistance, making the "erring sisters" less amenable to Northern reason, Adams was to stress that any step toward recognition would be looked upon by Washington officials as an act hostile to the Union, as a manifestation of an unfriendly disposition toward America. From Britain, Seward wanted only benevolent indifference.

Unfortunately, this sensible policy was difficult to inaugurate because Northern leaders did not inspire confidence abroad—Europeans suspected something devious from the United States. In the early days of 1861 observers reported that untrustworthy hands controlled American affairs. Though President Lincoln seemed "well-meaning and conscientious," he had not given proof of any "natural talent to compensate for his ignorance of everything but Illinois village politics." So the British minister in Washington, Lord Lyons, reported to Whitehall, adding that "neither he nor any man in the new cabinet seemed to possess talent or regard for foreign affairs." The secretary of state came under heavy suspicion, for he had a long record of anti-British speech and sentiment, and had made a profitable political career of twisting the lion's tail for his New York Irish constituents. With a willingness to insult Britain and apparent readiness to wrap the world in flames, he seemed the sort of person from whom any intemperance might be expected. Lyons lived in fear of some recklessly bellicose act toward Britain; his London superiors looked upon Seward as the personification of all that was obnoxious in the American character.[24]

In these circumstances it was indeed fortunate that a first-rate man represented the Queen at Washington. Richard Bickerton Pemell, second Lord Lyons, a bachelor of much patience and perseverance who, after some twenty years of foreign service experience, had come to the still unprestigious post on the Potomac in 1859, worked tactfully throughout the war to prevent misunderstanding between Britain and America from erupting into conflict. On several occasions—most notably during the *Trent* crisis of late 1861—Lyons used his considerable talent to arrange accommodations between the two countries. In time, he came to a finer appreciation of the mettle of the president and secretary of state, though in the war's early months, Seward's apparent willingness to stir up animosity toward Britain gave him many anxious moments. His own sentiments, especially a violent antipathy toward slavery, led him to favor the Union and to wish it well in his unofficial capacity, but fearing that a "soft line" with Washington might lead to more aggressive demands, he advised superiors to follow the tested rule, *si vis pacem, para bellum,* if you wish peace, prepare for war. Friendship with America seemed to him a legitimate objective of his diplomacy, but not one to be purchased at the cost of surrender to unjust demands. That, he recognized, would be folly. In this, as in much else, (as, for example, recognition of the need for strict neutrality), he faithfully reflected the views of his London superiors, who relied upon his "wisdom, patience, and prudence," to steer them through the dangers of the American imbroglio.[25]

The American war presented Lyon's immediate superior with an intricate problem in political philosophy. At a critical point in the struggle for Italian unification, on October 27, 1860, Lord John Russell had written a memorable dispatch in which he stated that Her Majesty's government would look with approval on the "gratifying prospect of a people building up the edifice of their liberties, and consolidating the work of their independence amid the sympathies and good wishes of Europe."[26] Behind that message, it was reported, Cavour, that most unsentimental of men, saw through tearful eyes "the Italy of his dreams, the Italy of his hopes, the Italy of his policy."[27] As a patron of Italian independence and an architect of that nation's liberty, Russell stood pre-eminent in the ranks of European spokesmen for what our generation calls national self-determination. With some justification, one might assume that in his mind the American South should have an equal right to determine its destiny, to establish its nationhood. The matter was not so simple, for there was in the foreign secretary, as in the prime minister, a deep antipathy to slavery.[28] Palmerston once told Sir John Crampton, British minister in Madrid, that Britain had no "more determined enemies of slave trade than Lord Russell and myself, and . . . we have both labored assiduously & with much success for the extirpation of that abominable crime." Pam went on to note that no project in all his career was more important: "The achievement which I look back to with the greatest and purest pleasure was the forcing of the Brazilians to give up their slave trade." And, Pam concluded, so long as Spain refused compliance with prohibitions against slave trading, she could never "take or hold her proper and natural position among the powers of Europe."[29] To these sentiments Russell would have given a hearty "Amen"! To them he would have added a sense of moral responsibility for having foisted slavery on America in the first place. To his highly developed sense of honor it did not seem just to reproach Britain's offspring "with an evil for the origin of which we ourselves are to blame."[30] Holding such views, the Queen's foreign secretary would not be likely to do business with a nation whose vice-president proclaimed to the world "the great truth that the Negro is not equal to the white man; that slavery, subordination to the superior race, is his natural and moral condition."[31] Between the two contradictory pressures of aversion to slavery and Whig ideals of nineteenth-century liberalism and independence, a long torment began in Russell's mind: "The Englishman in Russell could not conceal the feelings of a lifetime when slavery was mentioned, the Whig recognized frankly that in another aspect the struggle was for independence on one side and for empire on the other. Between those conflicting ideals the old Whig was more likely to be attracted by the call of independence than empire, and the old Englishman who had sat in a Cabinet that had freed the West Indian slaves was more likely to be attracted by the call of emancipation than secession."[32] That dilemma, perhaps as much as anything else, explains—even if it does not always excuse—his reluctance to grapple with the problems posed by the war. Because he could sympathize fully with neither the North nor yet with the South, he took refuge in the straight and narrow neutrality mapped out by his chief. Described by one of his successors as "a compound of a giant and a little child," he often displayed "the simplicity and directness of both."[33] All who came in contact with this attitude during the war were a bit nonplussed by it; they assigned to it a deviousness it did not possess.

Russell, third son of the Duke of Bedford, brought to his office a noble name and several impressive achievements in a long and distinguished political career dating back to 1813. His had been a prominent part in piloting the Reform Bill of 1832 through the House of Commons—but alas, he became so attached to its soon outdated provisions that critics fastened on him the nickname of "Finality" John. His mind was straightforward, not subtle, and, Henry Adams to the contrary notwithstanding, he had no liking for beating around the bush, no talent for dissimulation: his was a highly developed ability to speak directly, often disconcertingly, to the point. By personality, training, temperament—in every way he was well equipped to transmit Palmerstonian policy to the American representative.[34] Moreover, he was able to recognize the utility of the advice from Lord Lyons that it might be impolitic openly to receive or rebuff the Confederate commissioners.

One final item remains in connection with the problems facing Her Majesty's government as it sought to penetrate the dilemma posed by the American war, and that is the purpose

and personnel of Confederate diplomacy. About a month
before the attack on Sumter, that is, on March 16, 1861,
Davis' first secretary of state, Robert Toombs, sent a three-
man mission to Europe in search of commercial treaties and
formal recognition. Their instructions incorporated lengthy
legal justifications for Southern action, stressed the advantages
to other nations of proposed import duties "so moderate as to
closely approximate free trade," and pointed out the danger
to Britain "if the supply of our staple [cotton] should suddenly fail or even be considerably diminished." A "delicate
allusion" to this last-mentioned possibility, Toombs said,
might be in order. The Confederate States, for these and
other reasons, presented "themselves for admission into the
family of independent nations and ask[ed] for that acknowledgment and friendly recognition which are due to every
people capable of self-government and possessed of the power
to maintain their independence."[35]

William Lowndes Yancey, Ambrose Dudley Mann, and
Pierre A. Rost, the men selected to carry these arguments
to Europe, were, according to a later historian avowedly
partial to the South, "about the poorest choices possible."[36]
Yancey, "prince of fire-eaters," had led extremists at the 1860
convention of the Democratic party and had played a large
part in bringing about the disruption of that party. Though
a person of some ability (rumor said he had been sent abroad
to be kept out of the president's hair), he had a fatal defect
for the task at hand. He was too ardent a spokesman for
slavery and too active a proponent of the international slave
trade. To appoint as head of a diplomatic mission "a man who
advocated a militant attitude on the slave trade was extremely
naive or extremely arrogant and, whether the one or the
other, very disregardful of the strong antislavery sentiment
of both England and France."[37] Of his henchmen nothing
need be said.

Their efforts, as might have been predicted, proved disappointing. They did not secure the use of European ports for

privateers; they did not negotiate commercial treaties; they did not secure recognition; they did nothing to bring about recognition of the South's belligerent status; and most importantly, they did not convince foreign statesmen of the wisdom of intervening on behalf of the South. Russell, after perfunctory interviews, refused to see them again, having decided, as he told Lyons, "to keep them at a proper distance."[38]

Nor did Davis' subsequent representative in London fare any better, as will be seen. James Murray Mason, who exemplified the more bucolic aspects of Southern character, was rather a "strange choice" for so sensitive a post. Arrogant, "provincial to an absurd degree,"[39] a little dense, he was too heavy-handed in negotiation and too sure of his own opinions to be a good diplomat. Frequent lapses from British standards of decorum aroused animosity, as did his strong commitment to slavery. Nor did his handling of parts of the naval business do much to aid Confederate progress. All in all, he probably did the South more harm than good.[40] Certainly he was no match for his Northern adversary.

* * * * *

It was the splendid fortune of the United States at this time to be represented at the Court of St. James's by a man who bore the name of Adams, "itself a guarantee of courtesy, common sense, and discretion."[41] For the first hundred years of America's national existence the Adams family of Massachusetts rendered invaluable service to the nation. John Adams helped bring the new nation into being at Paris in 1783, and later represented it at the hostile British court. During his presidency in 1797–1801 he helped prevent war with France—at great cost to his political fortune. His son John Quincy participated in the negotiations at Ghent in 1814 which ended America's second war for independence. Later John Quincy took up residence in London to smooth Anglo-American relations. The second Adams was America's greatest diplomat during the years when the nation's foreign policy was set in "classic form," to use the phrase of Samuel Flagg Bemis. In the third generation history repeated itself: Charles Francis followed in the footsteps of his father and grandfather by becoming minister to England in 1861, and in time of national peril performed important service for the United States. For several critical years he proved himself perhaps the ablest diplomat in the family line and a worthy foe for Europe's most skilled statesmen. Few men out of uniform, save Lincoln himself, could match his contribution to Union victory in the Civil War.

The third son of John Quincy Adams was born August 18, 1807, and before his second birthday had embarked with his parents for the Court of the Tsars at St. Petersburg. Life in diplomatic circles had its advantages, even for the very young. Charles Francis became proficient in French, the language of court and polite society, which his parents spoke fluently; the language of diplomacy became almost the child's native tongue, and for many years he preferred it to others. Formal education came haphazardly, much of it from not-too-happy experiences with boarding schools, including one in England. That experience (if we can believe his son Henry) gave him a lasting insight into English character, if not much sympathy for it. Upon return to the States he enrolled in the Boston Latin School and later, Harvard. In January, 1829, at the age of twenty-two, after being subjected to the "uncommonly good" training of reading law with his father and Daniel Webster, he gained admittance to the Massachusetts Bar. Destined for a public career, the young Adams read history and political science, subjects that his father considered necessary training for civic responsibility. "My sons," John Quincy once told his oldest boy, "have not only their own honor but that of two preceding generations to sustain."[42] National service was an indispensable part of the education of every Adams.

The advantages which birth had given to Charles Francis

were offset in his generation by the preponderance of a family heritage of greatness. John Quincy did not achieve public stature until after his father had left the national scene; Charles Francis was less fortunate, for he had two ancestors against whom he could be measured, and one of them remained uncomfortably prominent in national affairs. The son resented being pointed out as a facsimile of his father; he felt that it had no justification. Differences of opinion strained relations between father and son, but did not prevent the elder Adams from recognizing the younger's talents. John Quincy Adams died in 1846, confident that his son would continue the family tradition, would take up the cause of human liberty at the approach of the "most portentous crisis" in the nation's history.[43]

After the death of an older brother in 1829, responsibility for upholding the family reputation for public service had devolved on Charles Francis. For a time he assisted his father in the House of Representatives; later he served a five-year term in the Massachusetts legislature. He joined friends in publication of the Boston *Whig,* which boldly proclaimed that the only way to save the Union was "total abolition of slavery—the complete eradication of the fatal influence it is exercising over the policy of the general government."[44] The year 1848 was memorable in his life for it marked him as an antislavery man, a position that had not come easily. He accepted appointment as a delegate to the bolt-Whig convention which met in Buffalo in August, 1848, and was nominated for vice-president on a ticket with Martin Van Buren. This change from Democratic to Whig (later to Republican) affiliation reflected his shifting stand on the issue of slavery. By the end of the 1850s, Adams had narrowly missed important public office, but then, with the help of Charles Sumner and others, he finally won election to the House of Representatives in his father's former congressional district, and during his first term supported Seward with moderation and good sense.

On the day of Lincoln's election Adams had returned to the House to sit in the so-called Secession Congress. Despite the heated atmosphere, he labored to bridge the gap between the sections. In one of the rowdiest sessions on record he remained calm, reasonable, amenable to compromise, winning thereby praise from Southern congressmen, one of whom described him as the "member never out of order."[45] Adams in the House and Seward in the Senate tried to detach the northern tier of slave states from their more impetuous brethren in the Deep South; they sought to slow disintegration of the Union until the new administration could take office. But in the troubled days between Lincoln's election in November, 1860, and his inauguration in March, 1861, Adams and Seward, like many of their countrymen, grew restive about the president's unwillingness to provide leadership: his seeming reluctance to grapple with the problem of rebellion, his "want of decision," caused apprehension in the North and led Adams to believe that the president-elect was not equal to the challenge confronting him. Adams and Seward did what could be done nevertheless. At the risk of shattering Republican party unity, and at some cost to their own popularity, the two men fought to retain the loyalty of Virginia (Seward once told Adams that if this policy succeeded, they were both ruined politically). Adams never wavered from the course he considered right. In his diary he outlined his objectives: to combine "the preservation of our principles with a policy sufficiently conciliatory to bridge over the chasm of rebellion."[46] Somewhat later in a letter to George Sumner, he justified this stand and argued that it had been made necessary by President Buchanan's weakness and vacilation. Adams set forth what might be called a moderate Republican view of the impending crisis in a carefully prepared speech which he delivered in the House of Representatives on January 31, 1861. This effort at conciliation paralleled one made in the Senate by Seward some weeks earlier and was, according to some observers, "the speech of the session." He began with an appeal for reason and after a lengthy review of the unfolding tension chided the South for its attempt to extend slavery into the territories, calling such efforts chimerical, like trying to get wool out of goats, but he made clear his sympathy for Southern fears and reminded Northern colleagues that refusal to listen to just complaints did not enhance prospects for peace. All problems between the sections were not susceptible to legislative solution, he warned, stressing the oft-neglected truth that a popular prejudice might annul the most beneficial law. And if he were willing to use force to coerce South Carolina, that seat of sedition, he also urged that the North attempt to lure the other disaffected states back into the Union by compromise and concession. Pointing out the essential justness of Lincoln's election, he appealed to the Southern sense of fair play. If disunion came, he said in closing, it would come because some upholders of slavery demanded that lovers of the Constitution surrender principles for which their ancestors had fought and died. Extremists demanded a boon beyond the government's power to give: they ask us to "stain our standard with the symbol of human oppression, and to degrade ourselves, in the very hour of victory, before our countrymen, before all the civilized nations of the world, and before God." To persist in such demands was folly, for they could not be granted, even if refusal brought down heaven itself.[47]

The uneasy peace between the two sections of the country lasted long enough for Lincoln to take office on March 4, 1861, to make his magnificent inaugural plea for reconciliation, and to announce his intent "to hold, occupy, and possess" the property and places of the government. He then set about putting his official house in order and gathering the reins of power into his own hands. The days of drift were coming to an end.

The early weeks of the administration were a period of confusion, marked by, among other things, intra-cabinet squabbles for power and patronage and, more importantly, a serious difference of opinion between the president and secretary of state about the conduct of domestic and foreign policy. Naturally, it took some time for the president to assert himself and to convince his colleagues that his would be the dominant voice in determining the government's course.[48] While they grappled with the problem of beleagured Fort Sumter, Lincoln and Seward had to select the men who would represent America abroad. If war came, the European response to it would be a factor of immense importance, though one could hardly guess that from Lincoln's casual, almost cavalier, handling of appointments to the major diplomatic posts in Europe.

In keeping with time-honored America practice, the new administration had incurred a number of political debts on its way to office, and the president, as was the custom, hoped to pay off some of these by appointments to government posts, including some in the diplomatic service. Prior to the inauguration, Lincoln had kept a little black book in which he jotted down names of deserving friends of the party. Without consulting his secretary of state, he selected William L. Dayton of New Jersey as minister to Great Britain and John C. Frémont as minister to France. When Seward objected to this arrangment, the president consented to a reshuffle that moved Dayton to Paris and put Adams in London. Seldom has an important appointment been made so offhandedly. Lincoln later joked that the change had been made because Seward had begged for it, and that the secretary really "had asked for so little." But then one could never be too sure of Lincoln's motives, for he often masked important decisions with laughter. Perhaps Thurlow Weed's warning that Britain and France might join forces to exploit American troubles had taken effect; perhaps Lincoln realized the importance of filling key legations with antislavery men; perhaps he recognized that Adams was pre-eminently qualified for the post, or perhaps he simply understood that such a selection lay in the secretary's province.[49]

Adams, who had little confidence in the president's ability, chose to regard his appointment as a sign of Seward's influence in the cabinet. The awkward Midwesterner had not made a favorable impression on the aristocratic New Englander. At a presidental reception, Lincoln had stepped out of a receiving line during presentation of the Adams family. Horrified by the breach of etiquette, Adams recorded his impression of the incident in his diary: "Were Mr. Lincoln a gentleman, this would have been intentional insult. As he has no training, I construe it simply as ignorance of social courtesy."[50] Soon after his appointment, when he visited the president, Adams found confirmation for this low opinion of Lincoln. The president seemed indifferent to the problems of Adams' mission, and when the minister attempted to thank him for the appointment, he replied, "Very kind of you to say so Mr. Adams but you are not my choice. You are Seward's man."[51] Then, almost ignoring Adams' presence, he went on discussing patronage plums with the secretary of state. It was a long time before Adams regarded Lincoln as anything better than a rough country oaf, a backwoods bumpkin.[52]

The selection of Charles Francis Adams as minister to Great Britain was a stroke of genius, however haphazard. The prudent Brahmin had an intuitive grasp of the subtleties of human nature and of the complexities of international relations; he was, in addition, a person of wide experience, wisdom, and restraint. He met the British as they liked to be met—on their own terms. He could be and often (too often, perhaps) was as cold and aloof as any noble lord—as Palmerston once discovered to his cost. Adams also proved an excellent foil for Victoria's foreign secretary: temperamentally much alike, they were able to conduct business with icy propriety; their frigid imperturbability allowed them to conduct negotiations calmly, without ire or anger. Adams undertook to create and sustain amicable Anglo-American relations, to mediate between the occasionally bellicose Secretary Seward and the sometimes wrathful protector of British prestige, Lord Palmerston. Throughout his mission, despite severe provocation, he was "never in a passion, never in a panic." He conducted a diplomacy of watchful waiting, of patience, of smoothing easily ruffled feelings, while at the same time pressing the Queen's ministers for compliance with the obligations of neutrality.

The secretary of state did not object when the new minister proposed to remain in America until late April to attend the wedding of one of his sons. The fifty-four-year-old minister, his wife, his son and private secretary, Henry, a younger son, and an eighteen-year-old daughter then embarked for England.

*   *   *   *   *

Minister Adams' arrival in England coincided with the opening step in Victoria's struggle to define the responsibilities of her subjects to the American war. Landing at Liverpool like some early martyr "about to be flung into an arena of lions under the glad eye of Tiberius Palmerston," Adams was confronted with the royal proclamation of neutrality. The Queen, on May 13, 1861, had announced recognition of Confederate belligerency—"a bitter bit of marmalade for the minister's first English breakfast."[53] This commonsense reaction to the outbreak of fighting was widely misunderstood across the Atlantic; many Americans looked upon it as part of a plot to dismember the Union; others saw it as a move to give aid and encouragement to the Confederacy.

But Britain's public announcement of policy capped long weeks of consideration of the proper response to transatlantic affairs. A debate in the House of Lords, soon after news of the attack on Fort Sumter had reached London, attempted to define the government's position: had the ministry, Lord Malmesbury asked on April 29, tried to prevent hostilities, had it expressed willingness to open a path toward peace? A cabinet spokesman replied that in view of the well-known American resentment of foreign interference in domestic affairs, the British minister at Washington had been instructed to refrain from advice unless the contending parties requested it. Behind the scenes the government was working out guidelines for policy, and these the prime minister defined in a bit of doggerel: "They who in quarrels interpose will often get a bloody nose; and if you would keep out of strife, step not in twixt man and wife."[54] In a more serious vein he reminded Russell that Her Majesty's government ought to remain aloof and allow the combatants to resolve their differences in their own way. On another occasion he expounded his views in a long letter to fellow parliamentarian Edward Ellice. As Pam saw the situation, Britain ought to do everything possible to help bring the fighting to an end, and he and his colleagues would be happy to do what could be done. There were obstacles, however. An offer of good offices might excite American sensitivity toward European interference, might do more harm than good. Moreover, it would be difficult—almost impossible—to arrange any sort of compromise agreeable to both parties which would not be "repugnant to British principles and feelings." And while England might propose amicable separation, she could not enmesh herself in any acknowledgement of slavery. Palmerston therefore thought any move toward intervention premature; it seemed wiser to allow the Americans to take some of the "wiry edge" off their craving for conflict before trying to arrange any peace by mutual concession.[55] Soon thereafter, Lord Russell set the keynote of British policy when he told Parliament that "we have not been involved in any way in that contest . . . and, for God's sake, let us, if possible, keep out of it."[56] Nonetheless it seemed sensible, even necessary, to recognize Southern belligerent status as the best means of forestalling maritime incidents which might embroil Britain in the war. The mistress of the seas suddenly found herself neutral in a war that showed every promise of becoming a maritime war. The press quickly reminded readers that issues raised by war in America were likely to be of considerable importance "to the shipping and commercial interests of the kingdom," that the impact of the blockade would be "most serious" and "more felt in the port of Liverpool and in the cotton districts of Lancashire than in any other part of the world."[57] As *Punch* put it, the American difficulty was "beginning to create English difficulties."[58] Her Majesty's government also realized that it could not treat some five million insurgents who had declared their independence as mere renegades or pirates. To Russell the question was not one of principle but of fact: "The size and strength of the party contending against a government, and not the goodness of their cause, entitle them to the character and treatment of belligerents."[59]

Early in May the Foreign Office informed its Washington representative of the decision to confer belligerent status on the South. Though hedged by regret and sympathy, the message made clear that the Queen had no choice but to regard conditions in America as a "regular war." The ministers who conducted the Queen's foreign affairs then sat back, for Victoria was not yet ready to welcome the South to the family of nations. The Confederate States had to earn that accolade by a convincing demonstration of ability to maintain the independence they had so rashly proclaimed to the world. Britain could not recognize the South, Russell later said, until the "fortune of arms" had clearly substantiated its claim to nationhood.[60]

To the North, Britain's initial reaction had a sinister appearance; it had an air of heartlessness toward a friend; it seemed to foreshadow recognition of the Confederacy; and above all, it threatened to convert the Queen's domain into a Confederate naval base.

Early in April, after President Davis had authorized letters of marque and reprisal, Lincoln announced his plan to set on foot, at a subsequent date, a blockade of the entire South. Thus he had himself technically recognized Confederate belligerency and unwittingly encouraged the British government to do the same thing. According to international law, a nation could not blockade its own ports because blockade was a recognized part of war only between independent nations. "If your ports are blockaded," Bright told Sumner, "then there is war, if war, then there are belligerents,—if belligerents, then we cannot change our position." Lincoln should have *closed* the ports. Sumner later charged, with considerable exaggeration, that the president's hasty declaration "opened the gates to all those bountiful supplies by which hostile expeditions were equipped against the United States," and Secretary of the Navy Gideon Welles charged that Lincoln had placed America "in a most embarrassing position in the eyes of the whole world."[61]

But was it fair to accuse Britain of unseemly haste in establishing Confederate belligerency prior to the arrival of the American minister? Did that act show "unfriendly animus" toward the Union? One must note that Britain attempted to steer a difficult middle course between rival claims of the contending parties. As one newspaper put the matter, "no very keen sympathy has been awakened in Great Britain either on behalf of the North or the South."[62] And again *Punch*—that marvelous mirror of the time—caught a prevailing mood by pointing out that "Yankee Doodle is the Pot, Southerner the Kettle."[63] From December, 1860, when South Carolina seceded, until May, 1861, when Victoria announced her policy, Britain had scrupulously refrained from any interference in the dispute between the States. The Queen's ministers had followed a strict hands-off policy, partly because the American problem was too opaque to permit any reasonable estimate of future events, and partly because Lord Palmerston, recognizing the need for prudence in transatlantic affairs, wished to provide no pretext for a quarrel with Washington. By mid-May, however, the threat of Southern privateering, Lincoln's decision to treat such activity as piracy, and the myriad problems raised by the blockade gave every promise of spreading the war to the ocean, so the mistress of the seas attempted to set limits to neutrality by granting belligerent status to the South. But it is important to remember that events in America and not a predisposition toward the South forced the British hand. The royal proclamation of neutrality was, as E. D. Adams pointed out long ago, "simply the natural, direct, and prompt notification to British subjects required in the presence of a *de facto* war."[64] (Of course, Britain conferred important advantages on Davis' government by that act, for, according to international law, the Confederacy "could now solicit loans and arms, bring captured vessels into prize courts, and in general be regarded as a quasi-political entity.")[65] And if, from the Union point of view, notification came too soon, it seems unlikely that any more propitious time could have been found. For however long Britain delayed recognition of belligerency, as Martin Duberman has written, "there would still have been some to wax wrathful at her 'untimely' interference."[66] In retrospect, it probably was fortunate that the Queen acted before Adams arrived: had she hesitated, he might have had to protest an act he had no power to prevent, and his mission might have ended with a quarrel over the "legal" existence of war in America. Seward's mythopoeic conception of the war as local rather than international in scope complicated the minister's task, as did the violent outcry of his countrymen to the initial British responses to the war.

What had Her Majesty's government done to anger the North? For one thing, in mid-April, even before news of the attack on Fort Sumter reached London, a partisan of the South introduced a parliamentary motion for recognition of the Confederate States. And though the House of Commons, at Russell's request, postponed action on the motion, it did so only temporarily. The foreign secretary elected to meet, albeit unofficially, with representatives of the Richmond government who had arrived in London in early May seeking recognition. The ministry also informed Parliament that royal naval forces in American waters would be augmented to protect British shipping and announced that Her Majesty's government could not treat Southern privateers as pirates. Britain and France, moreover, had agreed to act in concert on American matters, and, as noted, Britain accorded belligerent rights to the South. It soon became apparent that Britain, one of the major commercial and trading nations of the world, would place few restrictions on the sale of war materials to the Confederacy (though, as will be seen, there were some ambiguous restrictions on the sale of ships). Many Americans found ample evidence in all this to justify their suspicions that Palmerston intended taking a hand in the game, that he contemplated an aggressive American policy.[67]

Seward shared the apprehensions of his countrymen, and the drift of events overseas intensified his contentious disposition. It appeared that European leaders were disregarding admonitions against interference in America; more than that, the secretary saw a danger that Britain and France might get "committed" in the war, might, as he told his wife, try to "save cotton at the cost of the Union." To forestall that threat, Seward drafted a vigorous set of instructions for Adams, the famous Dispatch #10 of May 21, 1861. While Seward looked upon this note as "bold and decisive," it is perhaps more properly described as "reckless and inflammatory."[68] In it the secretary launched a long diatribe against the course followed by Her Majesty's government: he strongly criticized reception of the Confederate commissioners and ordered Adams to "desist from all intercourse whatever, unofficial as well as official with the British Government, so long as it shall continue intercourse of either kind with the domestic enemies of this country"; he told Adams to show the dispatch to Russell and to await further instructions from the State Department. He noted that America would not complain about "the combination now announced by the two leading powers," but said the United States "had a right to expect a more independent if not a more friendly course from each of them." Moreover, Lincoln's government would maintain its blockade of Southern ports and would expect Her Majesty's government to respect it. Recognition of the Confederacy by Great Britain would be, Seward said, tantamount to "British intervention to create within our territory a hostile State by overthrowing this Republic itself." If the Queen chose to recognize Southern privateers as lawful belligerents, if she chose to afford them protection from Union pursuit and punishment, then the United States might seek "an adequate and proper remedy" under the law of nations. The secretary of state acknowledged the seriousness of the situation, recognized the "grave importance of this occasion," but asserted that if war came, it would come because Britain had provoked it by her unwise fraternizing with the domestic enemies of the Union.

Fortunately for the course of Anglo-American relations, Seward took this document to the president, who toned it down in a number of sensible ways. He deleted a reference to enmity between the two countries and made several other modifications in phraseology. Most importantly, he converted the note from an official to a private communication, one that Adams was not to show Russell, though he might convey the "sense" of the message.[69]

Adams, who had a high regard for Seward's sagacity and statesmanship, was somewhat taken aback by the dispatch, even in its softened version: it seemed to presage "war with all the powers of Europe"; it seemed to throw "the game into the hands of the enemy."[70] Having no wish to provoke the British needlessly, Adams took advantage of the latitude granted by his instructions to convey only a muted version of the note to Russell. His own reaction to the dispatch was mixed. Though shocked, he attributed the dangerous policy to the influence of demented men and continued to think of

Seward as "calm and wise." Surely, he thought, the secretary had not taken leave of his senses. But he later confessed that had the original tone of the message been communicated to Russell, it might have ended his mission on the spot (his son and secretary, Henry, thought that literal compliance with it would have "made a war in five minutes"). But the minister also thought that the note had had a salutary effect: its strong tone warned foreigners against hasty action toward America and may have helped "shock the British Ministry into a more cautious policy."[71] When the dispatch was published some time later as part of the diplomatic correspondence, it provided reinforcement for British mistrust of Seward, even though in time the secretary learned to leash his bellicose tendencies and had, in fact, developed a finer and more subtle feeling for the power and potential of his post.

In the opening months of Adams' mission, however, the British had specific reason to keep a wary eye on the secretary's maneuvers. The sudden interest of the United States in the Declaration of Paris had a suspicious look, and the course of negotiations, which anticipated subsequent American adherence to the convention, did little to raise the British estimate of American integrity.

At Paris in 1856 the European powers, particularly Britain and France, had again attempted to define the rules of maritime war and to set forth the commercial rights of neutrals in wartime. The convention signed there embodied four provisions: (1) privateering remained abolished, (2) a neutral flag protected enemy goods, not contraband of war, (3) neutral goods—except contraband of war—were not subject to capture under an enemy flag, (4) no "paper" blockade, i.e., in order to receive international sanction a blockade must be "maintained by a force sufficient really to prevent access to the coast of the enemy."[72] When invited to subscribe to this international agreement, the United States had refused, holding out for addition of a fifth article which would have protected all noncontraband private property at sea. Then, soon after the outbreak of hostilities in 1861, for a variety of motives which were, to say the least, subject to misunderstanding in Europe, Seward moved to open discussions seeking American adherence to the Declaration. The initial instructions to representatives abroad had been issued on April 24, partly as an attempt to forestall European recognition of Confederate belligerency, but that maneuver failed. Seward, nevertheless, continued to press for American participation in the international accord, seeing in such a course some advantage for the North. Whatever his avowed objective was, the course he followed had, according to his most recent biographer, a secondary, scarcely veiled purpose: "to obtain an international consensus outlawing southern privateering."[73] After weeks and months of frustrating and unfruitful talks, the American maneuver failed. Negotiations had been marked by many disagreements, some important, some trivial. There was confusion over whether Washington or London was the proper place for them, and over whether the negotiators had power to bind their governments. There was uncertainty about the scope of the agreements and about which nations ought to participate in them. And there was more than a little suspicion on each side that the other was pursuing selfish ends. Finally, in late summer, the British wrote finis to the talks by insisting upon inclusion of a rider to the convention. In it, they disclaimed all intent of undertaking any action which might have direct or indirect bearing "on the internal differences now prevailing in the United States."[74] That statement made explicit the British decision to exclude the South from prohibitions of the Declaration's first clause. It served notice that however distasteful she might find the practice of privateering, however anxious she might be to spearhead a worldwide move to abolish it, Britain would not revoke the permission she had earlier granted the Confederates to arm such ships. Nor would she treat as pirates those who acted on that permission under duly authorized letters of marque and reprisal. The negotiations did little to lessen British suspicion of American opportunism, nor did they do much to enhance American faith in the openness of British diplomacy: both sides came away from the meetings with a residue of mistrust and misunderstanding.

By the summer of 1861, both Adams and Seward had settled into their respective jobs, had tested the mettle of their adversaries, and had handled, with greater or lesser success, a number of tricky diplomatic problems. If they had received some hard knocks in the Declaration of Paris negotiations, they could take some consolation from two decisions reached by British officials in June. On the first of the month the Admiralty issued an order which forbade both belligerents to bring captured prizes into any port in the Queen's dominions, and about two weeks later Russell informed the American minister that he did not intend to have any further official contact with the Confederate commissioners. With these matters out of the way the State Department could turn its attention to one of the most critical tasks confronting it. In the months ahead that task would tax all resources of mind and spirit, to it would be devoted endless time and patience. Adams and Seward turned, in the summer of 1861, to that confusing confrontation of Crown and Confederacy then developing in the shipyards of Great Britain. Throughout the war it became a major objective of American diplomacy to thwart the South's program of naval construction in the Queen's realm.

THREE | CRUISERS: PART ONE

*S*EVERAL MONTHS before war broke out, the experienced naval captain, Raphael Semmes, outlined a Southern strategy in anticipation of hostilities between the sections. In a letter to a congressman friend he suggested a well-organized system of attacks by armed vessels on Northern shipping. Semmes knew that unless the South could somehow compensate for it, Federal naval supremacy might prove decisive in a war. To even the odds, he told his friend, enemy commerce must be hit hard and often. Semmes's plan envisioned an irregular naval force free from any taint of piracy and operating under the restraints of international law. He proposed a militia of the sea—privateers under government license—to destroy the North's merchant marine and to decrease its naval efficiency.[1]

The idea had merit, and the South moved to put such a plan into operation when war came. President Davis made the first move when on April 17, 1861, as head of the provisional government, he issued a proclamation offering letters of marque and reprisal to owners of private vessels (hence, "privateers") who would seek out and destroy enemy shipping. Such authorizations were a handy and time-honored weapon for small navy powers, and the United States had used them with considerable success in the wars of 1776 and 1812. American reluctance to give up such a convenient and

inexpensive weapon of naval war explains in part its unwillingness to subscribe to the 1856 Declaration of Paris. Technically, the authorization from a sovereign state—the letter of
marque—exempted privateers from prosecution as pirates,
but in 1861 the North, naturally enough, refused to recognize
either the sovereignty of the South or its right to issue letters
of marque. Lincoln's initial proclamation of blockade contained a threat that interference with Union shipping would
be regarded as piracy and that those who participated in such
activity would be subject to prosecution for that crime, with
its possible death penalty. This called forth counterthreats
from Davis and led the British to announce their refusal to
concur in the narrow Northern definition of maritime law.
This unofficial form of sea war, however, did not play an
important part in Southern resistance. On June 1 the British
closed their ports to prizes captured by privateers, and the
Union blockade soon became effective enough to keep them
out of Southern ports. The opportunity to profit from the
sale of captured ships and cargoes was thus removed, and the
privateers, having no interest in burning ships merely to
harass the North, became almost totally inactive. The essential function of the privateer—destruction of enemy commerce at sea—was soon taken over by another class of ship:
commerce raiders officially commissioned by the Confederate
navy, operated by its sailors, and commanded by its officers.
With this activity the name of Raphael Semmes is forever
associated.

Semmes resigned from the Federal navy on February 15,
1861, and immediately travelled to Montgomery to join the
new navy of the Confederacy. Then in his early fifties, he
brought with him many talents and much experience. He
was "of medium stature, small, compact, erect, but despite
his usually quiet and reserved manner endowed with a perceptive mind and an arresting personality. The martial bearing developed through years afloat and ashore in one naval
assignment after another was punctuated by military mus-

taches like iron spikes in a fashion of the day. It was from these aggressive-looking mustaches that sailors nicknamed him 'Old Beeswax.' Semmes was a man of action by training and occupation; he was an intellectual by avocation, a lawyer, a linguist skillful enough to serve as a Spanish interpreter, and author of *Service Afloat and Ashore During the Mexican War.*"[2]

Less than a week after Major Robert Anderson surrendered his ill-fated fort in Charleston Harbor, Mallory sent Semmes to New Orleans to command a small steamer renamed in honor of that initial victory of the new nation. That vessel, the *Sumter,* became the first warship of the Southern navy, the first Confederate cruiser. Though ill-equipped to be the prototype of a new class of fighting ship—five hundred tons and five guns—the vessel captured eighteen ships during a five-month cruise and set a pattern for the more famous raiders that followed it.

While the cruise of the *Sumter,* properly speaking, does not belong to these pages, it may be instructive to glance at some of the problems connected with its outfit, to examine its mode of operation, and to sketch the nature of its challenge to the Union.

When Semmes arrived in New Orleans on April 22, to start his task of converting the *Havana* into a cruiser, he found it "as unlike a ship of war as possible." Still, there was potential, and he liked its general appearance: "Her lines were easy and graceful, and she had a sort of saucy air about her which seemed to say that she was not averse to the service of which she was about to be employed."[3] It took about two months of unremitting toil, and a good deal of imagination and ingenuity, to complete the conversion, which, like so much else the South undertook, was a model of improvisation. By mid-June, Semmes was ready to try his luck with the blockaders, but not until the end of the month did a favorable opportunity for escape present itself. Then, on June 30, while the guardship (known as the *Brooklyn*) was off in pursuit of another vessel, Semmes elected to make a run for it. The *Brooklyn* was both faster and more heavily armed than the *Sumter,* and for a time after it took up the chase, it looked as if the new cruiser's career might end before it began. But at the critical moment the *Sumter's* engines began to pick up steam, the wind freshened, and Semmes, with superb seamanship, was able, as sailors say, to eat his adversary out of the wind. Once it fell into the wake of the *Sumter,* the Federal ship had to slacken sail, while Semmes continued to supplement his steam power with wind. That was the decisive advantage. "I have witnessed many beautiful sights at sea," Semmes later said of that moment, "but the most beautiful of them all was when the *Brooklyn* let fly all her sheets, and halliards, at once, and clewed up, and furled, in man-of-war style, all her sails, from courses to royals."[4]

During the first week of July, 1861, Semmes and the *Sumter* provided an impressive demonstration of the consequences of that escape. In the mid-nineteenth century the bulk of the world's seaborne commerce moved with the wind, and this simple fact of maritime life gave the raider an advantage of considerable import. For the winds and currents marked out ocean paths of heavy traffic, and on these paths there were points of convergence, certain crossroads where, because of peculiarities of shoreline, current, wind, market, and the like, large numbers of ships plied their way so frequently as almost to wear a path on the water. Naturally, Semmes knew this, and he immediately headed for one such spot, a place where he knew trade routes funneled to fairly narrow limits. Cruising in that area in which the Gulf of Mexico may be said to merge with the Caribbean Sea at the Straits of Yucatan (off the southwest coast of Cuba), he waited for his quarry to come to him. In no time at all, he had a full bag of prizes and more.

The cruiser employed a simple technique. Upon sighting a vessel, Semmes would attempt to lure it into range by flying false colors; then a shot or two brought the victim to a halt;

an officer from the cruiser went on board to establish identity (often taking captain and papers to Semmes for on-the-spot adjudication) . When the fact of enemy ownership had been established and if there were no complicating questions about cargo ownership, and after removing the crew and whatever supplies and equipment might prove useful, Semmes destroyed the vessel. His first act of aggression against the old flag took place on July 3, at 21° 29' N. Lat. and 84° 06' W. Long., when he fired the *Golden Rocket*.[5] But if the cargo of an enemy ship were owned by a neutral, as happened in the following days, Semmes tried a different tack. He entered the port of Cienfuegos with six prizes on July 7, astutely assuming that he might be able to maneuver Spain into broadening her definition of neutrality by allowing him access to her ports. Spain had responded to the war with a proclamation of neutrality very much like that of Britain. Queen Isabella's proclamation contained the usual prohibitions against enlisting in foreign service and supplying privateers, and it stipulated that the belligerents could not bring prizes into Spanish ports except in stress of weather. While these prohibitions applied to both contestants in North America, they worked a greater hardship on the non-maritime and blockaded South, and they brought into sharp relief that old argument over actual versus theoretical impartiality. When Semmes brought his covey of prizes into port, he tried to convince the Spanish officials that his status as a duly-commissioned naval officer exempted him from the prohibitions of the Queen's proclamation; he tried "to persuade Spain to give *Sumter* the maximum in belligerent rights." But the Spaniards would not play that game. The captain general of Cuba, already briefed on the Northern interpretation of Semmes's activity, informed him that all prizes were excluded from Spanish ports and that those he had brought in would be detained until home authorities could rule on their disposition. It was later decided—by a rather clever sidestepping of the issues raised on points of international law—that the prizes had been taken in Cuban waters (hence, illegally) and would be returned to their owners.[6]

Semmes, of course, could not wait for the slow machinery of justice to produce a decision. He had other work, other problems. When news of the raider's exploits reached the North, two things would happen: first, captains of commercial vessels would grow more cautious, selecting new routes and making captures more difficult; secondly, the Union navy would take up the chase. Thwarted by Spain's definition of neutrality, checked by American consuls throughout the Caribbean, pursued by the Federal navy, hampered by defective engines and lack of coal, the *Sumter* finally came to bay at Gibraltar in early 1862, and its commander was then removed from his command and given more important duties.

* * * * *

Meanwhile, the South had turned to Europe for warships, assigned priority to cruisers, and put James D. Bulloch in charge of their procurement. The naval secretary of the Confederacy knew that the kind of ship he needed might require a special construction program, for he did not want the discarded junk of European yards. Whether bought or built, his ships must answer the South's peculiar purposes. Mallory envisioned a small fleet uniting the best qualities of sail and steam; the ships were to be no larger than necessary "to combine the requisite speed and power," and small enough to provide economy in purchase and operation.[7] Such ships, potentially faster than anything in the Federal navy, could strike without warning and slip away to reappear at other unexpected and unprotected spots. Because technical means to forestall widely dispersed attacks did not exist, these raiders could cause endless trouble for the enemy: without worldwide telegraphy the Union fleet would be unable to cope with hit-and-run tactics. With Southern ports blockaded and foreign ports restricted, the raiders would remain at sea, living off their prey. Such arrangements, Mallory thought, would bring a large return on a limited investment and endless woe to his adversary. It must be remembered that the raiders were not designed to challenge the enemy's control of the sea; their unprotected sides could not withstand the battering of heavy guns; their purpose was to avoid conflict, not seek it. Unarmed and defenseless merchantmen were their targets.[8]

The efficacy of the Southern plan was soon demonstrated when the specially designed ships that Bulloch and his associates procured in British yards—gray ghosts, one author called them—began to roam the oceans of the world, "turning them into a furnace and melting pot of American commerce."[9] From the Atlantic to the Arctic, from the Clyde to the Caribbean, these corsairs of a century ago proved extraordinarily effective: eventually there were hardly any Northern ships left to capture. Late in the war, the commander of the C.S.S. *Tuscaloosa* reported that out of more than one hundred vessels seen by him in the South Atlantic, "only one proved to be an American," and in relaying this information to Richmond, Bulloch testified to the effectiveness of the cruisers by noting: "There really seems nothing for our ships to do now upon the open sea."[10] In the Pacific Ocean results were similar. "The master of a French ship reported not one American ship at the Guano Islands off Peru, where in 1863, seventy or eighty had waited impatiently for their profitable cargoes."[11]

Upon his arrival in England, however, Bulloch discovered that his job was far more difficult than even he had anticipated. In every direction and under every guise obstacles loomed to hamper his work. At the very outset of his mission he encountered one problem that remained a constant companion throughout the war—Northern counterintelligence. "Almost simultaneously" with his arrival he suffered that most ignominious fate of a secret agent: the press published full and accurate accounts of his work. It was all there—the precise assignment, the amount of money available, the names of his banker—almost as if the enemy had had access to his own instructions or to Confederate Treasury Department records. As a consequence of these disclosures, all persons suspected of being in Southern service were watched by special detectives hired by American consuls. The date of Bulloch's first dispatch to Mallory illustrated still another difficulty. Though he had arrived in early June, it was not until mid-August that a reasonably safe means of communicating with superiors was available. In addition, he soon found that he was competing with well-heeled Northern agents who were buying all available military supplies, and in their eagerness were bidding against each other and inflating prices. Then, too, the Queen's proclamation of neutrality was "almost an exclusive barrier against shipments to the South." Merchants "very generally" declined shipments of contraband goods, and the circuitous maneuvering necessary to overcome that reluctance usually created more problems than it solved. And of course there was the problem of finances. Funds from Richmond did not reach him until late July; this initial amount was quickly eaten up by the first contracts. The generous assistance of the Liverpool branch of Fraser-Trenholm partly circumvented that difficulty, but the problem of money, like the problem of Union countermeasures, plagued him throughout the war. His superiors had a devilishly difficult time making available to him the funds appropriated for his work. Another impediment to smooth functioning was that deplorable tendency of the Richmond government to duplicate its efforts abroad, and Bulloch soon had his hands full trying to coordinate the work of other agents, many of whom were unnecessary. The shoals of official and not-so-official representatives multiplied at an astounding rate. Bulloch later confessed that many careful plans went awry because of "lack of prudence" and "want of self-control" by men completely dedicated to Southern interests, but who were unfit for the delicate work of outwitting adversaries who held most of the high cards.[12]

American consuls quickly set in motion a broad program of countermoves that taxed Bulloch's resourcefulness and ingenuity to the utmost for the duration of the war. And it was not too long before the chief naval agent of the South met an adversary worthy of even his great talents. In the autumn of 1861, Thomas Haines Dudley of New Jersey took up his duties as United States consul at Liverpool, with a consequent multiplication of the South's troubles: as Philip Van Doren Stern has put it, he "combined the aggressiveness of a terrier with the tenacity of a bulldog in the performance of his duties as the American consul at that port."[13] Throughout the remainder of the war, these two men, Dudley and Bulloch, carried on a struggle of epic proportions that played no small part in the outcome of the war. It was, of course, an unequal struggle, given the resources of their respective backers, but marvelous to watch. If Bulloch had a slight edge in audacity and virtuosity, his opponent matched him with a relentless determination that would not be stayed or turned aside.

Tall and thin, Dudley's sharp-featured, narrow face was elongated by the downward drift of his Smith Brother's beard and mustache. This inelegant, but intelligent, dour-faced patriot soon proved a splendid representative of American interests. The forty-two-year-old consul had been born in Burlington County, New Jersey, of English Quaker parents and from his mother had acquired that sect's deep aversion to slavery, a feeling he retained all his life. He earned his first legal fee by disguising himself as a slave trader and going South to return a kidnapped Negro mother and her three children to freedom. In the temper of prewar America, stirred by abolitionist agitation, such an act—it need hardly be said —required rare personal courage, as did his struggle to recover from near-fatal injuries suffered in a steamboat explosion that pemanently impaired his health. Dudley, like many others in America, made the transition from Whig to

Republican affiliation, and by 1860 had worked himself into the higher echelons of the state party machine. He was a delegate-at-large to the Chicago convention that nominated Lincoln, and he played a key part in the behind-the-scenes maneuvers that made the nomination possible. Soon after the administration took office, Dudley was offered a choice of diplomatic posts, minister to Japan or consul at Liverpool. His choice of the latter was a bit of good luck for the Union.[14]

Shortly after his arrival in Liverpool in late November (about a week before news of the *Trent* affair reached Britain), he learned that he had stepped into the center of Southern shipbuilding activity; the remainder of his mission was largely devoted to forestalling Bulloch's plans. He soon displayed a considerable talent for the cat-and-mouse tactics required by secret service work. "To watch the movements of the Southern Agents who are here purchasing arms and munitions of war and engaged in fitting out vessels for the so-called Southern Confederacy," he explained in an early report to the secretary of state on December 11, 1861, "it is necessary to employ one or two detectives and occasionally to pay money in the way of traveling expenses to the men so employed. They are not as a general thing very estimable men, but are the only persons we can get to engage in this business, which I am sure you will agree with me is not a very pleasant one."[15] Pleasant or no, it had to be done, and Dudley was just the man to see it done. He soon found the man to do it: one Matthew Maguire, a local detective, who in time supplied much good and some not-so-good information about Confederate activity (the ubiquitous Maguire provided one of the best descriptions of the interior of the *Alabama* available). Still, the dirty work that Maguire and his ilk did in the dockyards, pubs, and boarding houses of Liverpool provided much of the material Dudley needed to document his charges of violations of the Queen's neutrality. The efforts of Dudley and his associates posed a continual threat to the safety of Bulloch's ships, impeded his work, and drove him to devise elaborate subterfuges that slowed but did not stop his adversary.[16]

There was, of course, good reason for Northern concern. Henry S. Sanford, later consul in Belgium and an early architect of Federal surveillance abroad, admitted that the Southerners worked with "system, energy, and discretion." Sanford considered Bulloch the South's most dangerous agent, "fully up to his task," and the consul spent £150 per month to have him watched. "Unless vigorous measures are speedily taken for discovery and effective suppression of the enterprises of the rebels here," Sanford told Seward, "we shall soon have . . . more serious losses on the seas than any our citizens have yet suffered." His detectives watched every move by the Southerners. Recognizing Bulloch's threat to Northern security, Sanford went so far as to recommend his "arrest"—kidnapping is what he had in mind—if he left England.[17]

Perhaps Bulloch's most difficult problem in building a navy for the Confederacy revolved around the attitude of Palmerston's government. The conservatism of Crown legal advisers, imprecision in neutrality statutes, Foreign Office indecision, ministerial vacillation—all these gave an aura of insecurity to his mission. Creation of a favorable climate of opinion became a necessary adjunct to his work, for Mallory had stressed the importance of refraining from acts that might compromise the Queen's neutrality. Success depended in large measure on Britain's definition of proper neutral conduct. The proclamation of May, 1861, the subsequent Admiralty rulings attempting to describe official responsibility toward the war, and—the basic statement of British obligation—the Foreign Enlistment Act of 1819 set out the rules of neutrality, though many ambiguities remained. If they could be exploited, tremendous advantages would accrue.

The British did their best to take a correct neutral stand. American vessels, Union and Confederate, could use port

facilities only for repairs; they could not increase their crews
or armament, nor take on contraband; and without permission from the Admiralty they could purchase enough coal
to take them to a home port just once in any three-month
period. The Queen's government attempted to treat both
sides impartially. The Foreign Office conceded President
Davis' right to issue letters of marque, but denied President
Lincoln's right to treat Southern privateers as pirates. The
middle-of-the-road position, especially in wartime, is seldom
popular, so either North nor South appreciated Britain's
definitions of neutrality.[18]

The Confederates naturally sought to take advantage of
loopholes in the law. When Bulloch contracted for his first
ships in the summer of 1861, the limits of neutrality had not
been defined; there had never been a case involving forfeiture
under the Foreign Enlistment Act. Even Lord Russell once
admitted that the cabinet hardly knew what the law was.[19]
But the South, with its limited resources and pressing priorities, had to know what the law was, to gauge the response of
the government to construction. It could not afford mistakes
which might lead to expensive, time-consuming litigation.

Bulloch hired a prominent Liverpool attorney, F. S. Hull,
to determine the restrictions under which the Confederates
had to operate. If the Enlistment Act forbade building ships
for belligerents under all circumstances and required con-
structors to prove a lack of intent to arm ships outside British jurisdiction, the subterfuge of concealing their "ultimate
purpose" from the builder would not protect property from
confiscation and consequent legal troubles. Hull was competent in legal matters, a "prudent, cautious, conscientious
adviser," but this problem gave him pause because the statutes were silent and there were no precedents for what Bulloch had in mind.[20] He submitted a hypothetical case to
legal experts in hope of ferreting out a reasonable estimate
of the Crown's position vis-à-vis Confederate construction.
To assure impartiality he concealed his client's name and

connections. The reply gave a full explanation of the Enlistment Act as it stood in 1861, and defined the responsibilities of citizens and aliens. It was not illegal, Hull thereupon explained to Bulloch, for the Queen's subjects to equip
a ship outside British jurisdiction, provided there was no
intent to use it against a friendy state; building a ship within
Her Majesty's dominions by any person—subject or alien—
was no offense because the offense was not the *building* but
the *equipping*.[21]

The interpretation which Bulloch received from Hull
apparently conformed to the best legal thinking on an extremely complex subject that had received insufficient attention. Somewhat later, when the legal adviser to the Board
of Customs, Felix Hamel, reviewed British legal responsibilities under the Foreign Enlistment Act, he concluded
that building any kind of ship was no offense, but if a ship
were equipped the person "so equipping with the unlawful
intent or who shall knowing[ly] aid, assist, or be concerned
therein" would be liable to penalties under the act. In his
view three things were necessary to bring a ship within the
realm of unlawful activity: that it be within the United
Kingdom; that it be "equipped furnished fitted out or armed
with intent to cruise or commit hostilities against any state or
country or against persons assuming to exercise the powers of
government in any state or country or part of a state or
country not being at war with Her Majesty;" and that the
intent be "clearly established and that the persons equipping
etc do so knowingly."[22] And still later, when the Lairds
sought to establish their responsibilities under the law,
George Mellish (later lord justice) advised them as follows:
"I am of opinion that the simple building of a ship, even although the ship be of a kind apparently adapted for warlike
purposes, and delivering such ship to a purchaser in an English port, even although the purchaser is suspected or known
to be the agent of a foreign belligerent Power, does not constitute an offence against the Foreign Enlistment Act (59

Geo. III, c. 60, s. 7) on the part of the builder, unless the builder makes himself a party to the equipping of the vessel for warlike purposes." A postscript endorsement of this statement bearing the signature of H. M. Cairns and J. Kemplay indicated their concurrence with this interpretation.[23]

Bulloch used the reply furnished by Hull as a guide for all his shipbuilding activity, and practiced every precaution to protect contractors against prosecution and loss by court action. Contractors never received information about Bulloch's intent, so he later claimed and there is no reason to doubt his word; no ship under his supervision ever received any war equipment in the Queen's realm. He insisted that all operations conform to the letter of local law. It was Hull's opinion that assembly of the component parts of an expedition outside the three-mile limit of Her Majesty's jurisdiction fulfilled all legal requirements. The best known Confederate cruisers were sent to sea in compliance with the restrictions imposed by Hull's interpretation of proper neutral conduct. Until the British closed these loopholes the Confederates hoped to sail a fleet of ships through them.[24]

* * * * *

After a hurried search of Northern and Canadian ports had demonstrated the impossibility of getting adequate ships in North America, the Confederacy perforce turned to Europe for its navy. Quite naturally its chief agent concentrated his work at Liverpool, a city ideally suited for the task at hand. In addition to being the home of Davis' fiscal agents, Fraser-Trenholm, the city was a major entrepôt for cotton and an export center for manufactured goods sent to the American South. Over the years, the city's business and financial interests had developed close economic ties with the cotton kingdom. The American consul, Thomas Haines Dudley, did not exaggerate when he later complained that Merseyside was a hotbed of pro-South partisanship, and ardent in its support for that section. The city soon came to fly more Confederate

flags than Richmond itself—if we may believe one not entirely
unbiased witness. When Bulloch arrived there, Liverpool was
a busy, bustling port with nearly five miles of quays and docks
and yards snaking seaward along the River Mersey. The dock
area of some three hundred acres handled much of Britain's
trade with East Asia, Australia, and America: in 1861 about
five million tons of shipping used the port facilities of Liverpool. The population of approximately 440,000 made a de-
cent living in local industries, especially soap, chemicals, glass,
and, most importantly, in shipbuilding and its subsidiary
trades. Just across the river from the city proper and connected to it by ferry was Birkenhead, home of one of the most
up-to-date shipyards in the country. Since its founding in
1829, the yard of John Laird and Sons had built fine ships,
and it continued to do so even after John Laird, Senior,
turned the business over to his two sons in order to run for
Parliament.[25]

Bulloch's first order of business at Liverpool was a conference with officials of Fraser-Trenholm, the designated financial agents of the Confederate government. On the day
following his arrival, he called at 10 Rumford Place to see
the resident manager, Mr. Charles K. Prioleau. The two men
quickly established an intuitive bond of trust and friendship
that was to last throughout the war and beyond. The agent
soon found that the company would do everything possible to
aid his work. Indeed, Prioleau already had given proof of his
devotion to the South by advancing credit to Major Caleb
Huse, who had come to Europe on an arms-buying mission.
Prioleau immediately provided Bulloch with the information
and credit he needed to begin work. Long before authorities
in Richmond could send funds to Europe, Bulloch was in
business, backed by the credit of this firm. The smooth start
of the building program owed much to the generosity of
Fraser-Trenholm; throughout the war the company remained
one of the Confederacy's chief foreign assets.

After establishing credit, investigating facilities, and conferring with the diplomatic representatives, Bulloch set to work. The first weeks and months of his mission were a gloriously productive time for him. Within weeks of his arrival he had arranged construction of the first raider; within two months he let contracts for the more famous second raider; and in five months he had demonstrated the feasibility of transoceanic shipments to the South by way of Bermuda, while at the same time pointing up the porous ineffectiveness of the blockade by running past the Federal cordon at Savannah. In Europe after the first battle of Bull Run, many people believed that President Davis had created an army, was creating a navy, and might yet create a nation. All this was heady wine to Mallory's men.

Because available ships cost too much or did not meet Southern specifications, Bulloch set in motion that special building program foreseen by Mallory. Despite advances in technology, wooden construction continued to offer advantages: it cost less and, more important, presented a less open challenge to neutrality by making more difficult the task of determining the builder's purpose. When equipped with a retractable screw, such ships could use the wind for power and stay at sea for long periods without coaling, no small advantage in view of Admiralty regulations.

Bulloch and William Cowley Miller, an experienced shipbuilder and designer of Merseyside, entered into negotiations for the first cruiser soon after the captain's arrival in England. With some modification, especially an increased spread of canvas, Bulloch accepted one of Miller's designs for a vessel of 191 feet overall length, 27-foot beam, and 14-foot depth, with a device for lifting the screw out of the water and into a well so that the ship could operate under canvas without a dragging propeller. Miller and Company did not have facilities for marine engineering, so it was necessary that another firm, Fawcett, Preston, and Company, undertake the design and building of the ship's power plant: two 100-horsepower steam engines with a double-blade screw propeller. With the

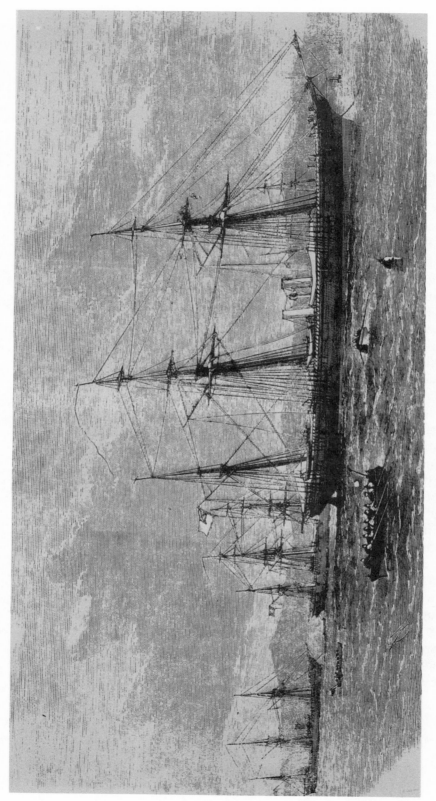

CONFEDERATE CRUISER *FLORIDA*

cooperation of Fraser-Trenholm, financial arrangements were worked out to pay the *Florida*'s cost of $225,000. Engines could propel the ship at an average 9½ knots (in smooth water it might make 10 knots) ; sails and favorable wind might kick speed up to 12 or 13 knots. The three-masted, twin-stack ship had a rakish appearance and gave the illusion of speed even when riding at anchor. Bulloch, of course, conducted his business with the builders in an unofficial capacity; under the dockside name of *Oreto* the ship was destined, rumor said, for an Italian port, or a Spanish one, or a Southern one.[26] Before long it attracted the attention of Union representatives.

Soon after arrangements for the first British-built cruiser were completed, Bulloch turned to another vessel. While waiting for funds the agent spent time improving its design, and in the process developed a fondness for this second ship. In late July, 1861, he signed with John Laird and Sons for construction of the 290th ship to come off the stocks at their Birkenhead yard. Number 290 (or the *Enrica*) soon attracted worldwide attention under its more famous name, *Alabama*. Almost a sister ship to the first cruiser, this one was slightly larger, measuring some 220 feet with a 32-foot beam, a displacement slightly in excess of 1,000 tons, and a draft of about 15 feet. Twin engines—with a capacity of 300 horsepower—could drive the vessel at a steady 10 to 12 knots in smooth water. Long, gently curved, built for speed, the ship "sat upon the water with the lightness and grace of a swan" —and carried the sting of a whip-ray. According to one report it was the "smallest, with the largest guns and greatest speed afloat." Bulloch sacrificed safety for speed: this trim raider was designed as a scourge of enemy commerce, and effectiveness depended on ability to outrace stronger chase vessels. Appropriately, the motto on the great wheel read, *Aide toi et Dieu t'aidera*.[27]

Construction of these two vessels overextended Southern resources, and Bulloch had to return to Richmond to consult with his superiors. In the autumn of 1861, when work on the first two raiders was well under way, and after the Confederate commissioners in London had approved the plan, Bulloch purchased a small steamer, the *Fingal,* stocked it with war material of all kinds ("probably the largest shipment of purely military and naval supplies ever brought into the Confederacy") , and ran it through the blockade, arriving home in mid-November. Details of the voyage are set out below (see pp. 243–44) , but it is worth noting that this early venture in government-sponsored blockade running gave a clear example of the benefit to be derived by eliminating the profit-seeking middleman from the business. But at the time too little attention was paid to the lesson. It was during this voyage that Bulloch discovered that perfect rendezvous for the raiders and their supply ships at Terceira in the Azores. Oddly enough, the agent, who was so scrupulously careful about adhering to the letter of Her Majesty's law when out-fitting ships for others, was more than a little careless about carrying guns and munitions when he left in the *Fingal*—a lapse perhaps explainable by the early date of this particular adventure.[28]

Bulloch's absence from England (from October, 1861, to March, 1862) caused a minor crisis in Mallory's overseas arrangement. The hastily improvised Confederate government did not operate efficiently; among other shortcomings it had serious defects in the naval department chain of command, and generally no dependable means of transmitting orders to personnel abroad. The time lag between issuance and execution of orders coupled with overlapping authority, hampered foreign missions and led to a contretemps over command of the first British-built ship.

Originally Bulloch's orders had instructed him to take the first cruiser to sea, while the special naval agent, Lieutenant James H. North, was to command the second ship. But Bulloch, before leaving Liverpool, had given Charles Prioleau of Fraser-Trenholm power of attorney to deliver the *Florida* to any available Confederate naval officer, and had briefed his co-worker North on plans for that ship, hinting that North might be her "fortunate" commander. While Bulloch was in Richmond, naval authorities did in fact transfer command of the *Florida* from Bulloch to North because they were certain that the first ship would be ready for sea before Bulloch could get back to England. This order did not reach North, and he continued to prepare himself for command of the second cruiser, as his original orders had directed. When Prioleau proffered command of the *Florida,* North declined, thinking it was still Bulloch's ship.

Upon return to England, Bulloch once more offered North command of the *Florida.* Again North refused, this time apparently out of pique at Bulloch's recent promotion to the rank of commander. Relations between the two men already had become strained, because Bulloch, before departing for Richmond, had refused to surrender his papers to North, a mere naval officer, and had hinted that North had been something less than zealous in working for Southern success. There was some justification in the charge because North, who also had come to England in the summer of 1861, took until May, 1862, to arrange construction of the ship he had been sent to build; and his refusal to take the *Florida* to sea resulted in part from Prioleau's insistence that no armament or war material of any kind be put aboard, while North unwisely refused "to take charge of an empty ship."[29]

* * * * *

North's refusal to take the *Florida* to sea exposed it to the danger of detention by port officials. The American consul at Liverpool had become very interested in the vessel, and his agents were poking around the pubs and dockyards of Merseyside picking up tidbits of information, good and bad, about it. Dudley, who was just beginning that war-long task of ferreting out information about Confederate shipbuilding activity, began asking pointed questions, began to work out techniques

for unraveling Southern strategems. He found that money
penetrated the most elaborate subterfuge, and was soon convinced that the ship had a sinister purpose. He knew that
the ostensible Italian ownership and destination was a blind;
with Adams' assistance, suspicions about the ship were
brought to the attention of Her Majesty's government. When
customs officers investigated the complaint they found that
the ship, though suspiciously sturdy, could not be considered
a warship within the technical meaning of that term because
it was not armed. It had neither guns nor munitions aboard,
not even a signal gun. The Foreign Office, consequently, had
no legal justification for detaining the ship. Russell informed
Adams that the government could not impose restraints on
the lawful economic activity of the Queen's subjects. There
was nothing illegal in the sale of an unarmed ship, he said;
nor was he convinced by American evidence that the vessel
was a warship intended for use against the United States. One
may note, *en passant,* that the official interpretation of Britain's neutrality statutes closely paralleled the one that Hull
had worked out for Bulloch: a ship could not be condemned
for a violation of neutrality unless it were equipped, that is,
actually armed.[30]

Meanwhile, Bulloch, who had arrived back in Liverpool on
March 10, was growing fearful for the safety of his ship. He
had no way of knowing how the government might respond
to American complaints, but he wished to take no chances.
The probing questions, the whispers and the warnings, made
him apprehensive and anxious to get the ship away. As soon
as he could, he arranged for an English captain, James Alexander Duguid, son-in-law of William Miller, to take the vessel
out of the country. Neither captain nor crew enlisted for
Southern service, for that would have contravened the Foreign Enlistment Act, though Duguid knew that the vessel
was not bound for Palermo, as its papers stated, but for Nassau. He knew, too, that the vessel was in custody of its "civilian" passenger, one John Low. When all arrangements had

been completed, and after another search by customs men, the *Florida* left Liverpool on March 22, 1862, under an English captain and flag.

Score one ship for the South—almost.

The intricate maneuver that would bring the vessel into the Confederate navy was not yet complete. Bulloch's trusted aide, Master John Low, CSN, now secretly in charge of the South's first British-built warship, carried detailed orders for the next phase of the plan. First, he was to compile a careful record of the ship's performance under steam and sail; then, when he had reached his destination, he was to turn the ship over to John Newland Maffitt, one of the most intrepid blockade runners shuttling between the British islands and Southern ports; but if he were not available, the vessel might be surrendered to any qualified Confederate naval officer awaiting assignment in the Bahamas.[31]

In addition to his own orders when he left Liverpool, Low carried two letters from Bulloch. The first of these, addressed to Mallory, summarized the difficulties of getting the ship out of Britain and expressed a hope that because of strict compliance with the letter of the law, the ship might be safe from further interference, though he warned of British and Federal suspicions about its ultimate purpose. The second note contained instructions for Maffitt and apologized for the ship's shortcomings. Bulloch explained that only the most circumspect course had warded off seizure, and that circumstances compelled him to omit all equipment suited to the ship's true character. But he said he had every expectation that Maffitt would succeed in arming it and putting it to good use. Then he explained his plan to get to sea in the second cruiser already under construction, and asked Maffitt to appoint a rendezvous for the two raiders. While recognizing that two small ships could do little to change the course of the war, Bulloch thought they might do much to demonstrate the spirit and energy of the Southern people and might repay the enemy for some of the damage inflicted on the South by superior force.[32]

As ill luck would have it, Maffitt was not at Nassau when the *Florida* arrived on April 28, after an uneventful but most promising shakedown cruise of thirty-seven days and approximately four thousand miles, during which it showed itself the equal in seaworthiness of any ship of its class, able to perform beyond expectations under steam or sail, independently or in concert. Low reported an average sail speed of 12 knots, with a top of 13½ knots; average steam speed of 9½ knots, with a top of 10½. (The ship later logged 14 knots under steam and sail.) Its appearance caused Union representatives in the Islands to step up efforts to have it seized. Contrary to Confederate expectations, the Americans had complete information about the raider, as well as about the supply tender *Bahama,* then en route from Liverpool to Nassau with stores and equipment, including four seven-inch Blakely (rifled) cannons. Seeking to forestall trouble, Low moved the ship but could not escape omnipresent Union agents who importuned British officials for seizure of the ship, and continually reminded them of neutral responsibilities, Northern style. A British naval captain finally inspected the ship on May 1. He conducted a minute search, but found no warlike equipment. Though the ship seemed suitable for conversion to a warship, he reported it unarmed, and hence not liable to detention. At about this time a dozen or so Union warships began patrolling nearby, keeping close watch. Then, to add to Confederate woe, a large number of the crew left the *Florida,* bribed, it was said, by Yankee gold, and they carried some interesting information to port officials: they knew the ship to be Confederate; they knew Captain Duguid to be in league with the rebels; they knew that the ship would be armed in Nassau. Money, apparently, had talked.[33] So apprehensive had Low become, that when the raider's supply tender finally arrived in early May, he thought it wise to store its cargo in a bonded warehouse.

When Maffitt finally arrived, on May 4, with the usual cargo of cotton, much valuable time had been lost, and the *Florida* was in serious danger. Acting with characteristic boldness, he took charge of the "waif on the water," albeit secretly, with Low as cover man. Maffitt was determined to get the ship to sea, whatever the obstacles, little dreaming how complicated that task would become. For one thing, Union representatives expressed great interest in all phases of the ship's activity; for another, he had neither officers nor crew for the raider; for still another, there was some mixup about who would command the ship (at this time Mallory still thought James North was coming from England to take command of it). Maffitt promptly called upon the Confederate Navy Department to confirm his command and to send money and men to get the ship away before the British, under American pressure, impounded it. But before he could escape, Admiralty officers, amid some confusion, detained the ship for violation of the Queen's proclamation of neutrality; legal advisers found that act illegal and insisted upon releasing the ship. Whereupon the officials again seized it, this time for violation of the Foreign Enlistment Act of 1819, and in early June turned it over to a Vice-Admiralty court for adjudication.

During the trial in August, 1862, the judge, John Campbell Lees, held that the Crown had to prove three facts before the court could condemn the vessel: that the "equipping" had taken place within the court's jurisdiction, that there had been intent to employ the ship in the service of the Confederacy, and that there had been an intent to commit hostile acts against citizens of the United States. Because Crown lawyers could not prove any of these things, Judge Lees released the ship to its owners on August 7, but to protect the government from damage claims for illegal seizure, he ruled that there had been reasonable grounds for detention and directed each party to pay its own costs.[34]

That decision dealt a serious blow to the Queen's neutrality regulations by demonstrating that they were inadequate to cope with the fine legal points raised by Confederate construction. It did not seem likely, as Governor C. J. Bayley wrote to the Duke of Newcastle on August 11, that the Crown would ever secure stronger proof of an intent to arm as a belligerent than had been produced against the *Florida;* therefore, he said, "We may assume that no prosecution of the same type will be instituted, or if instituted, that it will fail."[35]

Maffitt immediately took advantage of the decision and had the ship away within twenty-four hours, but its troubles were not over: they were just beginning. Sailing to deserted Green Cay, some sixty miles south, Maffitt met his new supply ship, the *Prince Albert,* with the raider's equipment, or most of it. After back-breaking work trans-shipping supplies under the tropic sun, it was discovered that parts vital to the operation of the batteries had been left behind: the guns were useless. Then a greater disaster struck. Yellow fever began its ugly work, decimated an already too-small crew, and put the captain temporarily out of action. After the ship had been commissioned into the Confederate navy, and after a trip to Cuban ports for supplies and medical assistance, Maffitt decided to take his waif into Mobile for recruits and repairs. On September 4, in late afternoon, he approached that blockaded port with useless guns and a daring plan. Running up a British flag, he steamed straight for the guardships, hoping that the audacity and appearance of the ship would cause the Federals to hold their fire long enough to give him the running start he needed to get past them. When he failed to heed the warning shots of the Federals, they poured a truly murderous barrage into the defenseless ship, a veritable *feu d'enfer,* as Bulloch later put it. But Maffitt made it through to Mobile, where he remained for the rest of the year, recruiting a crew, repairing damage, and preparing for a cruise of destruction.[36]

Early in the following year, Maffitt took his ship out past the blockaders, relying upon stealth to get him through without incident. He took his first prize on January 19, 1863, the brig *Estelle,* worth about $130,000; three days later two more vessels were taken and burned; and on February 12, Maffitt captured and burned his most valuable prize, the clipper ship *Jacob Bell,* valued with its cargo at nearly two million dollars.[37] One further facet of the raider's activity is perhaps worthy of note at this point. In late March, Maffitt captured a vessel, put a crew on board, and sent it out to destroy commerce; he did the same thing again in early May, with even more devastating results. "The *Florida,*" as one author put it, "was breeding offspring that were to be almost as dangerous as she was herself."[38] (One of these offspring took part in what has been described as "the most brilliant daredevil cruise of the war," but that is another story.)

Under a succession of captains in the months that followed, the raider and her satellites played a substantial part in raising insurance rates for Northern shippers by destroying, all told, some sixty vessels valued at over four million dollars. The *Florida* itself captured some thirty-eight ships, destroying in the process enemy shipping estimated at ten times its own cost. The raider's career ended under peculiar circumstances when a Northern warship illegally captured it in the neutral waters of Bahia in October, 1864. After strong protest by the government of Brazil, and a tacit admission by the United States that a breach of international law had indeed been committed in the capture, the first foreign-built raider went down mysteriously at Hampton Roads: in death, as in life, an acute embarrassment to the men of Mr. Lincoln's navy.[39]

FOUR | TWO CRUISERS, TWO CAPTAINS

*T*HE STORY of Bulloch's second cruiser—the *Alabama*—requires some preliminary consideration of a crisis in diplomacy that was created by an imprudent Northern naval captain in late 1861. In the mid-nineteenth century, the heyday of gunboat diplomacy, the impetuous naval officer was often an international troublemaker, but it remains doubtful "whether in modern times any naval officer has ever been guilty of a more ill-considered and thoroughly unjustifiable proceeding."[1] His precipitous actions brought Britain and America to the brink of war and had a considerable, if indirect, impact on the course of Confederate shipbuilding.[2]

In November, Captain Charles Wilkes of the United States sloop *San Jacinto* seized two men, James Murray Mason of Virginia and John Slidell of Louisiana (newly-appointed Confederate commissioners to England and France respectively) from the deck of an English mail-steamer in the Caribbean. By this hasty act Wilkes threatened to disrupt Anglo-American relations, bring about European intervention on the side of the South, and assure permanent dissolution of the Union. To a discouraged, disheartened, and victory-starved North, Wilkes' act seemed a great triumph, fit retribution for British insolence. To proud England, it seemed degrading to royal dignity, insulting to the flag, and a stain upon national honor. Coming at a time of growing misunderstanding and fanned by an irresponsible press on both sides of the ocean, the *Trent* affair excited sensitive emotions and unleashed torrents of vituperative charges and countercharges. To Englishmen, the incident smacked of American arrogance, carrying it almost, as Russell said, to the point of a "direct slap in the face." Many of them, remembering Seward's penchant for foreign wars and tendencies toward expansionism, saw the incident as part of a plot by which the secretary of state sought to acquire Canada as compensation for lost Southern territory.

During the early months of the war, a major liability for the South was poor diplomatic representation in Europe, and that defect had to be remedied. Selection of replacements for the ineffectual commissioners indicated a growing realization of the importance of international affairs in Southern success. President Davis designated Mason and Slidell as his new representatives abroad. When news of the appointments reached the North, a shudder of apprehension was felt across the land —almost as if the selection portended danger for the Union.

The New York-born Slidell was especially feared, and rightly so. Possessing all the qualifications of a successful riverboat gambler, he was able, adroit, shrewd, and unscrupulous, a man of strong passion and iron will "who would conspire with the mice against the cat rather than not conspire at all." Minister Adams remembered him as the sort of person who would fit in well at the intrigue-ridden court of Louis Napoleon. After a visit to the Slidell residence in Louisiana, the well-known correspondent of the London *Times,* William Howard Russell, described him for British readers: "I have rarely met a man whose features have a greater *finesse* and firmness of purpose than Mr. Slidell's; his keen gray eye is full of life; his thin, firmly-set lips indicate resolution and passion. . . . He is an excellent judge of mankind, adroit, persevering, and subtle, full of device and fond of intrigue . . . what is called here a 'wire-puller.' Mr. Slidell is to the South something greater than Mr. Thurlow Weed has been to his party in the North."[3] Such a man, so it seemed, had power to do mischief abroad.

The pompous Mason, on the other hand, personified—with less cause than usual—aristocratic Southern arrogance. Born into a First Family of Virginia, he traced descent to George Mason of Gunston Hall, a Revolutionary War hero and opponent of the Federal Constitution (partly because it sanctioned slavery). James Murray Mason had no qualms on that subject: he became an ardent advocate of the South's "peculiar institution." Appointed to the United States Senate in 1847 to fill out an unexpired term, he soon came to regard membership in that exclusive club his birthright, looking, according to one observer, as if he "owned the Senate chamber." The great Southern statesman, John C. Calhoun, selected Mason to read his final speech on the compromise of 1850; Mason became, in fact, the heir-apparent to Calhoun's position, though without the South Carolinian's burning intellect. Much of Mason's popularity in the South stemmed from his vociferous support of states rights. In 1850 Mason had opposed compromise and supported secession, and in the following decade he worked assiduously to make separation a reality. By efforts to dissolve the Union, by loud-mouthed support for the extension of slavery, by authorship of the much hated Fugitive Slave Law, by defense of Preston Brook's assault on Charles Sumner in the Senate chamber—by all these things and more Mason had blackened his name in the North, and had made it odious to lovers of the Union. Much Northern jubilation over the *Trent* affair stemmed from Mason's part in it, from a feeling that he had been taken down a peg or two: newspapers gloated that the Union had bagged the most abhorrent of its enemies.

These men might have caused trouble in Europe, and their dreams of success very nearly came true—not, however, through their own efforts, but through those of an American captain who felt himself destined to be an admiral. Charles Wilkes played the South's cards better than Confederate statesmen could have.

Details of the incident are quickly told. The Confederates, slipping past blockaders, had travelled to Havana, waited there until November 7, when they boarded the mail-packet, *Trent,* en route to St. Thomas in the Danish West Indies, where they hoped to make connections for the voyage to Europe. Meanwhile, Wilkes was bringing his ship from African waters to join the Union naval expedition against Port Royal. Touching at Havana, he learned of the plans of Mason and Slidell and decided to arrest the two men. His executive officer, Lieutenant Donald Fairfax, tried to dissuade him but was overruled (Wilkes' habit of court-martialing junior officers who disagreed with him assured a high degree of shipboard unanimity). After forty-three years of service in the navy, Wilkes had a reputation as an "insubordinate, impulsive, overzealous, and yet fairly efficient officer"; he was known also for having "a superabundance of self-esteem and a deficiency of judgment."[4]

At five minutes past one on the afternoon of November 8, the *San Jacinto,* then in the Bahama Channel, fired a shot across the bows of a ship flying British colors; at seventeen past one a second shot followed, and the *Trent* hove to and prepared to receive a cutter of armed American marines. Lieutenant Fairfax requested the surrender of Mason and Slidell. When the men refused to leave, Fairfax called his marines on board and arraying *that* warrant neatly on deck, ordered his men "to lay hands upon Mr. Mason." With this application of token force, the Confederates surrendered. Passengers watched the proceedings with hostility, making frequent anti-Union comments: "This is the best thing in the world for the South," one person growled, adding, "England will open the blockade." While Fairfax carried out his part of the play, Rosina Slidell, daughter of the envoy, tried to protect her father. Commander Williams (custodian of the royal mail on board) later reported that the brave, brave little girl had slapped the lieutenant's face, crying, "BACK, BACK,

YOU **** COWARDLY POLTROON!" More probably, a roll of the ship caused her to brush against Fairfax as she argued with him over her father's fate.[5]

The seizure of the rebellious citizens, or the confiscation of the embodied dispatches, or the impressment of two civilians from the deck of a neutral ship having been completed, Wilkes allowed the *Trent* to continue its voyage, though originally he intended to take it into port as a prize. It was, in retrospect, unfortunate that he did not bring the ship into port for adjudication, for had he done so, much of the steam would have been taken out of the subsequent protest of Her Majesty's government. His change of mind had serious repercussions. Beyond doubt, he was guilty of a grave breach of international law. "He had a perfect right to search any suspected ship for goods contraband of war," Allan Nevins has written, "and to take a vessel carrying contraband into port to await the verdict of a prize court. But he had no right to decide the question of a violation of neutrality by fiat on the spot, without judicial process. Moreover, it was extremely doubtful whether persons, as distinguished from goods, could ever be deemed contraband. In impressing men from the deck of a neutral ship, Wilkes had committed precisely the kind of act that did so much to provoke the United States to fight the War of 1812."[6] The British did not exaggerate when they called the incident a flagrant violation of the law of nations.

Capture of the Confederates electrified Northern opinion. "Your conduct in seizing these public enemies," Secretary Welles told Wilkes, "was marked by intelligence, ability, and firmness and has the emphatic approval of this department." The House of Representatives thanked him for his "brave, adroit, and patriotic conduct" and voted him a gold medal. The governor of Massachusetts gloated that "Captain Wilkes fired his shot across the bows of a ship that bore the British Lion at its head." The *New York Times* suggested dedicating another Fourth of July to him. Even the president reportedly would "rather die than surrender the men." Fifty years later, Charles Francis Adams, Jr., could remember no other event which had swept the country so completely off its feet.[7]

News of the incident reached Britain on November 27 and set off an explosion of resentment. Palmerston reportedly erupted to his colleagues: "You may stand for this, but damned if I will."[8] Talk of war—"and with our own Bastards"—filled the land.[9] George Cornewall Lewis, secretary of war, told the prime minister that all signs pointed to the inevitability of war.[10] Undersecretary of State E. Hammond informed the British minister in Paris that the incident smacked of "a premeditated scheme to force us into collision."[11] The Queen, believing that the Americans had "behaved scandalously" and that they were unlikely to release the commissioners, asked to be "fully informed" of all that passed on this "grave affair."[12] On November 29, Palmerston spelled out to Russell the nature of the British response: he sought an apology and release of the envoys. In the event that these demands were not met, Lyons must be recalled, for the country ought not to tolerate deliberate insult.[13] "It all looks like war," Russell reported some days later.[14]

Americans, too, sniffed impending disaster. The minister felt that his mission might terminate prematurely; his son Henry thought their position "hopeless;" and he told his brother: "This nation means to make war."[15] From Liverpool, Vice-Consul H. Wilding reported great excitement over the seizure and said that he could find no one "to admit the wisdom of it."[16] On December 2, Thurlow Weed wrote to Seward that "if the taking of the Rebels from under the protection of the British Flag was intended and is avowed and maintained, *it means war*."[17]

The British press was nearly unanimous in condemning the outrage. The influential London *Times* predicted that the cabinet would fall if it allowed the insult to go unrebuked, and the *Illustrated London News* asserted on November 30 that public opinion would not tolerate tame submission to the forcible removal of passengers from the protection of the flag.[18] On the same day, the Liverpool *Mercury* flatly stated that the issue was "one of peace or war" and assured the government that in the event of American intransigence, it could count "upon the hearty and earnest support and approval of all sections of the community."[19] The seizure of Mason and Slidell, according to the Southampton *Times,* created a "universal feeling of indignation;" and it went on to insist upon reparation for the insult to national honor: "The British flag has been tarnished, its vindication is demanded."[20] Had the ministry desired war, it would have found the country ninety-nine percent behind it, and one newspaper in Scotland estimated the consequence of such an event: "Within a week after the appearance of a British fleet on the seaboard of the Southern States, the blockade would be at an end. . . ."[21]

To be sure, Prime Minister Palmerston had long anticipated some such incident, and even had attempted to avert it by hinting to Adams that there was no reason to interfere with the passage of the envoys because one or two more Confederates in London could make no appreciable difference in the British response to the war. The usually astute American failed to catch the minister's meaning. The attempt to forestall trouble took place after the capture of Mason and Slidell, but before news of it was known in Europe. It later looked as if the American had been indulging in some sharp dealing.

Adams, of course, knew nothing about the affair. He could "infer nothing, assume nothing, imagine nothing." The delay in communication between Washington and Whitehall proved a blessing in disguise, for it gave heated tempers a time to cool, allowed sober second thoughts to assert themselves. Given the tense atmosphere on both sides of the Atlantic, an instantaneous exchange of information might well have been a disaster. Still, the silence from the secretary of state sounded ominous. Adams could recognize that in this instance Britain was right, America wrong, but he did not expect his superiors to see it that way. He felt that the nation was in danger, with a chief "little fitted" to save it. From his vantage point he could see no alternatives except war or surrender, and the latter did not seem likely. He thought his days in London numbered.

There was reason for pessimism. On November 30, after the Queen and Prince Albert had softened it somewhat, Russell sent a strongly-worded note to Lyons in Washington. In it he outlined the government's position, called the seizure a violation of international law (which he hoped the United States did not sanction), and instructed his minister to demand an apology and release of the prisoners. Although stiff enough, the note left room for diplomatic maneuver, for it was accompanied by two private letters aimed at easing tension. One of these instructed Lyons to visit Seward informally, divulge Britain's demands, and request the secretary of state to discuss them with the president and cabinet before formal presentation of the British note. The second letter instructed Lyons to refrain from "anything like a menace," to allow seven days (from formal presentation of the British note) for a reply, and gave him full discretion to decide whether the Queen's demands had been "substantially complied with." But Russell made it perfectly clear that if the demands were not met, Lyons must close the legation and ask for his passport.[22] The British minister, who seldom receives proper credit for his role in this affair, was a first-rate diplomat with considerable sympathy for the North. He interpreted these instructions to give American officials the widest latitude; he did everything in his power to allow the secretary of state a graceful retreat, recognizing that it would "be fair to Mr. Seward, and desirable with regard to our future relations with this government that the compliance [should it come] shall have, as much as possible, the air of having been made spontaneously." The "very circumspect course" of the British minister in Washington did much to assure an amicable settlement of the affair.[23]

There were, in addition, several other forces working toward a peaceful solution of the problems raised by Wilkes. For one thing, the British North American garrison was woefully unprepared for war: London officials were more than a little chagrined to find that "two key forts in Canada had been converted into reformatories, another into a lunatic asylum."[24] More importantly, and despite her moral support in the *Trent* crisis, British government circles harbored a deep distrust of France. Had not the Queen herself warned "in the *strongest terms*" of the danger of being "made a cat's paw for the mysterious and selfish purposes and plans of the Emperor"; had she not noted a "state of alarm or rather more profound distrust in the conduct & purposes of our neighbor."[25] Britons in general, and Palmerston in particular, felt that Napoleon could not be trusted. Knowing the emperor's weathervane temperament and machiavellian inclinations, Palmerston believed that he hated England and cherished ambitions "to humble and punish" her for past humiliations of France.[26] That suspicion grew, fed as it was by the growing French challenge to British naval supremacy in the 1860's. Always, Her Majesty's government had to weigh the possible impact of its action on French policy, had to guard against the possibility that Napoleon might leave his cross-Channel neighbor in the lurch by indulging his penchant for things unexpected and embarrassing. It was possible, and—to some well-informed people in Her Majesty's government more than likely—that the emperor would engage in adventures inimicable to British interests. At the end of 1861, it seemed reasonably clear to Palmerston that the emperor had matured plans "to go to war on a great scale next spring," and, as he told Russell, "if we are engaged in a War on the other side of the Atlantic, as seems likely, he will think himself free from our interference."[27]

While unwilling to stand for Yankee insults—and who could expect *that* from a man who in his youth had thundered *Civis Romanus sum* in the House of Commons?—Palmerston was almost equally unwilling to turn his back on the Tuileries. Then, while the issue of peace or war hung in the balance, the Prince Consort died on December 14. The Queen's husband had been a well-known advocate of accommodation, and his death calmed tempers, brought men to reflection, stilled the war clamor. New York City flew flags at half-mast, and for a few days the press muted its bellicose tone.

Soon after Albert's death, Adams received his long-awaited note from the State Department. Written on the last day of November, it did not reach him until December 17. In it Seward expressed a wish that the incident be resolved in a "spirit of mutual forebearance"; he informed Adams that Wilkes had acted without instructions, and that Her Majesty's government might expect the "best disposition" from America. Adams immediately conveyed this information to Russell to disabuse his mind of any impression that the secretary of state contemplated warlike measures against Britain. Russell replied that much depended on Seward's response to the British demand of November 30 for surrender of the men, but he also expressed an opinion that an amicable settlement, honorable to both sides, could be arranged.[28]

Peace depended upon the American president and cabinet. Although initial praise for the seizure was hard to retract, an undercurrent of reappraisal had rippled across the country. Men, when they had had time to reflect, saw that a war with Britain would be a supreme folly that could only bring humiliation for the Union and independence for the Confederacy. Moreover, more and more people came to realize that on the basis of traditional American beliefs about the freedom of the seas, Mason and Slidell ought to be released, indeed, ought not to have been captured in the first instance. National consistency and national conscience, in Seward's words, combined to compel Americans to regard the British claim as "intrinsically right." Lincoln feared the men might become "white elephants"—or millstones.

The cabinet met on Christmas day to consider Seward's

reply to the British note. Sumner attended in his capacity as chairman of the Senate Committee on Foreign Relations in order to read letters from John Bright and Richard Cobden advocating a peaceful settlement. "If you are resolved to succeed against the South," Bright wrote, *"have no war with England;* make every concession that can be made"; despite this advice, the cabinet could not agree and adjourned until the next day. They then accepted Seward's draft with a few minor revisions and sanctioned the surrender of Mason and Slidell.[29]

America had backed down. Many things entered into that decision: the threat of British naval supremacy, fear of a permanent disruption of the Union by a double war, and, perhaps most important, recognition of the intrinsic rightness of the British claim, which, after all, was based on long-standing American contentions concerning neutral rights and impressment. National principles dictated release of the men, however disagreeable the task, although Seward carefully camouflaged surrender under the guise of winning Britain to America's position on impressment. But then, Seward's note had been written with at least one eye on public opinion, and had been composed largely for domestic consumption: it had just the right chauvinistic tone to bring joy to jingo hearts. If the nation's safety had required custody of the Confederates, Seward said, they would have been retained, but since national security did not so require, they would be released. He then justified this decision by pointing out that Wilkes had left the capture unfinished, and that under maritime law a naval officer was not entitled to act as an arbitrary substitute for a legal tribunal. All in all, it was not an impressive state paper, but it was an effective one. It provided a nice face-saving formula, lessened domestic dissatisfaction with the decision, eliminated, for the moment, any possibility of British aid to the South, and, surprisingly, even enhanced the secretary's reputation somewhat. Lyons, at least, recognized that

Seward had worked very hard and had exposed his political popularity to considerable danger.[30]

The end of the affair was something of an anticlimax. At the height of the crisis, in early December, Russell had told the Confederate commissioners that he could not "enter into any official communication with them."[31] The new commissioners fared little better: when they reached London they were largely ignored. The *Times* unkindly reminded them that they were "worthless booty" and that Britain would have done as much "to rescue two of their own Negroes."[32] There was, in fact, a sort of national psychological release that gave a serious setback to Southern hopes for a collision between Britain and the North, and caused the American minister to tell his son that the "current which ran against us with such extreme violence six weeks ago now seems to be going with equal fury in our favour."[33] The *Trent* affair, said Henry Hotze, public relations expert for the South, "has done us incalculable injury."[34]

In the months that followed resolution of perhaps the most critical incident of the war, the Confederates noted a ground swell of resentment against their cause. From Gibraltar, Captain Semmes, then bottled up in the *Sumter,* commented on the rising anti-South sentiment. "The whole British nation," he told James North on February 26, 1862, "were so frightened in their late quarrel with the Yankees, and have been so delighted to get out of it without a war, that I am afraid we shall never bring them up to the mark again."[35] Some weeks later, North reported a similar view to the secretary of the navy, noting a "tremendous reaction" against the South, which he believed resulted from the release of Mason and Slidell. "These people have received such a fright," he informed Mallory, "that it will take a long time before they recover from it, and the Yankees might, in my opinion, insult them with impunity."[36] He also told the secretary to expect increased difficulty in getting ships out of England because of

growing Anglo-American rapport. Southern agents saw that
even the limited depredations of the *Sumter* were stirring an-
tagonism to their work. Bulloch reported the government
"more determined than ever to preserve its neutrality." Naturally, he became apprehensive about getting his second cruiser
out of British jurisdiction.[37]

*   *   *   *   *

After the *Florida* was out of England, that is, in the weeks
after March 22, Bulloch concentrated on getting the *Alabama*
to sea. His lawyer assured him that all proceedings complied
with the letter of the law, that there was nothing to do except
hurry work on the ship and "get her away as soon as possible."
Experience with curious customs men and Federal spies
warned of danger, and he feared the British might strain the
law by detaining his ship, even without evidence of any violation of the Queen's regulations. He knew that the South's
diplomatic representation was weak and that he had no effective means of protest against arbitrary arrest.

Work on the vessel proceeded with irritating slowness,
partly because the builder insisted on quality material and
first class workmanship; workmen had to fit four different
sternposts before Laird officials approved the work. Another
cause of delay was that Bulloch's other work kept him away
from Liverpool for frequent and extended periods of time so
that he was not always available for consultation. As the hull
took shape, and the ship grew toward the sky, it became clear
that it was no ordinary vessel: Number 290 was, in truth, a
magnificent testimony to the shipbuilder's art. Bulloch, who
knew ships and loved them, considered this one as fine a vessel "as could have been turned out of any dockyard in the kingdom, equal to Her Majesty's ships of corresponding class in
structure and finish, and superior to any vessel of her date in
fitness for the purposes of a sea rover, with no home but the
sea, and no reliable source of supply but the prizes she might
make.[38] Dudley's spies reported it to be "a very superior

C. S. S. *ALABAMA*

(Reproduced with the permission of the Franklin D. Roosevelt Library, Hyde Park, New York)

MODEL OF C. S. S. *ALABAMA*
(Reproduced with the permission of the Smithsonian Institution)

boat," that its timbers were of the "best English oak," that every plank and timber had been hand picked with scrupulous care, that no expense had been spared in material or construction.[39] So fine a ship fully deserved its subsequent reputation as a sweet sailing ship, "the most perfect cruiser of any nation."[40]

Who would command the stately ship? Did the South have a man to match it? Originally Bulloch had orders to take the vessel into action against enemy commerce. What a combination that would have been! But as the cruiser neared completion, Mallory, finding Bulloch's skill irreplaceable, ordered him to remain in England as director of the major phase of ironclad construction.[41] Then the naval secretary again demonstrated his knack of matching men and mission by selecting Raphael Semmes for command of this cruiser: the *Alabama*'s career under his spirited direction is a legend of the sea a century after man and ship disappeared.

Getting the ship out of the country was presenting some problems. A captain certified by the British Board of Trade had to superintend preparations for departure and assume responsibility for compliance with maritime regulations. To take the ship out of British jurisdiction, Bulloch hired Matthew Butcher, a former Cunard first officer with a reputation for competence and discretion. Though Butcher did not enlist for Southern service, it was necessary to take him into the plot, and for a few critical days the success of Bulloch's plan depended on the captain's silent cooperation—a word to American authorities would have provided positive proof of the ship's Confederate connections, evidence to justify seizure. Bulloch's estimate proved sound. Consul Dudley at Liverpool got no information from Butcher.[42]

While the *Alabama* prepared for sea, other agents of the South gathered supplies and armament in London, purchased a supply tender, the *Agrippina,* stocked it with the equipment for the raider (coal, cannon, including one 100-pound Blakely rifle, uniforms, ammunition, everything for conversion to warlike purposes), and worked out details for a rendezvous. The cruiser's new commander was not then in England, and uncertainty about the date of his arrival hampered planning because it would be unwise to have the ship at sea without him. To dally in port was more dangerous, for it might subject the ship to an encounter with Union warships or, more likely, to detention by harassed port officials. The Confederates knew that Federal spies were gathering evidence against the ship, and guessed that this would soon reach the Foreign Office. Whether it would be sufficient to move the government to order detention was another question, but they could take no chances. They had to act before Lord Russell did.

As the second cruiser neared completion in the summer of 1862, a net of Northern counterintelligence surrounded the Confederates. As Federal representatives became more effective, their influence on Crown action increased. Learning from failure, Union agents increased surveillance, consuls grew more vigilant, reports to Minister Adams became fuller and more frequent. American diplomatic pressure increased. Slowly the North was coming to realize that a small, efficient secret service overseas might be more powerful than regiments before Richmond. Federal agents wanted a sort of central intelligence agency directed by a man familiar with the laws and customs, the people and business of Britain—they needed a spy network in arms factories, shipyards, and mercantile houses because they knew that only fully documented, first-hand information would move the British to action, only irrefutable evidence could force Russell to detain suspicious ships.[43] Adams had been unable to convince the foreign secretary that the *Florida* intended to cruise against the United States. This time he meant to be better prepared.

Adams had written Russell in April, 1862, that a cruiser more powerful than the *Florida* was near completion on the Mersey, and he requested that it be detained until he could assure himself that it intended no harm to Northern shipping. After consultation with local officials, the Foreign Office declined to act because in its view there had been as yet no violation of the neutrality regulations. In the opinion of officials who had investigated the matter—and one must remember that the matter had been subjected to a fair amount of investigation—there simply was no reason to detain the vessel.[44] At the end of June the solicitor of customs, Felix Hamel, had written a warning to the government that it ought to exercise extreme caution in the affair of the *Alabama,* that no move against the ship ought to be made "without the clearest evidence of a distinct violation of the Foreign Enlistment Act . . . the terms of the Act being extremely technical and the requirements as to *intent* being very rigid." Unwarranted detention, he thought, might have "very serious consequences."[45] While the syntax of the advice may be stilted, the sense is clear and sound enough. In mid-July Hamel again examined the American complaint, but still was not convinced that there was anything in it but hearsay, hence, inadmissible, evidence. There was nothing in American contentions about the ship "amounting to *prima facie* proof sufficient to justify a seizure, much less support it in a court of law."[46]

Uninformed about the deliberations taking place within governmental circles, American representatives looked upon British lassitude as indicative of sympathy for the South, part of that long-sustained international conspiracy against the Union. Adams nudged the Foreign Office once more in mid-July. Again, no action. Then, in a final effort to move Her Majesty's government to detention, he hired one of Britain's leading barristers, Robert P. Collier (later queen's solicitor) and presented the American case to him. Collier thought that the government ought to detain the ship, and he told Adams on July 23 that it would be difficult to make a "stronger case of infringement of the Foreign Enlistment Act, which if not enforced on this occasion is little better than a dead letter." Collier further believed that if Russell allowed the ship to leave England, America would have serious reason for complaint. This opinion and the evidence supporting it went to the chief law officer of the Crown, Sir John Harding. With the papers on his desk, Sir John suffered a stroke, giving Bulloch a few more days of grace. When the government finally issued a seizure order for the *Alabama*, it was too late.[47]

The South had its own sources of information, its own access to high-level decision-making conferences. Bulloch had "the means of knowing with well nigh absolute certainty" the policy of the Foreign Office. Three days before Russell's detention order, a "private but most reliable source" informed Bulloch that his ship must leave England within forty-eight hours. Bulloch acted. On the night that he received the warning, he wrote letters of instruction to co-workers in the subdivisions of the enterprise.[48] To the captain of the tender in London he sent orders to sail for the Azores and prepare for a meeting with the cruiser; he sent an assistant, Clarence Yonge, to sail with the *Agrippina,* telling him to excite the crew's interest in the forthcoming cruise with a view to enlisting some of them in Southern service; to Captain Butcher he sent confidential information about the ship's route and rendezvous, including directions for transferring the ship to Semmes; and to another assistant, John Low, he gave the task of securing a tug to go out with the *Alabama* when it sailed. Then, on the night of July 28, he anchored the vessel at the public landing stage in Liverpool, with all preparation for departure made. Early next day, that is, on Tuesday, July 29, loaded with local dignitaries, prepared for a day of wining and dining, draped with flags, seemingly unaware of danger, the ship glided down the Mersey without clearance, ostensibly for a trial run. Late that afternoon, when the food and wine were much depleted, Bulloch suddenly discovered that it would be necessary to continue the trial into the night. He suggested that his guests return to the city with him in the tug so thoughtfully provided by Low. When the guests departed, the *Alabama* went to sea, just whiskers ahead of a detention order issued by royal officials at Whitehall. On the day that the *Alabama* made its "trial trip" (July 29), the other two law officers of the Crown, Atherton and Palmer, acting without the incapacitated Harding, advised Russell that the vessel ought to be seized immediately. But valuable time was lost while this advice bounced from the Foreign Office to the Treasury and then on to customs officials in London. This latter group did not send the telegram authorizing seizure of vessel Number 290 to its Liverpool representative until July 31. While all this was taking place in London, Consul Dudley was trying desperately to get the local collector of customs, Samuel Price Edwards, to hold the ship until its status could be clarified. But at the time of the *Alabama's* departure, that official was mysteriously absent from his post.

How does one explain Bulloch's success in this affair? Parts of the story are still murky. There is, for example, no adequate identification of Bulloch's informer, nor is there any satisfactory explanation for the delay in executing the July 29 advice of Atherton and Palmer. Then, there is that rather curious matter of Mr. Edwards. It later became known that he was "a very warm sympathizer with the Confederates and their cause." Perhaps more to the point, it also turned out that the collector of customs was a heavy speculator in cotton, and there is reason to suspect that he was "purposely out of the way" when the *Alabama* sailed.[49]

So, incompetence and inefficiency, plus cupidity and chicanery, on the one side teamed with audacity and good luck on the other to permit the raider's escape. But however one explains it, the fact remains that again Bulloch had outmaneuvered his adversaries.

Once on the high seas, the *Alabama* proceeded to its appointed rendezvous at Terceira Island in the Azores—the place Bulloch had spotted during his earlier voyage in the *Fingal*. There the raider met its supply ship, took aboard equipment and armament, filled out its crew by offering well-paid adventure, and on Sunday, August 24, 1862, was commissioned into the Confederate navy under command of Raphael Semmes, who told his men: "Let me once see you proficient in the use of your weapons and trust me for very soon giving you an opportunity to show the world of what metal you are made."[50]

It took very little time for him to keep that promise and to demonstrate the efficacy of that trade which he had perfected during his service on the *Sumter*. His activity on the high seas soon caused much trouble for the Union navy, great damage to enemy commerce, and some serious second thoughts by officials of Her Majesty's government whén they realized what a destructive force they had unleashed. Semmes was to all intents and purposes his own boss, a law unto himself, and he soon showed the world what a talented commander of a first-rate commerce-destroyer could do: in his hands the weapon had unlimited potential.

About the time Maffitt was running the *Florida* into Mobile, that is, in early September, 1862, Semmes set to work, making his first capture in the region of N. Lat. 38° 27' and W. Long. 30° 40'. After providing for the safety of the crew and helping himself to whatever supplies might prove useful, Semmes set fire to the Yankee whaler *Ocmulgee*. Thereafter, the victims fell with monotonous and terrifying regularity, so that in some six weeks the value of prizes taken totalled approximately $400,000—about twice the initial cost of the raider.[51] Semmes did not enjoy the dirty work—few sailors enjoy burning ships—but he did what had to be done, and was as considerate towards prisoners, especially women, as circumstances permitted (though when some of the victims returned to civilization they carried hair-raising if inaccurate reports about that "pirate" Semmes). He weathered a hurricane, quelled a mutiny, maintained discipline, eluded pursuit—all the while continuing attacks on merchant shipping. Then, in mid-January, 1863, he impudently lured a Federal gunboat, the *Hatteras*, from its post off Galveston, Texas, and destroyed it in a duel lasting less than fifteen minutes. It was the only time a Confederate naval vessel destroyed a Union

warship at sea, and as Bulloch later said, it was "a creditable
performance for the first effort of a hastily improvised cruiser
with a green crew."[52] One must not make too much of the encounter, however, for victory over the "good for nothing"
Federal ship proved very little about the raider's fighting
qualities. Bulloch's verdict may stand: "a creditable performance," nothing more.

The raider continued its ugly work, burning or bonding
ships with insolent ease, until the names of Semmes and the
Alabama were anathema to the North. The Federal navy sent
ship after ship in pursuit of the phantom, but, despite one or
two close calls, it went on its way unhampered, seemingly
invulnerable. It would appear in the South Atlantic or off the
coast of South Africa; then it might turn up in the China Sea
or Indian Ocean. During a twenty-two month cruise of
approximately 75,000 miles, this one Confederate corsair captured, destroyed, or ransomed some sixty-four prizes, account-
ing for the bulk of postwar damages paid to the United States
by Great Britain as a consequence of the international arbitration of the *Alabama* Claims in 1871–72.

The raider's last action, one of the finest sea fights of the
war, was a fitting climax to its career and is, of course, well
known to students of American history. While Semmes was
attempting to refit at Cherbourg, France, during the late
spring of 1864, the Union gunboat *Kearsarge,* under command
of Captain John A. Winslow, appeared at the harbor mouth
and waited for him to come out. The American minister at
Paris had summoned Winslow to this historic encounter, and
so brought to an end a search mission that had been in operation ever since the U.S.S. *Tuscarora* had missed the *Alabama*
when it slipped out of Liverpool in July of 1862.

Prudence might have dictated that Semmes stay in port,
at least until some badly needed repairs could be completed.
But he undoubtedly knew that such a course would have
aided the enemy, for a Union flotilla would then have as-

Duel off Cherbourg between the *Alabama*
and the *Kearsage*: Sinking of the *Alabama*

sembled at the harbor entrance, as it had done with the *Sumter* at Gibraltar. Perhaps Semmes, knowing he had no chance against a squadron, thought he might outmaneuver or outfight a single enemy vessel—though what he would have done had he been victorious is rather an intriguing question. The usually voluble author is strangely silent about events surrounding the fateful June day. It may be, too, that Semmes knew the game was up and wished to go down in a blaze of glory; or it may be that constant enemy insinuations about his propensity to run away, sly references to his reluctance to face armed foes, had wounded his *amour propre* and led him to seek combat deliberately. Or the decision may have been simply a matter of personal and professional pride. For all these reasons or for none of them, Semmes decided to fight the *Kearsarge*: "I beg she will not depart before I am ready to go out." Winslow did not depart.

In his diary Semmes predicted a stubborn fight and thought the ships evenly matched. He did not know that his adversary had an improvised coat of chain cable draped over its side, protecting its engines and vital parts; it was a sort of makeshift ironclad. In size and speed and armament the ships were much alike. But the Union ship was in better repair, its gunners had had more frequent practice, its engines were slightly more powerful, and its ammunition was first-rate. The *Alabama* mounted six 32-pounders, one 68-pounder, and one 100-pounder pivot rifle. The Union ship was armed with four 32-pounders, one 28-pounder rifle, and two 11-inch Dahlgren shell guns. These latter weapons, though already obsolete by back-home standards, packed a powerful punch, and Winslow knew how to use them to greatest advantage.

Shortly after 9:00 A.M. on Sunday, June 19, 1864, the best-known ship of the South, cheered by hundreds of Parisians who had come for the show, steamed slowly out of the safety of Cherbourg into the cold Channel. Among the crowd was the young artist, Edouard Manet, who sketched the raider's last moments. It was a thrilling fight, if short. Semmes's ship was not at fighting peak, its bottom was fouled, its engines decrepit, its powder defective. In the opening moments of the duel it did well, and the fight might have ended if one big shell that landed on the enemy ship had exploded. As the ships circled around a common center in opposite directions, starboard to starboard, Semmes tried to fight at long range; Winslow, whose guns were more limited in range, closed the distance, keeping out of boarding range. The Union ship fired less frequently—perhaps half as often as its opponent— but once the powerful Dahlgrens came into play, they literally demolished the unprotected raider plank by plank. Great gaping holes were punched in its hull, while the lighter Union guns raked the enemy deck with deadly effect. In about an hour, it was all over. The once proud *Alabama* began to settle. Semmes tried to dash for shore, but the ship could not respond. He struck his colors, piped "all hands save yourselves," and shortly after noon the great ship slipped stern first into the Channel.[53]

The British yacht *Deerhound,* a spectator to the battle, rescued Semmes and some forty crew members and took them to Southampton and safety. That incident and the subsequent warm welcome and hero's adulation that Semmes received in Britain touched off another acrimonious exchange of notes between Adams and Russell when the former tried to insist that the men from the raider were American prisoners of war. The British regarded such claims as extravagant and unworthy of consideration.[54]

Shortly after the famous ship's destruction, the London *Times* commented editorially on its career, providing, perhaps, the proper postscript to the story:

The *Alabama* could have found no more fitting grave, for she had lived on the waters, their child and playmate. She hailed from no Southern harbor, she was warned off from many a neutral port and went away to her wild work amid the loneliness of the watery waste. . . . She was a good ship, well handled and well fought, and to a nation of sailors that means a great deal. . . . Beaten in a fair but unequal combat by a gallant foe she has disappeared from the . . . ocean to take her place in history. . . . So ends the log of the *Alabama*—a vessel of which it may be said that nothing in her whole career became her like its close.[55]

FIVE | DIPLOMATIC INTERLUDE

*I*N OCTOBER, 1862, William E. Gladstone, then chancellor of the exchequer in Lord Palmerston's government, made a famous speech at Newcastle-on-Tyne in which he declared that "Jefferson Davis and other leaders of the South have made an army; they are making, it appears, a navy; and they have made what is more than either—they have made a nation." Seldom in modern times has a statesman put the cat among the pigeons with more devastating effect. Historians still disagree about the meaning and intent of that speech. A common interpretation holds that Gladstone, believing cabinet colleagues shared his views, had sent up a trial balloon to test public opinion, that his words foreshadowed a departure from neutrality, that they heralded a new initiative in foreign policy, that recognition of the Confederate States of America would follow in due time. But did this ministerial *obiter dictum* accurately reflect cabinet opinion? Had Her Majesty's government actually reached a point of intervention in American affairs? Perhaps no final answers can be given to such questions, although a re-examination of that famous confrontation of cabinet and Confederacy may illuminate some of the difficulties English ministers faced in arriving at an accurate appraisal of issues raised by the American Civil War and in relating those issues to the larger context of long-range British national interests.

OUR CABINET MAKER.

MR. PUNCH (OVERSEER OF WORKS). "WELL, PAM, OF COURSE I SHALL KEEP YOU ON,—BUT YOU MUST
STICK TO **PEACE WORK**!"

As 1862 wore on there remained a number of potential friction points in Anglo-American relations that, under changed conditions, might have led to serious trouble. Speakers in Parliament frequently expressed anti-American sentiments, which were usually accompanied by attacks on the blockade. Confederate naval construction in British yards annoyed Americans, as did the use of British Caribbean islands as way stations for ships supplying the South. More important in shaping the direction of relations during 1862 was growing distress in the textile manufacturing districts of England. Economic unrest began to generate sentiment for a reappraisal of policy. Further, Englishmen grew increasingly skeptical of Northern ability to force the rebels back into the Union, for by midsummer Federal forces were again in retreat from Richmond.[1] Widespread expectation of an extended war coupled with growing economic dislocation might subject the government to more public pressure than it could stand, making it amenable to mediation.

Indeed, in the summer of 1862 one such move was engineered by William S. Lindsay, an influential member of the commercial community and an avowed partisan of the South, who, on July 11, introduced in the House of Commons a motion calling for mediation in America. Ill-conceived and poorly executed as it was, the move revealed a strong undercurrent of pro-South sentiment in Parliament. Palmerston easily squelched the maneuver. He pointed out that meddling might mean war, reminded colleagues of the benefits of noninterference, called attention to the precarious state of Southern national aspirations, and urged that the ministry be given a free hand "to determine what to do and when."[2]

During the ensuing weeks the Confederate commissioner in London, James Mason, resumed his recognition offensive. He told Russell on July 24 that recent Southern military successes foreshadowed final separation of the American states. Restoration of the Federal Union was impossible, Mason argued. Had not the Confederacy given ample demonstration of its intent and ability to maintain independence? Was it not rightly entitled to a place among the family of nations? In a subsequent note he again urged recognition, reminding Russell that failure to grant it would encourage a war "hopeless in its objects, ruinous alike to the parties engaged in it and to the prosperity and welfare of Europe."[3]

Unconvinced that the time for recognition had arrived, the foreign secretary rejected Mason's plea.[4] Some days later, in response to parliamentary questioning, Russell again stressed his intention to maintain strict neutrality. He informed the House of Commons that any action taken toward America ought to be taken in conjunction with the major maritime powers of Europe, and if any change in policy were required during Parliament's recess, he would consult those powers.

In early August, then, the British foreign secretary publicly indicated that the time for intervention had not yet come. Behind the scenes, however, a sustained and serious reconsideration of government policy was gathering momentum. The cabinet, or more properly a portion of it, was exploring the pros and cons of a more aggressive response to the war. During the late summer and early autumn of 1862, and only then, Great Britain voluntarily approached the brink of war. Anglo-American relations were once again on collision course.

Lord John Russell, exploiting his position as foreign secretary, provided the major impetus for the new direction in policy. Though he had earlier suggested to his chief that a reappraisal of American policy might soon be necessary, he took no positive steps toward implementing a change until mid-September, when Northern military reverses and Lee's march into Maryland seemed to indicate that Stonewall Jackson "might end the war." With Southern prospects so much improved, Russell felt free to mature a plan that would permit a more active response to the war. First, he instructed his ambassador in Paris to sound the French unofficially about joint pressure to end hostilities. Then, after an exchange of views with the prime minister, but without cabinet consultation, he revealed the main features of his proposal in a letter to Gladstone on September 26. Russell's plan looked to an offer of mediation and, in the likely event of Northern rejection of that offer, recognition of the South—all this accompanied by a strong reaffirmation of neutrality.[5]

The war news had affected Palmerston as well. On September 10 he had been opposed to all meddling in transatlantic affairs; four days later he informed Russell of military dispatches which suggested Washington was about to fall into Confederate hands. If that happened, Pam wondered whether England and France "might not address the contending parties and recommend an arrangement upon the basis of separation." While commenting upon Russell's proposals, Pam had suggested inviting Russia (the most pro-Northern state in Europe) into the negotiations, apparently with the hope of sugar-coating a pill he knew the North would find unpalatable. He again stressed the interdependence of the American military situation and European diplomacy. He expected the battle raging north of Washington to have important consequences, for, as he explained to Russell, were the Union forces to be defeated "they may be at once ready for mediation, and the iron should be struck while it is hot." If, on the other hand, the Confederates did not win a decisive victory Britain might safely watch—and wait.[6]

On the 24th Palmerston gave Gladstone a long summary of his outlook on American affairs, and it differed in small but significant ways from that of the foreign secretary. The prime minister recognized the possibility that England, France, and Russia might propose mediation with some small promise of success, explained that arrangements were underway to seek French accord, stressed the need for cabinet approval of any policy shift, and guessed that the chancellor would support a more vigorous course. Palmerston told his colleague that any proposal would be communicated to both sides, and, if accepted by them, the European powers would then recommend an armistice, an end to the blockade, and negotiations on the

VERY PROBABLE.

Lord Punch. "THAT WAS JEFF DAVIS, PAM! DON'T YOU RECOGNISE HIM?"
Lord Pam. "HM! WELL, NOT EXACTLY——MAY HAVE TO DO SO SOME OF THESE DAYS."

basis of separation. If both combatants rejected the offer, the bloody conflict would continue. But if—and this was the more likely possibility—the South accepted and the North did not, then, said Palmerston, we should reaffirm neutrality and "acknowledge the Independence of the South." At all events, a crisis appeared imminent; the outcome of the battle north of Washington might trigger a decision. If the North were defeated, its cause would be hopeless; if the South were repulsed, its army might be destroyed: a few days might bring information of critical importance.[7]

To see this note as a strong stand for intervention, to regard it as an expression of full-blown cabinet consensus, is a serious misreading of the evidence. When taken with other expressions of a growing disenchantment with the scheme, the note suggests that Palmerston was playing his favorite game of watchful waiting. For whatever had been his inclinations in mid-September, he was having serious doubts by early October. Decades of crisis diplomacy had perfected his ability to detect the most subtle shifts in political currents. Conditions in America simply did not look ripe for intervention, certainly not without a convincing Confederate victory. Some intuitive feel for the sentiments of his countrymen counseled caution; some hidden sensitivity said the moment for mediation was not yet.

As September waned, other influences checked the move toward intervention. French reaction to the proposal was surprisingly cool, though that is perhaps explainable by a shake-up in Louis Napoleon's cabinet. More important was news of the Southern "stalemate" at Antietam. Palmerston, who had expected a clearcut Confederate victory, quickly adjusted to changed conditions. He reminded Russell on October 2 that an effective mediation depended largely on a "great success of the South against the North." Ten days earlier it had seemed that such a success was probable; now, one could not be sure. The cabinet's position was "full of difficulty." Time, another week or so, might shed additional light on the problem, but the dilemma could be resolved only by "more decided events between the contending armies." What had appeared an eminently sensible step before Antietam now seemed senseless and full of snares. Doubt delayed decision. The prime minister began to talk of an armistice, to weigh alternatives, to reassess transatlantic affairs, to realize that the American question required careful sifting. Did British interests really dictate involvement? Was the game worth the candle? In early October, there certainly was no cabinet consensus concerning the best course of action vis-à-vis America. In fact, Palmerston seemingly was in retreat from recognition.[8]

At that point, on October 7, 1862, Gladstone let his cat out of the bag. A frenzy of speculation shook England after the Newcastle speech: Was the chancellor speaking for the cabinet, or was he testing public sentiment? Had the government chosen this method to announce an official pro-South policy, and did the speech, therefore, signify a fundamental and far-reaching alteration in the ministry's assessment of Britain's future interests?[9]

Whatever the speech implied, it caught the American minister completely by surprise. Some days earlier, Adams had written to his Parisian counterpart that conditions in England were "as calm as a summer's night" and likely to continue that way. Caught off guard by the speech, he recognized its potential for mischief and saw its possibilities for adversely affecting Anglo-American relations. Strong words at Newcastle must, he thought, foreshadow recognition at London; they must indicate that the current of cabinet opinion had turned against the Union.[10] If so, America teetered on the brink of disaster. He toyed with the idea of asking for an official explanation from Russell but decided against it, electing to wait and see whether Whitehall would back up the speech.

Knowing Gladstone's pro-South proclivities and his tendency toward verbosity, Adams hoped that the chancellor had expressed a private point of view—one not sanctioned by the cabinet. This hope received substantial encouragement when, just a week after the Newcastle contretemps, another cabinet member, George Cornewall Lewis, declared at Hereford that the South had not yet established its independence according to existing criteria of international law. The interests of England, he asserted, were best served not by meddling but by inflexible adherence to the Queen's proclamation of neutrality and the government's policy of noninterference.[11]

When he learned of Lewis' remarks, Adams was much relieved, for he knew that if Gladstone spoke for the cabinet he did not represent a unanimous one. Perhaps, Adams mused, the chancellor had "overshot the mark."[12] But with no way of testing such speculation, the American realized that his country remained in danger; he knew that Lord Lyons was still in England and feared that the cabinet might decide to use its Washington representative as the instrument of a more aggressive American policy. Had Adams known the full story of what was happening behind the scenes, he would have had added reason for apprehension.

Six days after the Newcastle speech, that is, on October 13, Russell circulated a memorandum on American affairs in the cabinet. The foreign secretary apparently was attempting to exploit the Gladstonian *gaffe* to clarify cabinet opinion on intervention. He argued that the South had shown determination and ability to resist conquest, that sentiment for return to the Union was negligible in the Southern states, and that the Emancipation Proclamation, that "terrible plan," would result in a slave insurrection. Therefore, the European powers ought to propose a cease-fire to allow calm evaluation of the benefits of peace. This proposal—be it noted—fell far short of active mediation and recognition: Russell would not or could not spell out the specifics of an armistice or the means by which it might be implemented.[13]

As if in direct rebuff to Russell and his memorandum, Lewis, acting on his own initiative and without any prompting from the prime minister, spoke at Hereford the next day, the fourteenth. Although his speech had no more sanction than Gladstone's, Lewis tipped off the press and public that the cabinet had made no firm commitment to the Confederacy. He took this opportunity to expand on views he had already made known to Russell. The Hereford speech and a later memo prepared by Lewis were two important parts of a vigorous opposition to any departure from neutrality. Because Lewis did not speak as a partisan of either the North or of the South, and because he argued his case in terms of British interests, his words carried considerable weight, both in and out of the cabinet.

On October 17, Lewis repeated his objections to intervention, diplomatic or otherwise, in a long, carefully reasoned cabinet paper. While agreeing with Russell's diagnosis at many points, Lewis sharply rejected his colleague's proposed remedy. Any policy other than strict laissez faire was "full of dangers," some obvious, some obscure. For his part, Lewis doubted whether Russell's "philanthropic proposition" held any promise of success; he thought it more likely to result in evil than in good. Lewis argued that under existing conditions, Britain's attempt to arrange a settlement in America which was agreeable to both sides "would almost inevitably end in failure; while at the same time, it would embarrass her government, and perhaps tarnish her honour."[14]

Meanwhile, Palmerston, upon whom final responsibility rested, had indirectly sounded the opposition leader, Lord Derby, for his estimate of American affairs. The response to these overtures had indicated that the Conservative leadership strongly opposed intervention because it was chimerical, apt to "irritate the North without advancing the cause of the South or procuring a single bale of cotton." Given the passion of the belligerents, mediation could not succeed, even if the intervening powers "knew what to propose as a fair basis of compromise." England could not possibly derive any benefit from recognition unless she were prepared to sweep away the blockade, and that, Derby hinted, might mean war with the Union.[15]

Opponents of intervention were reinforced by timely support from an unexpected source. The cabinet received a report containing two important items of information from a special agent in America: (1) even if the war ended immediately there probably would be long delays before any appreciable amount of cotton reached England, and (2) the Northern states, especially those in the west, showed little inclination for a negotiated peace and were vigorous in support of the war. It therefore seemed likely that British intervention neither would ameliorate economic distress in the cotton districts nor find any acceptance in America.[16]

These facts strongly undercut the premise of Gladstone's argument at Newcastle. But Russell, who still believed that an armistice, even if rejected, could do no harm, grudgingly admitted only that recognition might be "premature," and that no move ought to be made without Russian participation.[17] Apparently the role of arbiter of American affairs exerted continued fascination for him, for like an English bulldog, he refused to let go of it.

If Palmerston sympathized with the foreign secretary's tenacity, he was too seasoned and too shrewd to ignore fact. The prime minister clarified his thinking on intervention in a letter dated October 22. While characterizing his colleague's view of overseas conditions as "comprehensive and just," Pam still tended to agree with Lewis that the time was not auspicious. Nor was timing the only problem. A premature armistice proposal (especially one seemingly motivated by economic distress) might weaken Britain's moral position, and Pam recognized his lack of leverage for moving the parties to a conference table. All Her Majesty's government might do was to ask the belligerents whether they would consider an "arrangement" between themselves—and it required no seer to predict the answer. To talk of peace to the contending parties would be very much like asking the recent high winds to leave the waters unruffled. Consequently, it seemed to the prime minister that the flirtation with intervention, justifiable perhaps when the Confederate offensive seemed to be carrying all before it, ought to be terminated. For his part, he had returned to the government's original estimate of transatlantic affairs: "We must continue merely to be lookers-on till the war shall have taken a more decided turn."[18]

Still refusing to give up on some form of intervention, Russell postponed a cabinet meeting scheduled for the 23rd, but met informally with some of its members to discuss an armistice proposal. He then turned from intra-cabinet politicking to meet with Minister Adams, who, after two weeks of rumor, uncertainty, and apprehension, had decided to seek official explanation of Gladstone's remarks at Newcastle. Russell informed him that the prime minister and cabinet regretted the speech because it conveyed an erroneous impression that the Queen's government had decided upon a change of policy. Russell could honestly say that no such decision had been made, though he did not think it necessary to disclose his own pique at his colleague's ill-timed revelation that discussion of a policy change was in fact underway. He told Adams that the government wished to adhere to a policy of strict neutrality and to allow the struggle to settle itself. He could, however, make no promises about the future of British policy. Yet, when Adams asked specifically whether Britain would continue her present policy, Russell gave an affirmative answer. Reassured, Adams perhaps took this remark more positively than Russell intended it. Since this interview coincided with the nadir of discussions seeking active intervention in America, Russell could straightforwardly say that no interference was then contemplated. Whatever mental reservations he may have had, he kept them to himself.[19]

The Russell plan was not dead. It lived partly because its architect did not believe intervention would lead to the dire consequences envisioned by Lewis or that such a move really required a departure from neutrality. Russell still sought a *modus vivendi* which would enable him to indulge his ambition to be the arbiter of America's destiny. Opposition to the plan, however, was forcing him to shift ground: first, he had favored a joint Anglo-French action, then, in response to the prime minister's hint, Russia had been brought into the scheme, and now, in late October, he saw that "no less than five powers" could implement mediation. In good diplomatic fashion the plan was being multilateralized. Meanwhile, he had drawn up a rejoinder to Lewis' memo, in which he insisted that his colleague had misunderstood the original proposal. The foreign secretary argued that he had always envisioned concerted action by the major European powers, that he was merely canvassing the possibility of securing such action, and that only if the cabinet approved and the powers agreed, did he propose going to the Queen with definite plans for a negotiated peace between North and South.[20] All parties save the belligerents figured in his calculations, possibly because he believed, with Gladstone, that the Americans could not resist "a general opinion on the part of civilized Europe that this horrible war ought to cease."[21]

But if the plan remained, so too, did opposition to it. Opponents of the plan received timely support from the influential Lord Clarendon, who, though not a cabinet member, kept close tabs on its discussions. A brother-in-law to Lewis and Palmerston's intermediary in the sounding of Conservative views, Clarendon was well briefed on all facets of the intervention imbroglio, and he came down strongly against any departure from established practice. He praised Lewis' opposition to involvement and credited him with a key role in alerting the cabinet and the country to its dangers, pointing out that the Hereford speech had done much to check the "alarm and speculation" touched off by the indiscretion of Gladstone; he emphasized that the cabinet memo of October 17 had played a large part in "smashing" interventionism. What Clarendon especially liked about Lewis's position was

ONE HEAD BETTER THAN TWO.

Louis Napoleon. "I SAY, HADN'T WE BETTER TELL OUR FRIEND THERE TO LEAVE OFF MAKING A FOOL OF HIMSELF?"

Lord Pam. "H'M, WELL, SUPPOSE YOU TALK TO HIM YOURSELF. HE'S A GREAT ADMIRER OF YOURS, YOU KNOW."

that it did not bind the ministry to any particular line of action but provided room for maneuver and left the cabinet free to modify its policy in response to changing conditions. That the Foreign Office plan lacked flexibility and committed the Crown to an exposed and potentially untenable position was to Clarendon a major defect. That plan, he asserted, would have placed England in an "idiotic" posture before the world; but then he thought that Russell had a tendency "to do something when to do nothing" was prudent.[22]

With so little to recommend it, the intervention plan seemed dead, at least to its opponents. But in late October it took on new life, primarily because the ministerial crisis in France ended with a new minister at the Foreign Office and a new aggressiveness on the part of Louis Napoleon. The emperor suddenly seemed very anxious to help terminate the American war. According to the British ambassador in Paris, Lord Cowley, plans were underway to approach England and Russia with proposals seeking "joint action by the three powers in suggesting an armistice of six months, *including a suspension of the blockade.*"[23]

The French proposal did not impress Palmerston—partly, one suspects, because it was French. Was it likely, he asked Russell, that the Yankees would agree to a cease-fire and a termination of the blockade? Was it likely that the cabinet and the Confederacy could reconcile their deep differences on the slave issue?[24] Dislike of slavery and distrust of the French prevented the prime minister from taking any interest in intervention.

Russell's response naturally included a willingness to discuss a plan that dovetailed so nicely with his own, even though he suspected that the Americans would reject any armistice offer. Again Lewis spearheaded opposition, countering with another long memo on November 7 which stressed past principles of recognition and examined traditional British practice, finding these inconsistent with current Foreign Office objectives. His argument was seconded in the

Times by one "Historicus" (another relative of Lewis!) who summarized the legal aspects of recognition in international law and argued, among other things, that premature intrusion by a neutral state in the internal affairs of another was a hostile act, construable in law as "a breach of neutrality and friendship."[25]

Once more cabinet opinion was divided, although by this time it leaned in the direction of indifference, if not downright hostility, toward any interference in America. For a last time Russell played all the familiar themes; Palmerston supported him with little enthusiasm; other members proceeded to "pick the proposal to pieces," as Lewis gleefully described the process. With but one or two exceptions everyone threw stones at the plan. Much opposition centered on its onesidedness, "it was so decidedly in favor of the South, that there was no chance of the North agreeing to it." With cabinet sentiment decisively against meddling, Palmerston "capitulated," and Britain rejected the French offer.[26]

Cowley conveyed this decision to the emperor, and almost simultaneously the English and French press published news of it. Soon thereafter, Adams and Russell met, though the former still knew nothing about the latter's involvement in the mediation maneuvers. Adams told him that the English note to Paris was certain to generate friendly sentiment in America. In turn, Russell asserted that the move had been sparked in part by a belief that Secretary Seward might have welcomed an international mediation. Adams stated in no uncertain terms that such was not the case, and informed his adversary of Seward's mid-August orders which forbade him to listen to any proposals of interference and to suspend his mission in event of recognition of the South. The foreign secretary complimented him on his discretion in not revealing these instructions sooner. "It is possible," one historian has argued, "that if Russell had known earlier about Seward's absolute opposition he might have thought twice before pursuing intervention plans."[27] This view, however, ought to be qualified by noting the more likely possibility that American intransigeance might well have rubbed British leaders the wrong way and have stimulated interest in intervention, just to take the arrogant Yankees down a peg or two. (Duff Cooper reminds us that Palmerston's vanity had been deeply wounded by a cartoon which showed him being led by Talleyrand—"that he of all men should be suspected of subservience to a foreigner was more than he could bear.") One should note, also, that throughout the discussions looking to some form of intervention, the British were not moved either by hatred for the North or sympathy for the South. Like many of their countrymen, Russell and Gladstone saw separation as the only possible destiny for the Americans. In the autumn of 1862, primarily because of severe economic distress in the cotton districts and repeated demonstrations of Northern military ineptness, Russell and some of his colleagues felt that the time had come for concerted European pressure for mediation. That the maneuver did not succeed was due largely to Palmerston's acute sense of the danger of intervention with force and the folly of interference without it, to his reluctance to take that last fatal step: in short, to his preference for peace.[28]

SIX | CRUISERS: PART TWO

*M*UCH HAS, of course, been written about the two most famous of the Confederate raiders—the *Florida* and especially the *Alabama*—but historians have largely neglected the stories of other Southern cruisers, though these lesser-known ships presented Her Majesty's government with some intricate problems and their fates accounted for many shifts in the fortunes of the Confederate cause in Europe. Commerce raiders were never numerous, a handful inflicted most of the damage on Union shipping; but the Confederacy built other raiders in addition to the famous ones, and though their names are strange and little known except to Civil War buffs, their histories illuminate both the troubles that faced President Davis' overseas agents and the difficulties that confronted Queen Victoria's ministers as they grappled with the issues raised by Confederate naval construction.

In the fate of these obscure ships one may also trace the effect of Southern military reverses on Palmerstonian policy. For, in the final analysis, failure of the Confederate construction program came as much from military defeat as from Union countermeasures. Minister Adams and his son Henry recognized the advantage of negotiating from strength.[1] John Bright, a friend of the North, told Senator Sumner that England's response to American affairs depended in large measure upon military results, that Union success on the battlefield would greatly reduce the Confederate capacity for making trouble abroad.[2]

As noted, it was not surprising that Lee's failure to win at Antietam in September, 1862, pushed the British to a crucial reappraisal of policy. The reversal of Southern military fortunes perplexed the Queen's ministers, for they had nearly decided that the North could not conquer the rebellious states. Then, as a result of conditions in America, the cabinet had decided to continue the hands-off policy adopted at the outbreak of hostilities. Britain's difficult problem of finding a proper response to the war, Pam said, could be resolved only by more decisive military results in America. Later, and in a different context, the prime minister again emphasized the close connection between Britain's position and the fortunes of war by telling his foreign secretary that any interference in the conflict seemed unwise while the South's military fortunes were less than prosperous.[3] With justification one might argue that if Lee had won in Maryland, if Pemberton had held Vicksburg, if Pickett's charge had succeeded, then naval procurement abroad would have been far easier. The construction program might have encountered fewer obstacles, might have been accelerated to a point where no effective countermeasures could have interfered. Timing was all important to the program; delay, whether because of money or inefficient communication or doubt about the British response, upset a timetable.

The cruiser question was fraught with trouble for Britain, and variations in official reaction mirror the government's dilemma. Southern business did no harm to the economy, indeed helped offset hardship caused by the cotton "famine." "As far as the trading and commercial interests of the country are concerned," the Liverpool *Mercury* told readers, "the policy of peace has proved to be also the policy of prosperity."[4] That same policy, however, had also permitted armed ships of the South to pursue Northern commerce, and Russell and his colleagues in the Foreign Office grew wary of the consequences of continued depredations by British-built cruisers; their success proved harmful to the South by bringing them vividly to the attention of royal officials. The press, at least in part, was becoming critical of Confederate activity. The Southampton *Times,* for example, wondered why so many people connived at a practice "inconsistent with our neutral position," and pointed out that reasonable people could not condone "the wanton destruction and the terrible havoc which these Confederate privateers have committed."[5] Even the press of Liverpool, the center of Confederate construction, expressed concern over commerce raiding. It was becoming evident that an end to the business might serve English interests better in the long run.[6] Ministers became aware that England—as the leading maritime power of the world—had much to lose by lax morality on the ocean. The Duke of Argyll told the cabinet that in "the first war in which we are engaged 'Alabamas' will certainly be fitted out against us from neutral ports. It will then be found important to be able to say that we did our best to protest against the legitimacy of such proceedings."[7] The government saw the need for a stronger policy and a second look at the practice of unrestricted shipbuilding for belligerents.

Recognizing defects in existing regulations, the government had to be circumspect in seeking to change them, for centuries of constitutional conflict had devised safeguards for private property, forcing officials to operate in a narrow framework of national and municipal laws, many of them obsolete or inadequate to the times. Because of conditions in England and on the Continent in the early 1860s, the Foreign Office preferred inaction. Russell stalled and read dispatches from the South hoping to find a clue to action— perhaps he would not have to act.

Behind his reluctance stood the massive resistance of the imperturbable Palmerston, the political realist, serenely confident that his kind of neutrality was best for Britain. While his policy, or seeming lack of it, alternately angered or pleased people in America, it worked to Britain's advantage, and that, after all, was Pam's primary concern. In discussing the pros and cons of mediation, he doubted that England could find a basis of accommodation suitable to both sides in America. It seemed safer to stand aloof and allow those "raging Parties" to settle the quarrel. The best course "was to give no pretext for a quarrel with either side," while maintaining British rights. About a year later, in October, 1861, he repeated this advice on America, saying that the best policy called for avoidance of dispute with either side.[8] Here, as in so many other things, he was in harmony with his public; he judged their temper well. "If I have in any Degree been fortunate enough to have obtained some share of the good will and confidence of my fellow countrymen," he once told William E. Gladstone, "it has been because I have rightly understood the feelings and opinions of the nation, and because they think that I have . . . endeavored to maintain the Dignity and to uphold the Interests of the country abroad, and to provide for its security at Home."[9] With this sensitivity to the well-being of the Queen's subjects, Palmerston could gauge the effect of Confederate activity on domestic and international conditions and act to prevent serious danger to England.

*   *   *   *   *

The fate of the cruiser *Canton* illustrates many of the problems of Confederate construction; its loss demonstrates just how decisive a combination of Southern military failure and Northern diplomatic pressure could be.

The cruiser's story began auspiciously, and Mallory's men encountered little trouble in opening negotiations for the vessel. In the spring of 1862 the navy department sent George T. Sinclair abroad to buy or build a ship. Instructed to cooperate with Bulloch in design and finance, Sinclair soon found that Confederate funds overseas were not adequate. He called on James Mason for assistance, and the commis-

sioner suggested the sale of cotton bonds and assumed responsibility for advancing the agent funds to start work.
While this form of financing was to expand greatly in future
months, Mason was gambling on its merits, though he later
won Mallory's approval for it.[10] Everything went forward.
Bulloch assisted in technical matters by furnishing plans,
specifications, and sample contracts. Uncertain about British
reaction to this activity and anxious to keep his Confederate
connections under cover, Sinclair, in the autumn of 1862,
indirectly contracted for a ship to be delivered in nine
months. A British subject, Edward Pembroke of London,
acted as intermediary by ordering the vessel from the Clydebank firm of James and George Thomson.[11]

Designed to fit the South's purposes, the cruiser incorporated the recently patented technique of composite construction—wooden planking over an iron frame—pioneered
by Alexander Stephen and Sons of Glasgow.[12] This construction gave three advantages: increased strength with decreased weight, enlarged cargo space, and (when sheathed
in copper) resistance to bottom-fouling, a serious problem
to all-iron ships operating in warm waters. The ship fitted
nicely into Southern plans, for it possessed speed and maneuverability, a large power plant with retractable screw, and
an extended cruising radius. Designed to carry heavy guns,
this ship was to be a self-contained fighting unit—a super-
Alabama. Southern agents considered it a bargain at
£51,250.[13]

Soon after construction got under way the problems of
all Confederate shipbuilding began to plague the vessel.
Inefficient communication, lack of coordination, and delay
in construction created misunderstanding between Mallory
and Sinclair. In the weeks of uncertainty and apprehension
that followed seizure of the *Alexandra* in April, 1863 (see
pp. 161–77) , Sinclair, with the approval of Mason, decided to
slow work on his ship pending the outcome of proceedings
against the *Alexandra,* but Mallory, who had important plans

for the *Canton* and who was largely uninformed about the situation in Britain, thought his agent was not vigorous enough in pushing construction. He therefore placed the senior naval officer in Europe, Samuel Barron, in charge of Sinclair's ship with orders to get it to sea as early as possible. But after investigation, Barron could suggest only one change. Sensing increased hostility and fearful of Scotland's more efficient detention system, he advised Sinclair to take a "vacation" on the Continent so that he would not be available if the British started asking embarrassing questions.[14]

As the ship neared completion, Northern interest in it picked up. Union agents gathered bits of information, collated them, and forwarded items of interest to Adams, who pressed for investigation. As early as September, 1862, the American consul at Liverpool, Dudley, began compiling a dossier and channeling information to his superiors. To the consul, everything about the ship looked suspicious: the people who "superintend her construction, the secret manner in which she is being built and the refusal of the builders to state for whom they are building her."[15] Convinced that the ship was for the Confederates, but unable to prove it, Dudley watched the *Canton* closely.

Despite American complaints Russell took no notice of the vessel until March, 1863, at which time a preliminary investigation convinced him that no action could be taken. He informed Adams that the *Canton* belonged to a bona fide British subject who intended using it for peaceful purposes; he said the ship could not leave for some months and that it would be watched for violations of neutrality.[16] Beyond surveillance he could not or would not go.

Toward the end of 1863—a crucial year for the Confederacy —the pace of events affecting the fate of the *Canton* accelerated. Northern agents continued watching it, but could uncover nothing that would justify seizure. Dudley had no doubt about the ship's purpose and wanted a Federal warship at the harbor's mouth to capture it should an escape attempt

be made. He and the consul at Glasgow, Warner L. Underwood, repeatedly tried to find some pretext to halt construction. Underwood reported to Adams that Scottish law offered
"peculiar facilities" for ministerial investigation; he thought
that suspected persons might be examined under oath without trial.[17] When Adams mentioned this possibility to Whitehall, Crown law officers were horrified and indignantly
denied the allegation. The solicitor general told Russell that
the Americans were entirely mistaken, that the laws of Scotland gave no sanction whatever "to the examination upon
oath of persons accused of crimes." The solicitor did, however, indicate a technique by which the government, if it
wished, might delay departure of the *Canton* without committing itself to any definite line of action. A civil suit would
prevent the ship from leaving port "until the legal question
should be determined."[18]

If hesitant, the government was thorough. On November
10, 1863, the Royal Navy's chief constructor reported that
his examination of the ship's specifications disclosed no evidence that the ship was "designed for war purposes." He
added that "the plans afford some ground for suspicion."
The collector of customs at Glasgow, Frederick Trevor, informed superiors that the ship had been ordered for Patrick
Henderson and Company, highly respected city merchants,
as broker for Edward Pembroke of London. Captain A. Farquhar told Admiralty officials that there could be little doubt
that "the statements and surmises contained in the U. S.
consul's letter to Mr. Adams respecting her are pretty correct; she is evidently built for aggressive purposes, and from
her fine lines will probably have great speed. The description
of her appearance is exact." After a second examination the
captain reduced his estimate of size, but repeated that the
ship had possibilities for aggression and might be "a second
Alabama."[19] All this did not alter Russell's estimate of the
case; he advised continued surveillance.

Union agents enlisted the help of local citizens to try

goading the Foreign Office to action. A memorial from the Glasgow Emancipation Society implored Russell to act immediately so the ship could not leave until a "satisfactory investigation has been made into her character, ownership and destination."[20]

The Confederates were not insensitive to all this interest in their business: speeches by British political leaders and prying questions by customs officers made them apprehensive, anxious to unload vessels they now thought would not be allowed out of England. In late October, 1863, Sinclair and Pembroke agreed to cancel their contract, the former insisting that the government's stiffening attitude made the breach necessary. "The unconcealed hostility of your government," Sinclair wrote on October 21, and the "publicly expressed opinion of Earl Russell that he was prepared to go beyond and behind the law in order to meet the bullying demands of the Yankees can leave no doubt on a candid mind that he will not permit the unarmed vessel for which I contracted to leave England for fear she may find arms in some other part of the world and offend the Yankees."[21]

Meanwhile the fine points of international and domestic law raised by the *Canton* and her supposed purpose did not go unnoticed at Whitehall. Although the Foreign Office wished to do nothing, events pushed officialdom to action. Unobtrusively Russell took steps to prevent the departure of the ship. By mid-November the Home Office had a bulky file on the *Canton*, and with the concurrence of the Foreign Office decided to detain the ship. Officers at Glasgow received orders to enforce this decision, discreetly if possible, with force if necessary. Crown law officers, still hesitant, counseled against seizure by judicial warrant under municipal law and advised an injunction from the Scottish Court of Sessions against the vessel's departure.[22]

Again legal complications stymied action. Officials were unsure of their course, yet agreed that it would be inexpedient—though not necessarily illegal—to allow the ship to leave the British Isles.²³ Because it was not expected to be ready for sea for some weeks, officials followed a wait-and-see game. Customs officers placed a telegrapher on twenty-four-hour duty to alert the Admiralty guard ship, the *Hogue,* of any attempt to move the *Canton,* although the guard ship's captain had strict orders to take no action without orders from Scotland's lord advocate: the British did not want the vessel to leave but were unsure of their right to stop it. On November 19, 1863, the chief legal officer of Scotland summarized this situation for the cabinet. "It is clear that we must make up our mind immediately as to the course to be followed, and whether we are or are not to try the question of forfeiture of the vessel under the Foreign Enlistment Act." This was no simple question, and he went on to argue that "we are in considerable difficulty not only because we are of opinion that as yet no *prima facie* case has been made out against the vessel or its owners or builders, but because we have strong reason to doubt whether the most unlimited access to information would materially alter the legal question." He pointed out that the government lacked substantial proof of any connection with the Confederacy, and said this was not the only or the most important stumbling block. Moncrieff reminded colleagues of a simple but important point—that the *Canton,* according to all available information, "has not equipped and no one has attempted to equip her, and therefore it may be said with much force that no one can have aided, assisted, or been concerned in her equipment." Unless someone made such an attempt the ship could not be charged with violation of the Enlistment Act.²⁴

Officials saw unresolved difficulty in the *Canton* case. Then early in December, 1863, unexpected information from a routine inquiry suggested a way out. One of the new owners of the vessel told investigators that Pembroke had entered into the contract with Sinclair, "who represented himself as a subject of the so-called Confederate States of America." Customs men discovered a note from Sinclair written in

September requesting termination of the contract because of British determination "to yield to the pressure of the U. S. Minister and prevent the sailing of any vessel that may be suspected of being the property of a citizen of the Confederate States is made so manifest that I have concluded it will be better for me . . . to close the contract referred to and go where I can have more liberal action." At last the government had some proof connecting the *Canton* and the Confederacy. In the absence of anything better, the ministers decided to chance another confrontation in court with the Enlistment Act. At least the Sinclair letter might constitute reasonable grounds for seizure.[25]

In view of the circumstances surrounding the ship, frequent American complaints, and the evidence of Sinclair's connection with the Confederacy, Sir George Grey, on December 10, 1863, informed the Foreign Office that customs men, acting under instructions from the lord avocate of Scotland, had taken the *Canton* into custody.[26]

Early the following year royal surveyors examined the ship for induction into the Queen's navy, but found it unsatisfactory. In the months that followed, its owners, who were British, made several attempts to release their property, finding each time that the government was obdurate in its determination to bring the ship to trial.[27] Finally, during a preliminary hearing held to test the sufficiency of evidence in this case, Lord Ardmillan ruled that to justify a seizure under existing regulations, it was not necessary to prove either an "actual arming" or an "intention to arm."[28] Such an interpretation of the law greatly enhanced the government's chances of success in court, so the Confederates made no effort to contest the case, and the Crown won by default—possibly the only way it could have won. In the spring of 1864, the *Canton* was forfeited to the Queen for a violation of the Foreign Enlistment Act.[29]

*   *   *   *   *

In the autumn of 1862, at about the same time Sinclair started negotiation for his ship, Secretary Mallory sent another agent to Europe, this one a distinguished man of science, Matthew Fontaine Maury, an internationally known oceanographer whose work on wind and tides had won high acclaim. He had assisted ship captains in planning faster routes—his work may have cut more than a month from the New York-San Francisco run. He had made the world smaller. His appointment, partly the result of domestic politics, was an attempt to use Maury's reputation to raise Southern prestige. The mission also had a more practical aim, for besides purchasing naval craft, the agent was to put into operation a modified system of financing. Transfer of funds by bills of credit had become costly due to fluctuations in currency values, so Maury brought a plan for using cotton bonds to finance Confederate operations.[30]

After consultation with Bulloch, Maury decided that transactions by individual agents might upset the delicate cotton market; he authorized the South's fiscal agent, James Spence, to dispose of the bonds in cooperation with Fraser-Trenholm. When Maury arrived in England the South's financial affairs were messy and negotiations over the so-called Erlanger loan were taking place (see below, pp. 147–50), so that it was necessary for agents to move cautiously in all things that might upset the money market. They decided to await the outcome of Emile Erlanger's maneuvers before putting Maury's bonds on the market. Still, the plan had merit and enabled the agent to embark on the other phase of his mission. During 1863 he succeeded in getting two vessels out of England, the *Victor* and *Japan*. The misnamed *Victor* (under a different name) proved a most reluctant rebel. Only the *Japan* (also under another name) had any success against Union commerce.

Strictly speaking, Maury's *Japan* (also called *Virginia* and *Georgia*), was an ironclad, but because it sailed as a commerce raider for nearly six months of harassment to

Northern merchantmen and fell into the same category of complaint as the *Alabama,* one may conveniently classify it as a cruiser, whose purpose was not blockade breaking but destruction of merchant shipping. Other factors support such a classification: Maury's orders spelled out the ship's mission ("to cruise against the commerce of the United States"), and his cousin, William L. Maury, captain of the ship after its conversion into a warship, exhorted his crew by telling them "to sink, burn, and destroy Union vessels." Thus, by intent, action, and effect, the *Japan* was a commerce raider.[31]

While the ship was in British territory outfitting with Jones and Company of Liverpool, an agent of that company, Thomas Bold (another relative of Maury), retained title to the ship in an attempt to forestall seizure, for Northern agents quickly picked up the maneuvers of Maury and his associates. Consul Underwood communicated their suspicions to Seward. Newspapers in Scotland speculated that the ship would serve under a Southern flag. And once again, British officials who visited the vessel while it prepared for sea convinced themselves that the ship was designed for commerce, that "her framework and plating were of the ordinary sizes for vessels of her class," and customs men who inspected it shortly before she left port certified that nothing on board indicated warlike intentions.[32]

To allay suspicion the *Japan* cleared for Hong Kong and other Far Eastern ports. It then went to Greenock, Scotland, to fill out its crew, and left British waters just ahead of the detention order issued upon the presentation of new American evidence. The persistent Consul Dudley had ferreted out the ship's mission from an unimpeachable source—drunken sailors who had jumped ship because of concern about violating the Queen's neutrality.

The case quickly assumed a comic-opera potential. The by-now-familiar routine took on new twists, to the mortification of Northerners and the delight of British newspaper readers, who were treated to a rollicking account of the con-

tretemps in the *North British Daily Mail*. The story began
by putting pressure on a sensitive nerve. "A case has just
come to light which will be almost as mortifying to the
Federals as the escape of the Alabama." The report accurately
sketched in the background, told how many men had shipped,
their prior service, and the unhappy consequence of paying advance wages to thirsty British tars. When the crewmen
recovered their senses after a losing bout with John Barley-
corn, their patriotism or thirst—or quest for further riches—
had flared anew, and they rushed to tell the American consul
that they had been "shipped for service on board the Japan,
a vessel fitted out to 'burn, sink, and destroy all Federal
vessels she came up with.' " Here was a situation which the
Yankees could not tolerate. Dudley informed his superiors,
who informed the Foreign Office. Russell proved cooperative,
the paper reported, and without even waiting for Dudley's
deposition had ordered Liverpool customs men to detain the
ship. Alas, the reporter continued, no ship answering Dudley's description could be found. Again telegraph wires
hummed: Liverpool to London, Adams to Dudley and back.
Then the matter cleared. The consul shamefacedly admitted
that he forgot to mention that the ship was at Greenock. Officials tried there, but too late. The ship had sailed for an
"unknown destination."[33] The destination, as it turned out,
was the French coast and a rendezvous with a supply tender
from Aldernay that carried nearly £3,000 worth of supplies
and equipment for the new raider.

Curiously, attempts to detain the supply ship, the *Alar,*
also had failed. The New Haven board of customs stated
there was no evidence "to call for any interference on the part
of the Crown." Apparently there was confusion in government policy and procedure. The tender's departure was expedited when an "unaccountable mistake" caused the Foreign
Office's letter of instruction to port authorities to go astray
and then to be delayed five more hours because the commercial telegraph had closed for the day.[34] Several weeks later,

after American complaints about the partisan nature of this act, William Atherton and Roundell Palmer, as law officers of the Crown, advised the Foreign Office that as far as they could determine no violation of regulations had been committed by anyone connected with the *Alar*. They advised against any action on the complaint and specifically excused Captain Hitchcock of the *Japan* from violation of the Enlistment Act by pointing out that any "recruiting" he may have done took place in French waters, while the act was "expressly limited to acts done within the territorial jurisdiction of the British Crown."[35] It seemed to them that the American complaint was invalid.

Adams drew another blank when he later complained that a British subject, one Thomas Bold, retained ownership of the vessel, even after it had begun raids on Northern commerce. Again, the Crown's legal advisers were not impressed by the American argument; they believed that such ownership, even if proved, was no offense at law. One of Russell's advisers noted that notoriety was not proof, that it was first necessary to prove that the *Japan* and *Georgia* were the same ship: and that, he hinted, might not be so easy.

So haphazard and rapid had been arrangements for the departure of the supply ship that it had to be towed to its meeting with the *Japan*. Trans-shipment of supplies took three nights, for the Channel beyond the three-mile limit of France and Britain was not conducive to the smooth transfer of cargo. But when the transfer had been effected, William Maury took command, announced his mission, hoisted the Confederate flag, and invited volunteers to a life of plunder and adventure. Those who refused the siren call returned home in the supply ship, and the thrice-named ship, now the C.S.S. *Georgia*, began its cruise of destruction. Though neither as effective nor as long-lived as some of its more famous brethren, it inflicted a fair amount of damage on Northern commerce. It had, moreover, the distinction of taking part in the South's only foreign war. Van Doren Stern gives a lively account of the semi-comic incident:

The *Georgia* [in February, 1864] waited for several weeks at the appointed rendezvous for the *Rappahannock* to arrive. While near the coast of Morocco some of her crew were allowed to go on shore where they were met by 'hundreds of Moors armed with spears and old-fashioned guns. . . .' There were no casualties on the desolate beach, but there was a general melee from which the *Georgia's* sailors escaped by hurriedly taking to their boats. When they got back to the ship, the drummer was ordered to beat to quarters, the guns were cast loose and fired at the mob on shore. The surprised Moors vanished immediately, disappearing into cave dwellings cut into the cliffs that lined the beach. The shelling probably did no damage, but the incident became known among the young officers on the *Georgia* as "the Confederacy's only Foreign War."[36]

This cruiser was ill-suited for its work; after capturing only nine Northern vessels, the ship needed repairs and went to France for them. While there, the Confederates decided to transfer its armament to the C.S.S. *Rappahannock,* then waiting to be outfitted at Calais. A rendezvous was arranged, the *Georgia* steamed off to engage in its foreign war, and the French foiled the plan by refusing to allow the *Rappahannock* to leave port (see below, pp. 221–26).

About three months after its encounter with the Moors, the *Georgia* became the center of a slightly different international incident, one that brought a minor victory for Northern diplomats and dried up a source of Confederate funds in the late months of the war. Like its sister ships, this raider suffered from the inadequate harbor facilities of the South and was eventually forced to seek refuge in a neutral port. The cost of refitting proved prohibitive, and the Confederates decided to dispose of it. The disposition raised some interesting points of international law and resulted in new regulations for British shipyards, ship brokers, and port officials. After its Moroccan adventure the raider had returned to France, where it was granted the customary fortnight visit (and where Federal warships attempted to prevent its escape). Overstaying its welcome in France, it left to return to Britain. Treasury officials on May 2, 1864, received notice of its arrival at Liverpool. What was to be done with the pariah? Customs men wired Whitehall for instructions and received warning of a possible collision between the *Georgia* and the U.S.S. *Kearsarge,* then prowling the coastal sea lanes. After consultation among the departments concerned in such matters, the Foreign Office announced that the ship must leave, unless sold (offers of sale had appeared in the local press). If a legitimate warship, it was exempt from municipal law but subject to Admiralty regulations, and it could be denied access to port. These legal distinctions became important, for on May 19 the Liverpool *Mercury* announced the sale of the vessel to Edward Bates, one of the city's wealthiest shipowners. Although port officials thought the transaction aboveboard, London authorities warned that Southern agents could be given little credence.[37]

Americans were even more suspicious of the convenient transfer. Vice-Consul Wilding wrote Adams on July 26, 1864, of his fear that the sale was a sham, that there was "no intention of converting her into a merchant vessel." He reminded the minister that the new owner, Bates, had dissented when Liverpool merchants protested to the government about fitting out ships for belligerents. Wilding also noted that little had been done to alter the ship's warlike character, that the rails on which the gun carriages operated were still on board and easily reinstalled. Next day Adams complained to Russell that the sale was not bona fide, that the legal cover afforded to British subjects to "send out in their name this vessel in a shape fitted for further hostile operations" was creating ill will between Britain and America. Such activity, he hinted, ought to be stopped before irreparable damage to the two nations resulted from it.[38] Although reluctant to think that good citizen Bates would permit his vessel to be used for belligerent purposes, Crown advisers believed that in the future it might be wise to prohibit any sale of warships in British ports, and with full approval of the law officers, the government, on August 11, 1864, ordered that no ships of war "belonging to either of the ·Belligerent powers of North America shall be allowed to enter any of Her Majesty's ports for the purpose of being dismantled or sold."[39] Again, the prohibition worked proportionately greater hardship on the South by further restricting its overseas options and eliminating one more "out."

The new owner, with a bill of sale signed by Bulloch, tried to take some profit from his investment by chartering his ship for a voyage to Portugal. American naval personnel refused to regard the transfer as valid and considered the ship a vessel of the enemy. Thereupon, the U.S.S. *Niagara* took it into custody, put a prize crew aboard, and sent it to America for condemnation. When Bates protested this action, Lord Russell informed him that the United States court must decide the legality of the ship's transfer of title. Bates took precious little profit from his investment in the *Georgia,* while the Confederates fared somewhat better, replenishing their cash assets by some £15,000.[40]

SEVEN | SCOTTISH SEA MONSTER

*T*o counter Lincoln's blockade of Southern ports, the government of Jefferson Davis had two options. The first was to rely upon the coercive power of cotton to force an outright European intervention in the war. But it soon became clear that the major European powers — Britain and France—would not intervene without having strong assurances of Confederate victory over Union land armies. The second, and more feasible, alternative—construction of an ironclad ram fleet—had much to recommend it. With such a fleet, equipped with underwater piercers of great strength and armed with powerful up-to-date guns set in revolving. turrets, the South hoped to open its ports, get cotton to Europe, enhance its credit, and give assurances of military invulnerability.

If such ships could be procured in sufficient numbers to overpower blockading squadrons, the North's stranglehold would be broken and the end of the war would be in sight —on terms favorable to the Confederacy. With the blockade lifted, and having meanwhile cleared enemy commerce from the seas with its cruisers, the South would have a market for cotton and access to unlimited war materials; she could then hold back the Northern forces, prevent conquest of the seceded states (except at prohibitive cost to the North), and thus weary the Union into a negotiated peace and recognition of Southern independence. So reasoned the Richmond authorities, forgetting the many variables, ignoring the terrible "ifs."

It was, of course, a long gamble, but where danger was, salvation might also be. If the ram plan was a more risky venture than cruiser construction, it nonetheless had a chance of success that careful management might exploit. The South, at any rate, could not afford to ignore the challenge; and Mallory liked the odds.

The Navy Department had no doubt of the importance of steam ironclads, and early in the war Mallory had told his co-workers that possession of such vessels was a matter of top priority. Such ships, he explained to the chairman of the Confederate Congress's Naval Committee, could operate up and down the enemy coast, disrupt blockade stations, and almost singlehandedly disperse the Union navy.[1] Later, when the ram program was under way, Bulloch echoed these sentiments in outlining the duties of the powerful Laird rams. These ships might sail southward, he told Mallory, "sweep the blockading fleet from the sea front of every harbor, . . . prevent anything like permanent, systematic interruption of our foreign trade." In his imagination grandiose plans formed. He saw Northern cities, even Washington, prostrate before the rams, offering fabulous ransoms, begging for mercy. Portsmouth, New Hampshire, that hotbed of hatred for the Confederate cause, might pay $60,000,000 "insurance" against shelling. Then there was similar work on the Mississippi. Such operations, while greatly weakening the enemy's will to fight, might also have strikingly beneficial results abroad.[2]

Southern naval strategists hoped that Federal forces would be diverted from blockade duty to seek out and destroy the cruisers; the remaining squadrons, thus weakened, would then fall to the piercing rams.

The Washington government was much alarmed by the supposed power of the rams. Assistant Secretary of the Navy Gustavus V. Fox expressed a common fear when he wrote to a special overseas agent that the rams must be stopped at all cost because the Union had no defense, no guns to fend off their attacks. To detain them was, Fox thought, a matter of life or death. Northerners expected the rams to bring the war to coastal cities, to attack Boston or New York, and to scatter the blockading squadrons.[3] From Belgium, Henry S. Sanford described the rams as "the most formidable war-vessels that could be employed to do us injury," and he urged the uncle of Queen Victoria, King Leopold, to use his influence in preventing their departure from England.[4] At his post in France, John Bigelow soon came to realize that ram construction promised much danger for the Union. When he saw the little vessels that Bulloch was having built in France, Bigelow insisted that they were capable of opening every Confederate port to the commerce of the world and putting every important Northern seaport under tribute.[5]

* * * * *

Secretary Mallory moved quickly to put into operation the second phase of Southern strategy. The Confederate Congress, on May 10, 1861, had appropriated two million dollars for the purchase or construction in European yards of one or two warships of the most modern design and equipment. Well-informed about foreign affairs, the secretary had briefed congressional leaders on the naval rivalry between England and France. He told them that under Napoleon III the French had surged ahead by building over a dozen ironclad warships of up-to-date design, and that Britain was slowly closing the gap by an aggressive program. He explained to Congress the implications of the new naval technology, stressing that only with weapons of the most modern design could the South hope to offset Northern numerical preponderance, only with rams could the South hope to break the blockade. With congressional approval he sent James H. North to Europe to secure ships patterned after the French *La Gloire*, reputedly the world's most powerful warship.

North received careful instructions to assure the success of his mission. Because of France's supposed sympathy for the South, Mallory believed the agent might make arrangements there for the transfer of ready-made warships of the most powerful classification, but if that course should prove impracticable North was to seek permission to construct ironclads in England or France, keeping his Confederate connection secret. The secretary gave full details on specifications and armament for the vessels, and told North to examine Britain's newest ironclad, the *Warrior,* then under construction on the Thames, to see whether any of its improvements could be included in his own vessel. In addition he was to confer with Captain Cowper Coles, one of England's best naval architects, to ascertain Coles's views on construction and armament. What the South wanted was a ship which, while staying out of range of Union guns, could pound blockaders to pieces.[6]

There were many complexities involved in North's mission. Before returning home he had to face all the problems inherent in a foreign construction program: his difficulties mirrored those of the Confederacy itself. Money was a major worry, as was the lack of communication with Richmond. Imprecise responsibility and overlapping authority, the plethora of agents competing with one another, and the uncertain attitude of royal officials, kept him off balance and distracted him from the task at hand. Then, there was the sheerly human element. Despite unflagging enthusiasm for the Confederate cause, North was temperamentally unsuited for the cat-and-mouse maneuvering needed to outwit Union spies, suspicious customs men, and shrewd Scots. He was surprisingly naive, and years of naval service perhaps had made him petulant, hypersensitive, and inflexible—accustomed to command rather than compromise. He lacked the tact of Bulloch, the astuteness and skepticism of Slidell. A stickler for "going by the book," he could not adjust to a game in which there was no book. His refusal to take the *Florida* to sea very nearly led to disaster. Though well-intentioned, he could not put his mission into the general pattern of Confederate objectives.

Upon arrival in England in the summer of 1861, he found that no ready-made warships were available, either there or in France. When he set to work lining up construction possibilities he met an unexpected obstacle: the Anglo-French naval race, then in progress, had resulted in a scarcity of armor plate. The British attempt to restore the naval balance vis-à-vis France had a stimulating effect on the shipbuilding industry, giving most yards ample work. Admiralty needs took precedence over foreign orders. There was a way around that difficulty: for a modest margin of profit, contractors would squeeze in new orders. North, alas, had no money.[7] The appropriation for his work did not arrive. He received a cryptic, coded telegram from superiors: "buy an ironclad . . . upon any terms."[8] But in exasperation he told Mallory that money alone talked; without it builders lost interest.

Unsure of his ability to carry out the heavy responsibility of his mission, unable or unwilling to take advice from co-workers, handicapped by lack of funds, surrounded by suspicion, almost overwhelmed by his task, North took nearly a year to begin construction of the most powerful weapon in the Southern arsenal.

In the spring of 1862, after months of searching, North's persistence began to bear results, and in April he was able to inform Richmond of promising prospects for an ironclad. Soon thereafter, on May 21, 1862, he signed a contract for frigate Number 61, the mammoth and mysterious Scottish sea monster. Asking Mallory for funds to meet ten equal payments totaling £180,000, he promised delivery within a year.[9]

On the drawing board North's ironclad appeared a formidable ship, for it measured 270 feet with a 50-foot beam and a displacement of 3,200 tons, builder's measure. Plans called for reinforcement to withstand the stresses of ramming

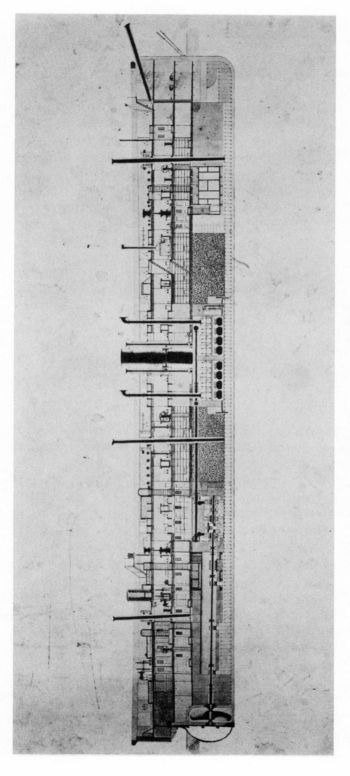

"THE SCOTTISH SEA MONSTER"

Longitudinal section of J. H. North's ram, No. 61. Built by J. & G. Thomson, Glasgow, and bought by Denmark. Commissioned into the Danish Navy as the *Danmark*. (Reproduced with the permission of the Huntington Library)

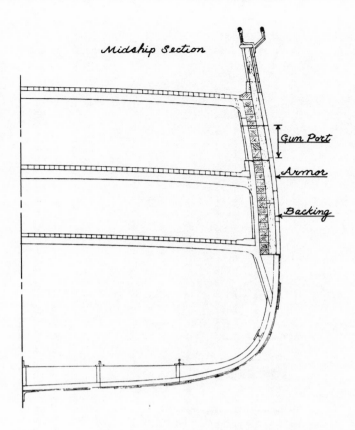

Midship Section

Gun Port

Armor

Backing

Above, a midship section of No. *61* (the *Danmark*); below, a longitudinal section showing the spur. Sketches by William E. Geoghegan, Smithsonian Institution.

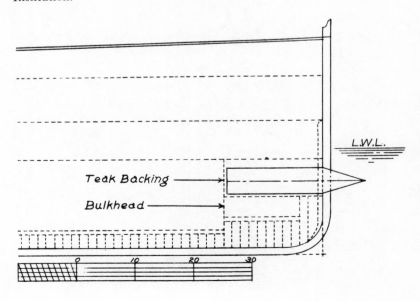

L.W.L.

Teak Backing

Bulkhead

0   10   20   30

under propulsion of two engines producing a nominal 500-horsepower. Plating approached Royal Navy standards, with a sheath of armor 4 and $\frac{1}{2}$ inches at midship, tapering to 3 inches at stern—all backed with 18 inches of teak in two nine-inch layers, one horizontal, one vertical. The protective covering extended from the 14-foot waterline to the gunwale at the spar deck. Under the counter and for 13 feet abaft the stem, the plate thinned to one inch. The plans also provided for a recessed shelf to be worked into the sides of the ship, to support the plate and backing and to bring them flush with the hull below the armor belt.[10]

Contrary to a persistent Civil War myth (the origin of which may have been a fanciful artist's sketch that appeared in *Harper's Weekly* during the war), frigate Number 61 did not have double turrets and a sleek profile. It was a stubby, rather unpleasant-looking broadside ironclad, pierced for ten guns per side, mounting all armament on the main or battery deck. The gunport shutters, 2 feet wide and 3 feet high, cut through plate and backing, were inconveniently pivoted from an upper corner of the port. In action such an arrangement would have been a handicap, for if the lifting chain were shot away, the shutter would fall closed and put the gun out of action. The old wooden-wall solution to that problem, *i.e.*, blasting the shutter away, might prove disastrous to the gun crew. North, an old navy man, suggested pivoting the shutters from the lower edge of the port, but for some reason did not insist upon this more sensible arrangement.

Plans of the ship show a plumb stem, overhanging stern, an almost straight sheer, and a flush spar deck. Above the level of the main deck, Number 61 was sharp-ended at bow and stern. In combat the rudder-head and post would have been exposed to shell damage, for they were not completely submerged. The bowsprit was hinged so that it could be lifted out of danger during ramming. Though neither handsome nor fine-lined, Number 61 was probably superior to second-line British ironclads; though smaller than the *Warrior* or *La Gloire,* it was much larger than the more famous Laird rams that Bulloch was building at Liverpool.

North had little bargaining ability and remained uncomfortable and off-balance in the complicated business negotiations surrounding this deal. His impatience to "do something" for the South resulted in several imprudent clauses and expensive omissions in the contract. The ship was far too large for the demands that the Confederate navy wished to make on it. Its displacement, if taken at 4,747 tons, would have given a draft of nearly twenty feet, thus cutting off access to shallow Southern harbors far more effectively than any Federal squadron could do. The number of men needed to operate the vessel was too large; North specified space for 500 men (the *Alabama* operated with a crew of about 150). North also forgot to specify a lifting screw,* an omission noted too late for correction, and allowed the builders to protect themselves by stipulating that failure to meet the third installment (£18,000, when the ship was half-framed) would entitle them, after two months grace, to terminate the contract. In spite of Bulloch's express warning on this point, North did not include a penalty clause for late delivery. By failing to insist that the builders provide protection against the elements, North allowed progress to depend on the vagaries of Scotland's weather.

There was one additional problem, the ram, a conical-shaped spur about six feet long that was attached to the stem some six or seven feet below the water line. The builders contended that this arrangement would permit Number 61 to strike an adversary below its protective plate, lessening shock and damage to itself. They took precautions to assure its strength, but in the unlikely event that the ram might be torn away on impact, provisions were made to confine the

*A rather ingenious arrangement by which the propeller might be disconnected and lifted into a well in the ship while it was operating under sail alone.

damage to the fore part of the ship by means of bulkheads sealing that portion off from the remainder of the vessel. As time went on, North became dissatisfied with the builder's design and wished to substitute a modified and (as it seemed to him) more practical arrangement, but by the time he made this suggestion, the ship was too far advanced to permit structural alteration without considerable expense; and the builders were able to convince him that the original plan would answer his requirements.

Initially all went well, and North's shaky morale improved, though he could not free himself from gnawing apprehensions about money. He intensified his entreaties to Richmond for funds; he was becoming painfully aware of the necessity for having cash in hand to meet the payments on his ship. Indeed, he had little opportunity to forget the need for money because the builders sent him frequent and pointed reminders of the schedule of payments. In response to his pleas, Mallory ordered Bulloch to assist in paying for the Clyde ironclad: "Not a day, not an hour," Mallory insisted to his chief agent, "must be lost in getting the rams over, and money is of no consequence in comparison to the speedy accomplishment of this work."[11] Responding as usual, Bulloch met North's third payment in September, 1862, but by so doing nearly depleted his own resources.

By the autumn of 1862, the overseas phase of naval procurement badly needed revamping, for the haphazard duplication of agents and missions had strained credit and disorganized priorities. Bills of exchange, letters of credit, and shipments of specie could not replenish the rapidly dwindling supply of available resources. On September 20, Mallory summarized his plight: the country's domestic exchange was nearly exhausted and could be procured only in small quantities; cotton was leaving the South in amounts too small to serve as an adequate source of foreign exchange; and he was "seriously apprehensive" about the treasury's ability to meet the demands of the European contracts. Mallory hoped, however,

that these conditions would quickly pass away, and he emphasized that they must not slow the construction program or
endanger credit in Britain. While stressing the need for Bulloch's assistance to other agents, Mallory authorized him to
pledge bonds, sell hypothecated cotton, or borrow on the best
terms available. Such arrangements, as Bulloch well knew,
were stopgap measures until the South's new fiscal coordinator, James Spence, could arrange the sale of the cotton bonds
by which the Confederacy hoped to finance its foreign purchasing operations.[12]

In this period of deepening economic crisis, North found
an opportunity to exploit that Southern financial panacea,
cotton currency. On September 19, he told Mallory: "If I had
Confederate bonds or authority to pledge cotton on the faith
of the Government, backed with the signature of our minister
out here, I think money might be raised, and on more favorable terms than you can in the Confederacy."[13] Cotton currency was a constant lure to Southerners, and North, of all
people, came close to setting up the means of supplying it.
But lack of cooperation from the commissioner in London
combined with communication difficulties and confused responsibilities to thwart the plan. North's currency plan was,
of course, not original; the idea was, so to speak, in the air,
and at one time or another most of the Southern representatives suggested some variant of it. The procedure was that for
an agreed-upon price for cotton, say five to ten cents per
pound, the Richmond government agreed to deliver a stipulated number of bales to a port of the customer's choice in
the Confederacy. The bonds, warrants, or certificates were
"futures." At the time North made his proposal to Mallory,
the latter had just completed arrangements for sending some
two million dollars worth of such certificates to Spence for
sale in Europe, and Bulloch, in collaboration with Fraser-
Trenholm, was sounding the Liverpool market for sale of
similar cotton warrants. North's plan had one advantage—
a buyer for the bonds. On his own initiative and indepen-

dently of other agents, North had (he said) stirred up enough interest in his plan in London business circles to be assured of funds with which to pay the balance on Number 61 and provide a surplus.[14]

Bulloch, who had many friends in the financial world, was taken aback by the ease with which North nearly managed this complicated transaction. Two days before Christmas, 1862, Bulloch commended his co-worker and confessed his own lack of success: "If any person or persons have offered to buy cotton from you at 10 or even 8 cents per pound, I earnestly advise you to sell without delay and irrespective of any anticipated means of raising money." The more experienced senior agent offered one caution. Sell for cash! "In plain terms," he explained to North, "if any man will pay you $40 to $50 per bale of 500 pounds, the cotton to be delivered to his order in any port in possession of the Confederates, I would close the bargain instanter." Five days later, after conferring with other agents, Bulloch repeated this advice, adding that the "character of the person buying is nothing if he purchases for cash." Warning that cotton brokers were apt to be "more than sharp," he urged prudence.[15]

By early December, North stood ready to conclude a deal needing only official endorsement from Bulloch plus final approval from the mysterious and still unnamed broker. A key member of the brokerage firm was away on business, but his associates expected authorization for the purchase of about £150,000 worth of certificates.[16] At this point, the chaos in Confederate fiscal affairs blocked North's venture, forcing him to abandon the scheme on the threshold of success. Bulloch told North that Richmond authorities had prescribed a special form for cotton bonds, ordered that they be signed by Mason, and that the proceeds from all sales be assigned to Fraser-Trenholm. Treasury officials in Richmond also insisted on a delay in bond marketing because of the impending Erlanger loan. In theory a wise—even necessary—attempt to reduce competition on the money market, in fact the decision

cut off a promising source of funds for North and slowed construction of the Clyde ram.[17] North acknowledged the new
arrangement and reported its effect: "Mr. Mason has received
such instructions from the Treasury Department that he
thinks I had better stop all proceedings. So, in obedience, I
have stopped and the result is, I have no money."[18]

With his excursion into high finance at an end, North was
thrown back on his own depleted resources, Bulloch's
thinned-out credit (Bulloch's January payment to Thomson
had exhausted current funds), and Minister Mason's bland
assurances of forthcoming funds.[19] The new year had not
brought any improvement in Confederate credit; and Southern finances, which badly needed overhaul, had to wait many
more months for the first step toward a sensible plan for the
coordination of purchasing and financial operations and the
appointment of a czar for fiscal affairs.[20] In early 1863, agents
begged Minister Mason for money or permission to raise
their own, but the minister counseled patience, believing it
inexpedient for naval officers to meddle in the cotton market.
Having "no hurry" in him, the minister remained unper-
turbed by their pleas. North sent a request for funds in early
February, pointing out that the builder might stop work.
"There will unquestionably be money to the credit of the
Government and in a very few days," Mason placidly replied,
"and if necessary you may say so on my authority." If in the
face of *that* assurance the contractors decide to suspend work,
why, "let them do it." On February 21, the same day that
Mason wrote the above note, Secretary Mallory sent a long
instruction to his chief naval agent couched in different terms.
Rapid delivery of the rams still held high priority with him,
for he hoped to use them for the recovery of New Orleans; he
again stressed that no money or effort should be spared in
getting them to sea quickly, and ordered Bulloch to complete
his ships and North's "as early as practicable."[21]

The autumn and winter of 1862–63 was a period of acute
economic distress for Confederates in Europe. Credit weak-

ened, debts mounted, and the senseless duplication of men and missions had brought fiscal affairs to the point of chaos. The South had overextended itself and the failure of cotton diplomacy was becoming painfully evident. But cotton did have a power that had not as yet been properly exploited: it could be used as collateral for credit. By hypothecating cotton, the authorities in Richmond might go a long way toward putting their overseas financial affairs in order, and the autumn of 1862 was a propitious time for them to do so; by then, surplus foreign stocks of cotton had been depleted, with a consequent increased interest in cotton speculation as its price rose on European markets. The Confederacy took two steps to stabilize its overseas finances: first, as noted, it approved the use of cotton as backing for bonds, warrants, certificates, and the like. Then, on October 28, 1862, the·government appointed as financial coordinator James Spence, a Liverpool businessman who had been active in the Southern cause. But it failed to spell out his duties, and again a good plan ran into trouble: it took too long to arrange, approve, and implement a system that might have gone a long way to alleviate foreign fiscal troubles. (One British firm reportedly was willing at this time to take nearly two million dollars worth of these cotton certificates.) Unfortunately, there were communication problems, personnel problems, and problems of assigning responsibility. Most importantly, there was the problem of the Confederacy's second fiscal maneuver, the so-called Erlanger loan.

*   *   *   *   *

On the same day that Spence was appointed coordinator of foreign finances, John Slidell at Paris sent to Richmond "certain propositions" for a loan that had been suggested to him by the famous international banking firm of Emile Erlanger and Company, one of the largest, most successful, and best-connected financial houses in Europe. The minister remarked that he would not have bothered bringing the prospectus to the attention of superiors if he had not had ample reason to believe that "in anticipation of its acceptance the very strongest influences will be enlisted in our favor."[22] What these influences were or what they would do he did not say.

The proposal sent to Richmond was a most interesting one. Secretary of State Benjamin, one of the shrewdest men in the South and sometimes called the "brains of the Confederacy," explained its features to the equally astute commissioner in Paris in a note dated January 15, 1863. Benjamin noted that the proposed terms were so onerous that the Confederate government could not possibly approve of them. It was immediately plain to the secretary that though nominally a loan, "the contract was really one for the purchase of cotton and that cotton would be demanded for the whole amount." The terms of the preliminary contract were rather complex, but as Benjamin interpreted them, they gave subscribers a right to buy cotton at about 3 and $\frac{2}{3}$ cents per pound. (At the time, cotton was selling for 16 to 22 cents per pound in the South and from 30 to 50 cents per pound in Europe.) While the original terms were rejected, a modification of them was negotiated by Benjamin and approved by the Congress of the Confederacy. Under the revamped proposal the amount of the "loan" was reduced from 25 to 15 million dollars and the interest from 8 to 7 percent; the South was to receive 77 instead of 70 percent of par value, and after due allowance for deferred payments, discounts, and commissions, it would net about 70 percent, or about $33.60 per bale of 400 pounds. It was a bad deal, as Benjamin well knew. "The profits by the takers of this loan will be enormous," he told Slidell with commendable restraint; but he went on to suggest that they should be "quite sufficient to effect the political purposes you anticipate."[23]

While these negotiations were going on, Southern agents in Europe were, as noted, encountering great difficulty in meeting their financial obligations. Minister Mason reported in early February that nothing had been done to dispose of the cotton certificates already in Europe, except to use a small portion of them to meet some pressing debts piled up by Caleb Huse on behalf of the Confederate war department.* Mason also called attention to the rising cost of money and warned that unless something were done, credit would be in a bad way. All this, of course, directly affected North's ram project in Scotland.[24]

Approval from the Confederate Congress to market the Erlanger bonds reached Europe on March 18, 1863 (the act of authorization had been passed on January 29), and the next day the brokers opened their books in a number of European cities. In two and a half days over £15,000,000 worth were sold, most of it in the British market. The initial demand drove the price up, so that the bonds sold at a premium of four or five percent on the first day, even though (as Spence and others recognized) the market price was dangerously high. Popular support seemed so strong that Mason crowed, "cotton is king at last."[25]

Mason, as usual, was wrong—or at least he spoke too soon. By early April the bond price began to sag, though there was little evidence to support Confederate contentions that Northerners were manipulating the market to depress prices. For the South two dangers would follow a sharp decline in the price of the bonds: First, the already shaky credit situation would receive a damaging blow, and secondly, bond purchasers might forfeit their initial deposits of fifteen percent rather than make the required second payment in late April. These considerations, plus some heavy pressure from Erlanger agents (one of whom hinted that the proceeds from the initial sale were in fact the profits of the company and not the property of the Confederates), led the South to that most dangerous of market maneuvers. With money just acquired from bond sales, they attempted to bull the market.[26] And in the weeks that followed, they poured some seven and one-half

*Huse was one of the first—and most talented—agents of the war department to operate abroad in purchasing military supplies for the Confederate States.

million dollars into the market to sustain bond prices. When the results of this flier into high finance were finally tabulated, it turned out that the South had purchased about half the bonds offered for sale, and realized approximately two and one-half million dollars out of a fifteen million dollar "loan."[27] No one knows how much profit accrued to the promoters of this scheme. If one could penetrate the enigma of Erlanger, much might be told about the collapse of the Confederacy. When men so shrewd and able as Benjamin and Slidell, two of the most sophisticated in Southern service, could be duped by the lure of chimerical "political advantages," what chance did the South really have in Europe? Perhaps, as has been said, the money was "pure profit to the Confederacy." One wonders what it was called by the French financial foxes who fleeced the South.

*   *   *   *   *

Meanwhile, in the early months of 1863, as the Confederates struggled to bring order to their tangled finances, they had to fend off mounting Union counter-efforts, for the American representatives continually gathered evidence of Southern activity and refined their techniques to make complaints about it more effective at Whitehall. Failure did not slow them down; disappointment did not turn them aside. Perhaps financial troubles made the Southerners more apprehensive, for they started noticing a subtle shift in the British reaction to their activity. At first it was difficult to define, but there was something in the air, something in the evasive answers to questions, something in the ease with which Yankees seemed privy to the most clandestine Confederate transaction. Confederates noted, or thought they did, an increasing British coolness, a seeming predilection for the North, and signs of collaboration between the British foreign secretary and the American minister.[28] By February, 1863, they saw more signs of a shift in British policy; by March suspicion verged on certainty, and fears received confirmation in April when Crown

officials seized the *Alexandra* at Liverpool (see pp. 161–65).
This development spread consternation. Did the seizure por-
tend more rigorous enforcement of British neutrality? "It is
evidently the object of the English government, knowing that
they can not legally stop our operations, to delay them to the
utmost," reasoned the officer superintending construction of
the seized ship, Lieutenant James Hamilton, and he added a
surprisingly accurate prediction of English policy: "I do not
think the *A.* will be condemned, but I do think it will be
hard to get her out of the clutches of the English government.
Lord Russell would pay twice her value rather than provoke
an angry frown from his terror, Mr. Seward. It is my impression every vessel now building in England will be seized and
subjected to the same injurious delay that mine promises."[29]

The Confederates tried to transfer ships to French registry
on the assumption that the emperor sympathized with Southern aspirations. It was a wise stratagem, provided its premise
held true: that autocratic France offered advantages denied in
democratic Britain.

James North felt the anti-Southern sentiment that accompanied seizure of the *Alexandra,* and on May 6 warned Mallory of fear for the naval program—all ships stood in danger
of confiscation, and Lord Russell had become an active partisan of the North, much under the influence of the American
minister. North wondered whether he ought to put his Scottish ship under French registry, an expensive step, but what,
he asked, were a "few thousand pounds" of added expense if
it would protect his vessel? A few days later he wrote to warn
the secretary about the seizure and publication of Confederate
despatches. Public attention to naval activity, he said, increased British determination "to adhere more strictly to her
rules of neutrality."[30] He had written to Slidell in Paris some
days earlier about these thoughts, asking whether his ship
might be changed over to French registry. The commissioner
replied that the expediency of such a move depended on the
speed of construction. If the ship could not be ready to leave

in six or eight weeks, it would be wiser to await the outcome of the attempt then in progress to transfer registry. Slidell told North that a conference would shortly be held in Paris to discuss the problem and promised to relay its decision to Scotland.[31]

Even when threatened with the seizure of Number 61 and the collapse of their entire building program in Britain, the Confederates were incapable of proceeding efficiently. The Paris meeting scheduled for May of 1863 did not take place until mid-June. On the thirteenth of that month Lucius Q. C. Lamar and Mason and Slidell sent a communiqué to North warning that Lord Russell might make it impossible to get Number 61 to sea, that recent British activity disclosed a determination to read the rules "in a manner not only injurious to the interests of the Confederate States, but so as to prohibit any further operations in their behalf within Her Majesty's dominions." After careful consideration of all facets of the problem, the Southerners had decided that North must sell his ship to protect the large investment in it.[32] There was no help for it, Mason told North, but to sell the ship in hope of realizing enough profit to operate without risk in France, beyond the reach of the hostile interference of the British government.[33] Bulloch later endorsed the sale of the ship for three reasons: the ship was far behind schedule and could not easily be transferred; it cost too much and required too large a crew; and it would be "practically impossible" to get out of England.[34]

Seizure of the *Alexandra* in April had intensified efforts to move the shipbuilding program to France. The court's decision in that case upset those plans. On the Confederacy's day of good omen, June 25, the Court of Exchequer ruled that the *Alexandra* had been unjustly seized and returned a verdict against the Crown. What impact would this decision have on their building program, Southerners wondered. Should they continue construction in Britain or intensify efforts to move it to France? Soon after the verdict, North asked Mason whether, in view of the judge's charge to the jury indicating that the South might build any sort of unarmed ship, they should not continue naval construction in Britain. Mason, too, was perplexed. He had written to Slidell that the court's decision seemingly made the sale of North's ship unnecessary. Slidell agreed with Mason and thought they could safely delay that operation. Mason then advised North to drop negotiations for the sale of his ship.[35]

North now hoped for the best.˙ In early July, 1863, he brought Mallory up to date on details of the ship's status. He told of the decision to sell and the reason for its reversal; he discussed the *Alexandra* verdict, reporting the view that ships could not be prevented from leaving the country. The speeches by Baron Pollock and the defense attorney during the trial also supported the South's legal right to build ships anywhere in the realm. And while constant shortages of materiels, labor unrest, and uncertainty about government policy had hampered progress on Number 61, everything would, he predicted, proceed to a successful conclusion.[36]

Mason, Slidell, and North agreed that work on the Clyde ironclad should continue, and they communicated this decision to Secretary Mallory in Richmond. But no one told Bulloch!

At a time when the entire British building program was under strain, at the moment when its director was deep in negotiations to transfer the operation to France, the chief naval agent was uninformed about a major decision made by his associates. Work on the largest ship under contract continued without his knowledge. Bulloch had been seeking investment opportunities in France for the funds he supposed would be forthcoming from the sale of North's ship. From Paris in late˳ July he sent news of splendid prospects. He had just contracted for two small rams, and his survey of France's shipbuilding resources convinced him that the sale of Number 61 could buy and equip two more rams. He did not like North's ship, and was unconvinced that the *Alexandra* verdict would make any appreciable difference in English difficulties.[37]

A host of problems converged on Confederate agents as the year 1863 drew to a close. Russell took "full possession" of the Laird rams, and displayed no enthusiasm for taking the case to court; the South's London representative, Mason, ended his ineffectual mission, indicating that President Davis had renounced hope of early European intervention; American pressure for a halt to French construction was making Bulloch apprehensive for the ships there; and finally, the British government seized Sinclair's ship, the *Canton,* in mid-December.[38] This last event brought home to North the need for disposing of his ship. The senior naval officer, Samuel Barron, financial agent, Colin McRae, and Commissioners Mason and Slidell conferred with North about the Clyde ironclad. All agreed that it must be sold. On December 14, North forwarded his decision to Mallory from Paris, promising to execute it as quickly as possible.[39]

North sold the ship in a transaction which turned into an incredibly complicated, time-consuming, inefficient operation that brought little profit to the South. After consultation with his lawyer, James Galbraith, and the distinguished legal authority, Sir Hugh Cairns, North decided to surrender his interest in the unfinished ship if Thomson would agree not to sell it to the Union navy. North and Thomson terminated the contract by "mutual agreement" on December 21, 1863.[40] Arrangements appeared simple: Denmark would get an ironclad and the Confederacy would recover its money. The transfer and settlement of accounts dragged on and on. North did not receive his first payment until May, 1864, and the builders did not complete the ship until August. They explained that government intervention, and a costly strike lasting more than two months, had handicapped their efforts. North requested a statement of account in June, 1864; it arrived in October, with an extensive list of supplemental charges, including expenses for the trial trip entertainment (tradition-

ally borne by the builder) and an unexpected and opportun-
istic demand for a commission on the Danish sale. North
demurred. The Thomson firm deducted the charges from the
unpaid balance. In face of the impending collapse of the
Confederacy—General Sherman then was marching through
Georgia—North did not contest these actions by taking them
to court. The balance, less commission and charges, he turned
over to Bulloch, completing his mission "in as satisfactory a
manner as seems possible under the circumstances."[41]

North was deeply disappointed at the turn of events and
regarded the loss of the ship as 'the result of Russell's pro-
North proclivities. It was obvious, as he told Mallory from
Paris in early February, 1864, that Her Majesty's government
"bitterly opposed" all Southern enterprise. The loss weighed
upon him, for he had been confident that the "noble" ship
under his command would have done valiant service.[42]

Perhaps North, who knew the ship as well as anyone, was
correct in his estimate. There is reason to believe, however,
that the ship might have proved a disappointment. Bulloch,
the most talented of Mallory's agents, did not think highly of
it, and his opinion was supported by another—one that is
entitled to respect, for it was expressed by the South's senior
naval officer in Europe, Samuel Barron. Shortly before the
decision to sell was made, that is, in early November, 1863, he
had surveyed the ships under contract to the South and reported his findings to Richmond. About North's ship he had
a mixed feeling. While he considered it a "splendid ironclad,"
a credit to the builder and the officer in charge of construction, he was forced to admit that it would prove impossible to
get Number 61 — a warship — out of Britain and that even if
that miracle should take place, the ship was too much of a
gamble, too little suited to Southern purposes: "She is so
large, has such a draft of water, requires so many men to man,
sail and fight her, will expend such an immense quantity of
fuel, and will be so altogether extravagant a vessel, that I am
forced to doubt very much the expediency or propriety of

ever owning her."[43] Barron's estimate was accurate, as the purchasers (to their sorrow) were later forced to admit, though this was no satisfaction to them, to the Southerners who had contracted for the ship, or to the Scots who had built it.

* * * * *

The autumn of 1863 was a time of unrest in Continental politics, especially in the duchies of Schleswig and Holstein. With the death of Frederick VII of Denmark in November, 1863, the troublesome problem of the duchies engaged the serious attention of European diplomats. It was a problem so complex that according to a contemporary story only three men in the world understood it: one was dead, one was insane, and one had forgotten about it. But the third man in the story, Palmerston, had not forgotten, even if he could do little about it.

Austria and Prussia, temporarily allied and hopeful that time would increase their influence in the duchies, had wished to prevent the Danish reunion with Schleswig, and they disputed the succession of the new king of Denmark, Christian IX, to the duchies. Austria had a remarkable sea force (as demonstrated some years later at Lissa), but it was stationed in the Adriatic. Denmark had a navy that was master of its territorial waters. Prussia had only a few gunboats and corvettes, and its first ironclad, the *Arminius*, was then under construction in London on plans drawn up by Captain Coles.

About a month before North cancelled his contract with Thomson, that is, on November 21, the Prussians began maneuvers to buy ironclads. Two officers were ordered to England to investigate the possibility of buying the Laird rams. The mission was to be secret, an object easily managed by disguising it as an inspection of Prussia's ironclad, then being built. Though it soon became evident that the rams were not for sale at any price, North's ship came to the attention of the Prussians. It had been offered by Erlanger, acting under orders from Slidell (another example of kinks in the Confederate chain of command). The suggested price, £250,000, seemed reasonable. The naval architect Guyot (then superintending the *Arminius*) undertook a survey of the vessel. His investigation convinced him that the ship was useless ("unbrauchbar"), a poor example of a covered corvette, scarcely differing from the Prussian *Arkona* (except that Number 61 had a ram). Nor did he trust the builder's estimates of speed or draft or date of completion. He strongly advised against purchase. When it became clear that no other ships were available, Guyot, after another look at Number 61, still could not convince himself: the erstwhile North ram looked no stronger than an ordinary merchant ship, too light in material, bracing, and reinforcement to withstand hard service at sea.[44]

The Danes meanwhile were also seeking additional naval strength. They sent Captain Otto F. Suenson, the director of shipbuilding at the royal dockyard in Copenhagen, and Carl F. Tietgen, a young banker, on a survey of British shipyards. They too had dreams of owning the Laird rams, and when that course proved impossible they also turned to North's ship. Perhaps they met the Prussians in Scotland: certainly Thomson would not have allowed them to remain unaware of Prussian interest in Number 61. On the same day that North cancelled his contract, the Danish Session appropriated funds for purchase of the Scottish frigate or a suitable substitute. Captain Suenson evaluated the ship somewhat differently from his Prussian counterpart. He saw its deficiencies, recognized them for what they were, and had few illusions about probable performance. His need was even greater than the Prussians', and he had no way of knowing that the Prussians had rejected the ship. He had to guard against allowing it to fall into their hands. He recommended purchase, and at the end of the year the Danes agreed to pay £240,000.[45]

With difficulty (including such things as digging away part of the bank, deepening the river, and installing special anchors and a powerful hydraulic jack) Thompson finally launched Number 61 on February 24, 1864.[46] But because Denmark and Prussia had been at war since the first of that month, Her Majesty's government could not permit the ship to leave. It remained in the Clyde River for outfitting under supervision of Lieutenant A. B. Munter, R. D. N., who undertook several major alterations in the ship's structure and specifications, chief of which were elimination of the ram and addition of an armored conning tower just abaft the mainmast. Several minor modifications in internal arrangements were also made. By mid-August the ship was ready for a trial trip. A festive occasion it was, with many members of the local shipping community on board, as well as representatives of the royal and Danish navies and distinguished guests. Messrs. Ferguson and Forrester added to the festive air by providing "a most sumptuous dinner," and the band of Mr. Banks "discoursed appropriate music at intervals." From all appearances and comments, the trial run was a huge success. The engines performed beautifully and the ship attained an estimated speed of nearly twelve knots.[47]

The war between Denmark and Austria-Prussia was settled at Vienna on October 31, 1864, though an armistice had been in effect since the preceding July. In late August, the British government finally granted permission for the frigate to transfer to Danish control, and H.D.M.S. *Niels Iuel* went to Scotland to escort the ship. Arriving after a stormy voyage in mid-September, the escort provided a crew for Number 61, then commissioned it into the Danish navy, and the two ships left the Clyde for a trip to the dockyard at Horten, Norway— the royal dockyard at Copenhagen at that time being too short to accommodate the new addition. At Horten the ship was given its new name, *Danmark,* and visited by the local public who had opportunity to appraise the new representative of the Danish navy and to compare its grim appearance to the pretty *Niels Iuel.* In early October the *Danmark* arrived at Copenhagen. The ship made only one cruise, from June to October,

1869; after visiting several Norwegian ports, it moved out into the Atlantic for trials in bad weather north of Scotland and west of Ireland. Gales and heavy seas buffeted the ship, causing rolls of 45 degrees. With coal bunkers empty and all sails blown away, it barely got into Queenstown Harbor, where by odd coincidence another Confederate ironclad (one of the erstwhile Laird rams, now H.M.S. *Scorpion*) had sought shelter from the same storm.[48]

Though the largest in the Danish navy, the North ironclad then was decommissioned, and never returned to sea, for naval technology soon rendered it obsolete.[49] It served in various unimportant ways in the last decades of the nineteenth century, was stripped of its rigging in 1893, and functioned temporarily as a reserve-receiving ship. In 1900 the Danes deleted it from the naval list, though it remained for some years in the royal dockyard. In 1907 the Scottish sea monster, the vanished hope of a long-lost cause, went to the scrapheap.

*   *   *   *   *

Some authorities argue that this ship, had it left the Clyde soon enough, "might have made a difference in the outcome of the war." It is difficult to see how such a view can be sustained. For one thing, the unbiased estimate of the ship's structural strength made by Guyot for the Prussians throws considerable doubt on its potential as a warship. This evaluation was echoed by Bulloch and Barron, two highly reliable and expert naval agents of the South. But much more important in arriving at a final evaluation of the vessel's potential is the evidence of actual performance in the Danish navy. Thanks to the researches of R. Steen Steensen, Royal Danish Navy, the estimate of the ship's capability made by North must now be discarded. For reasons that are natural enough, the agent overestimated its contributions to the Confederate war effort, and that error has been perpetuated by historians.

EIGHT | A CURIOUS CASE

*I*N THE spring of 1863, after repeated Northern remonstrances, the ministry of Lord Palmerston began to realize that, if the North won the war, Confederate shipbuilding in British yards might bring on an embarrassing diplomatic and legal confrontation with the United States. Her Majesty's government, seeking to forestall such a situation, took a step toward Union views of proper neutral conduct. Royal officials tried to sort out the ambiguities in the legal status of Southern activity. Was it lawful? Could the government draw a line between legitimate commercial enterprise and acts "hostile" to a friendly power? This search for the legal limits of neutrality resulted in the curious conflict between the Crown and the cruiser *Alexandra*.

* * * * *

The background of the *Alexandra* affair was complicated. It went back nearly half a century to a "single phrase in a statute, which [had] lain rusting so long that the oldest Judge on the Bench confesse[d] himself inexperienced and perplexed with regard to it"—to the Foreign Enlistment Act of 1819 which set out rules for Britain's neutrality in event of future war, but set them out with much ambiguity.[1] Those rules had proved entirely inadequate to the exigencies of history's first "modern" war. President Davis' naval agents had an easy time constructing and sending out the *Alabama* and *Florida*. They demonstrated that the South could, to use an expression of the day, "sail a fleet of ships" through the Queen's antiquated rules.

Foreign Office efforts to test the Foreign Enlistment Act—to obtain a favorable gloss on it by court action—centered on the seizure of a small steamer, the *Alexandra,* at Liverpool in April, 1863. The subsequent trial sought to clarify the responsibilities of British subjects toward shipbuilding for belligerents. And perhaps there would be something more important than a mere restatement of the prohibitions of neutrality: the case might become, as the Liverpool *Daily Courier* put it, a matter of "universal importance," marking a "new epoch in the history of international law."[2]

Government officials initially had moved into this situation with much reluctance. The seizure order signed by Undersecretary of State for Foreign Affairs Edmund Hammond had been issued uncertainly because officials suspected that they had no right to issue such an order and that the courts would not sanction it. Three days before the decision, Russell had written Adams that the government could not interfere with "commercial dealings between the British subjects and the so-styled Confederate States, whether the subject of these dealings be money [Adams had complained about British indifference toward Confederate efforts to raise money on the London market] . . . or even ships adapted for warlike purposes."[3] On the day the order was issued, April 5, 1863, the collector of customs at Liverpool, Samuel Price Edwards, had reservations about its legality, and asked whether the ship "if registered and duly cleared is detainable, having, as yet, committed no offence against any law as far as I am competent to judge."[4] Experience had made Edwards familiar with ramifications of the rules, but this case gave him pause.

Russell's decision had in part been prompted by the American minister. In March, 1863, Anglo-American relations, following the harmonious interlude left by resolution of the

NEUTRALITY.

Mrs. North.—"*How about the* Alabama, *you wicked old man?*"
Mrs. South.—"*Where's my rams? Take back your precious Consuls—there!!!*"

15

Trent affair, had once again gotten out of kilter. The escape of the *Alabama* and its career of depredation, coupled with English reluctance to prevent the floating of a private loan of three million pounds to the South, had raised Northern tempers. There seemed a reluctance to heed the American warnings about Confederate naval activity. Adams complained that the government practically ignored the subject, issuing no strong warning against such activity. Unless Britain took a stronger stand he feared that President Lincoln might issue letters of marque. He knew that there was much sentiment for such a move, for Secretary Seward had warned that the destruction of commerce could only be halted by the Queen's more rigorous enforcement of neutral obligations or use of adequate forces "under commissions of marque and reprisal."[5] Congress had granted the president power to carry out this measure, and according to Seward, public pressure for it might become "unanimous and exacting"—unless Britain mended its international manners.

It had taken much time to press the British to action. In Liverpool, Dudley had been flooding the customs office with warnings about the ultimate destination and purpose of the *Alexandra*, though the Confederates had tried to keep them secret. A year earlier, in fact, Dudley had picked up the first bits of information and had written Seward that he would take all legal steps to force detention. At that time he warned that there seemed little likelihood of success, because English legal advisers did not think the evidence strong enough. It seemed as if British officials were not zealous in securing evidence, or aggressive when presented with it. But Dudley told his chief that he would keep the vessel under surveillance.

Federal persistence was finally rewarded. By late March, 1863, Dudley had collected enough evidence, he thought, to justify seizure, and though it was incomplete he knew that any delay would lead to the risk of an escape. One of his informants, Oliver Mumford, reported the *Alexandra* nearing completion, while John DeCosta, a local shipping agent and the source of much news about dockyard activity, deposed that the builder, William Miller, had said that it would be faster than the *Florida*. Dudley recognized the danger. On March 28, 1863, he requested the collector of customs to detain the ship, on the ground that it was "being equipped, furnished, and fitted out in order that such vessel shall be employed in the service of the persons assuming to exercise the powers of Government and called the Confederate States of America and with the intent to cruise and commit hostilities against the Government and citizens of the United States of America, with which Government Her Majesty the Queen is not now at war."[6] Two days later Adams forwarded Dudley's evidence to Russell, promising to keep the Foreign Office informed of developments, and he included a plea for cooperation between the two countries. He casually noted that the same people who had helped in the departure of Number 290 were now active in outfitting this vessel. This trouble in Liverpool, he asserted, was no isolated violation of the rules but part of a network of Southern naval activity masterminded by the Secret Service of the Confederate States. Such activity was dangerous, threatened cordial relations between Washington and Whitehall, and must not go unchecked.[7]

Because issues were not clear—neutrality was no matter of black and white—Crown officials had to move cautiously. They had to balance forces: to discharge England's international obligations, while interposing no impediments to the lawful economic endeavors of Her Majesty's subjects. They needed proof before they could move—proof that would withstand the hammering of lawyers in court. Americans were not producing that kind of proof. Officials suspected that the *Alexandra* had been built by pro-South Englishmen as a gift for Jefferson Davis (it was in fact built by Fraser-Trenholm for that purpose). They knew that technically a British firm retained title to the ship. But in early April, 1863, they had no proof of a Confederate connection, and on the crucial question of warlike preparation the American evidence was weak.

Conflicting viewpoints within the government hampered Foreign Office decision-making. Customs officers affirmed that the ship was for the South, that detectives were gathering evidence that would permit action, and that it might be detained "unofficially" for a short time if London authorities wished greater security. After an investigation in late March, the solicitor of the treasury reported that the ship, though more strongly built than a merchant vessel, violated no rules: he knew of no law against building specially reinforced ships.[8]

Russell received a report from law officers on April 4 which recommended seizure. "We regard this case as fairly raising an important question as to the true construction of the seventh section of the foreign enlistment act," the lawyers informed the foreign secretary, adding that "it would be proper for Her Majesty's Government on this opportunity under all the circumstances of the case to bring [it] to trial." They argued that the words of the act were that "if any person shall equip . . . with intent or in order that such ship . . . shall be employed in the service of any foreign Prince, the penalties of the act shall be incurred!" As they saw the case, intent constituted the essence of the offense, but they went on to argue that the ship's structure might afford reasonable ground for seizure and that the time for a test case had come.[9]

Signed by Roundell Palmer and Robert Phillimore, this opinion seems to have moved the foreign secretary to action. He knew that the owners would probably try all means to recover their property, but thought that the case might clarify the rules. And if the court sanctioned seizure merely upon suspicion of intent, the Southern construction program would end or, rather, might end at the discretion of the Crown.

The good news of seizure elated Adams, who expressed a lively satisfaction and promised to assist in preparing the case for trial. The move, he said, would defeat the hopes of evil men trying to sow dissension between Britain and America, and would convince people back home of England's determination to remain neutral.[10] This was exactly the result desired by the British.[11]

To Southerners there seemed unpleasant overtones in a seizure made on Easter Sunday. They noted the cheers of local pro-Union committees, but took little solace from the Liverpool *Courier's* comment about them: "these sticklers for neutrality show no concern whatever about . . . recruiting for the Federal service going on in Ireland, and the wholesale shipment of warlike stores from this port for New York."[12] Confederates noted a minor alteration in legal procedure. It had been the practice in such cases to give defendants a preliminary hearing before a magistrate, but officials had by-passed this step. Bulloch feared the ship might be exchequered—a legal technique which promised a long delay (the government retained the option of initiating proceedings) and which, even if the ship were not condemned, usually prevented defendants from collecting damages. Another reason for Southern apprehension was the confusion and delay in bringing the case to trial. Because of local sentiment (Liverpool had a heavy economic interest in continuation of the construction program) the government insisted upon a change of venue to London.

The period between seizure of the vessel in early April and the trial in late June vexed everyone concerned in this case. On one hand Russell's reluctance to state a position in public and to move against persons or firms accused by Northerners as violators of neutrality exasperated Union representatives and made them see pro-South tendencies everywhere. The secretary of the legation in London, Benjamin Moran, felt that sympathy for the South prompted the procrastination. "These people have acted as though they were bound to shield and defend the rebels," he wrote in his diary, "in all their violations of municipal and international law—to excuse . . . all their crimes—while they believe every slander uttered against us and try to make us prove that we are innocent of charges against us."[13] As for the Southerners, they too suspected British intentions. They complained that Queen Victoria's government was enforcing the Enlistment Act "in a manner most injurious and damaging to us." Bulloch informed his superiors that all shipbuilding had become suspect. No vessel could leave England, he said, "without enquiry, interruption, and delay, and a ship building anywhere in private yards . . . is not only watched by Yankee spies but by British officials, and is made the subject of . . . protests from lawyers and men of position, and even petitions from the Emancipation Society." He complained that the neutrality of Britain aided the Yankees. By early June, James North, frightened by the lack of progress on the Clyde ram, was jumping at shadows, convinced that "no ship built for the Confederate States would be allowed to leave the country."[14] Pessimism extended to Richmond, and just before the trial Secretary Mallory told Bulloch, "We have long since abandoned all belief in English intervention, and have learned to regard the settled policy of the ministry as hostile to us."[15] Filled with presentiments of disaster, aware of the precarious nature of their undertaking but lacking resources for alternate programs, Southern agents could do nothing but await the trial. Naval contractors, fearful of liabilities and suits, hesitated to continue construction for the South until the court gave some clarification of their status. Attention centered on the law courts at Westminster.

* * * * *

At this time, on June 22, 1863—the Southern *dies fastus*—the British Court of Exchequer, sitting at Westminster before the Lord Chief Baron and a special jury, opened the trial of the *Alexandra*, charging its owners and agents with violation of section seven of the Foreign Enlistment Act. The ninety-eighth and last count of the indictment held that the defendants "did equip, furnish, and fit out . . . and did knowingly assist and be concerned in the equipping, furnishing, and fitting out of the said vessel, with intent to employ her in the service of certain foreign states . . . with intent to cruise against the republic . . . of the United States of America."[16] It soon appeared that in this confrontation of Crown and cruiser the inexperienced solicitor general, Roundell Palmer, prosecuting his first major case, was no match for the defense. One of Britain's most gifted barristers, Sir Hugh Cairns, teamed with one of Britain's best trial lawyers, George Mellish, for a sophisticated show of courtroom virtuosity in pleading the cause of the Confederate sympathizers. Cairns cleverly cut out the ground from a key witness and reduced the issues to terms which British hearts held dear—appealing in turn to nativism, an inherent sense of justice, and sheer economic self-interest. At times, he even made it appear that the prosecutor was one of the attorneys for the defense. Sir Hugh, with delicate irony, quoted an opinion of the Queen's solicitor general in an earlier refusal to act against the *Alabama*. "The United States have no right to complain [the solicitor general had affirmed on that occasion] if the act in question is enforced in the way . . . laws are usually enforced against British subjects on evidence, and not on suspicion; on facts, and not on presumption; on satisfactory testimony, and not on the mere accusation of a foreign minister or his agents."[17] Palmer meekly said that those remarks did not apply in the present case.

Cairns again quoted that speech: "It would be a great mistake to suppose that the foreign enlistment act was meant to prohibit all commercial dealings in ships-of-war with belligerent countries. It was not intended to do so."[18] Why had the Crown reversed itself, why had the Queen's solicitor changed his mind? Why, Cairns wanted to know, was not the law of the *Alabama* applicable to the *Alexandra*? He returned to the legality of selling ships to belligerents, asserting that there was no lawful reason why a person could not build a ship which could be converted into a war vessel and sold to a coun-

C. S. S. ALEXANDRA

try at war. He pointed out the anomaly of the Crown's position, and played to the jury:

You have power by your decision to paralyze the commerce and industry of our ports. You may fetter honest and straightforward ship-building in the country, and drive it to a neighboring country which is quite open and willing to accept it [France]. You have it in your power to rejoice the hearts and quicken the energies of the spies and informers who infest our dockyards and appear to throng the ante-chamber of the American minister. You have it in your power to do all this by finding a verdict for the crown; but, on the contrary, you have it in your power to achieve a far better and higher result. You have it in your power to show the American government—and in all courtesy, good feeling, and good fellowship—that upon one thing you are determined, and that is, to have our laws applied, not upon suspicion or presumption, but upon clear legal proof. You have it in your power to show that the neutrality we have adopted in this unfortunate war has been adopted not to hamper and destroy, but to foster and promote the development of our commerce. Above all, you have it in your power to show that just as we will not change our laws, so also we will not stretch or strain or warp our laws to suit the temper of a foreign minister, or the exigencies of a foreign state. You can do that, and I trust you will do it in this case, by returning a verdict against the crown and for the defendants.[19]

The South found another ally in the judge, Sir Jonathan Frederick Pollock, a veteran of nineteen years as chief baron of the exchequer. Pollock's charge to the jury showed some bias for the South. During the trial he had given hints of his sympathy; once he interrupted counsel to ask whether it was lawful for a neutral nation to furnish ships to a belligerent for use "against a power with which we are at peace?" If the law did not prohibit sale of munitions and muskets, why should the sale of ships be prevented? Answering his own question, he informed the court that "in point of law they are not [prohibited]." Stressing this fact, "the importance of which was impossible to exaggerate," he asked the jury whether they

thought the vessel was to be delivered in pursuance of a contract perfectly legal or whether there was intent in the port
of Liverpool, or any other English port, that the ship be fitted
out, equipped, and armed for aggression. If the jury were
convinced that the contract was *to equip* the vessel within
Her Majesty's dominions, that was a matter "justifying conviction," but if they believed "the object really was to build a
ship in obedience to an order in compliance with a contract,
leaving to those who bought it to make what use they thought
fit of it, then it appears to me that the foreign enlistment act
has not been broken."[20]

"Without hesitating for more than half a minute," according to a reporter from the Liverpool *Mercury,* the jury
returned a verdict against the Crown in favor of the defendants.[21]

The reaction of the British press was as varied as political
and economic interests could make it. The Liverpool *Courier*
carried a long résumé of the trial. "Everybody in England
who cares to know about such things knows today that the
steamer *Alexandra* is legally declared to have been illegally
seized by the British Government. . . . In the North there will
be gnashing of teeth and denunciation of England's 'dis-
honesty'; in the South a corresponding amount of rejoicing,
for both sides are singularly affected by the slightest appearance of English favor in balancing their great contention."
The paper informed its readers (in an area with large financial stakes in supplying belligerents) that the case hinged on
the definition of "equipping" and that the court's decision
allowed sale of both ships and munitions—but not in the
same package! There was a larger issue: "In effect this makes
construction and supplying of the *Alabama* and *Florida* . . .
as those vessels left our shores, perfectly legal acts." The paper
chided the North by pointing out that the decision had been
based on non-English authorities. "The Northerners ought to
appreciate this thoroughly, for there is a smack of Yankee
smartness and humor in Baron Pollock's adoption of Ameri-

can law and learning in virtually deciding the case of the *Alexandra.*"[22]

The *North British Daily Mail* also stressed the choice of precedents: "It is a satisfaction to feel that the Lord Chief Baron has acted in accordance with a high American authority in his interpretation of the law, and it will be impossible for the American Government to question the soundness of his opinions without impugning that of the greatest of their lawyers, Mr. Justice Storey." The *Daily News* pointedly remarked that "Americans may take advantages of the convenient doctrine now enunciated."[23]

Several London papers took pleasure at the result. The *Morning Post* noted that it "may be a great hardship to the Federals that their opponents should be enabled to create a navy in foreign ports, but, like many other hardships entailed on belligerents, it must be submitted to."[24] The influential *Times* wondered why so much time had been spent on "so simple a question," and contented itself with noting that the verdict sanctioned the sale of both ships and munitions.[25]

The Southampton *Times* gave a judicious review of the trial, stressing its long-range implications. The case, it said, "furnishes one of the most important decisions ever recorded in the annals of British jurisprudence. It declares that according to the present state of the law we can build & send out as many vessels as any belligerent party may require, provided that they are equipped elsewhere. . . . It is evident that the law is in a very unsatisfactory state, and that if the recent decision be taken as precedent we may find it someday very inconvenient to ourselves."[26]

American representatives were not pleased. Benjamin Moran accused the judge of sneering at the Union and championing the South. According to Pollock's charge to the jury, Moran wrote in his diary, contractors might build warships, "sell them to a belligerent, and send them forth to be armed at sea from another vessel from the same port, and that . . . act is not a violation of either law or neutrality."[27] Minister

Adams feared the decision would hasten construction of fleets of ships to prey on Union commerce. "Without the interposition of some new barrier," Adams reported to Seward, "Great Britain must, from this time, appear as ready to furnish the means for any and every enterprise that may be undertaken, within her limits, against nations with which she professes at the same time to be under the most solemn engagements to keep the peace.[28] In his diary he recorded disappointment. "It seems as if circumstances were always destined to prey upon us in this fearful struggle, from abroad as well as at home." The decision puzzled him, for he realized that Britain had "as much to lose by lax morality on the ocean as any nation."[29]

In retrospect, no simple explanation can be given for the *Alexandra* affair. Until April, 1863, many people believed that the South had a right to procure ships abroad; at least there were no legal prohibitions. International regulations and Anglo-American precedent sanctioned such activity: custom and law merely forbade using a neutral port as a base from which to send out armed land or armed naval forces directly against a friendly power. As a result Britain found herself in an awkward position because the depredations of the Southern cruisers were showing just how inconvenient such an interpretation could be. The Crown, seeking a new policy, had proceeded unwisely in choosing the *Alexandra* as its excuse for having a legal confrontation with the Confederacy.

Some years after the war, Roundell Palmer, a leading participant in that affair, recalled the ambiguity of the law as it stood in 1863. According to one point of view, he wrote, the prohibitions of the Enlistment Act applied only to ships of war which were equipped within British territory "with such means of offense as might enable them at once to cruise or commit hostilities against an enemy at sea." Other men thought this too narrow a construction, one unwarranted by the letter and unsanctioned by the spirit of the law, and they put forth an alternate view of the rules in which "any equipment whatever" within Her Majesty's jurisdiction fell under the prohibitions of neutrality and furnished just cause for confiscation, even if the builder's interests in the vessel were strictly commercial and even if the "equipment" which it received failed to permit immediate participation in warlike operations. However, this postwar exposition of policy seems full of hindsight. Legal advisers recommended seizure in April, 1863, partly because they thought that in certain details of appearance and construction the vessel was obviously suitable for use as a warship and that these characteristics furnished prima-facie evidence of warlike intent. A recent student of this unique event in the British response to Confederate construction, has concluded, after a close examination of the evidence, that "the Polish crisis, coincident with the rising temper in America, and possibly a fear regarding Britain's place in future wars, caused [Crown officials] . . . in April, 1863 to test the theory of the law officers regarding the structure of vessels as evidence of their intent."[30] It did not escape official notice that so convenient an interpretation would arm the Crown with a weapon of great potency, for it would require no evidence but the vessel itself and a professional statement that it could be used as a ship of war.

One cannot avoid contrasting this case with the controversy over the escape of the *Alabama*. About a year earlier, in the summer of 1862, when protests against the departure of that vessel were becoming insistent, legal experts had attempted to argue that its physical appearance and the evidence produced by the Federals made it seem reasonably clear that the vessel had been constructed as a warship.[31] But, as we have seen, before the government accepted that view, the ship had escaped. In response to subsequent parliamentary criticism Palmerston reminded his colleagues that the act of 1819 required "evidence on oath confirming a just suspicion" before preventive measures could be taken. The Crown needed, and by inference did not have, evidence from reliable, first-hand witnesses that would stand up in court. The prime minister excused vacillation by pointing out some anomalies in the rules. According to the official interpretation of the incident, the *Alabama* "sailed from this country unarmed and not properly fitted out for war; and she received her armament, equipment and crew in a foreign port. . . . her condition at that time [on the eve of her departure from Liverpool] would not have justified a seizure." Such an action, Pam said, "would have been altogether unwarrantable by law."[32] During this debate the solicitor general had set out the government's position with much eloquence and precision (to his later embarrassment, as noted). He argued that the government's policy had been "strict, impartial, and honest from beginning to end," and that there was no truth to the allegation that the vessel had left Her Majesty's dominion "as a ship armed for war." He told the House of Commons that the vessel might have been legally built for a foreign government, and "though a ship of war, she might have formed a legitimate article of commerce, even if meant for the Confederate States." Nor was there any justification in the charge that Her Majesty's government bore any responsibility for actions of the ship subsequent to her departure. "The *Alabama* might have been *intended* to be a ship of war, and *intended* to be delivered to the orders of a foreign government at war, but so long as that government was not at war with the United Kingdom and so long as the vessel was not actually armed *when she left Liverpool,* there was no offence in either English law or international law."[33] According to one recent evaluation of the evidence in this escape, the Crown did all that could legally be done. Mr. Rupert Jarvis, formerly of Her Majesty's Customs and Excise Library, argues that at the time of the vessel's departure from Britain "no case could have been sustained," for thorough examination by customs officials certified that the ship was not equipped or fitted out for war purposes and therefore did not come under the prohibitions of the law as it then was.[34]

* * * * *

Seizure of the *Alexandra* marked an attempted reversal of the
rules of British neutrality, a change during the game, for detention was made upon a new interpretation. Russell had
written Adams during the *Alabama* affair that it was not
British policy to deprive any person of liberty or property
without evidence of legal violation, and reminded the American that such evidence was difficult to secure.[35] The *Alexandra's* owners had been denied their property because the
vessel apparently was for use against the North—not the same
thing as requiring conclusive evidence. A dispatch from the
Foreign Office to the British minister in Washington, two
days after seizure, stressed the change in procedure and offered a reason for it: "The orders given to watch, and stop
when evidence can be procured, vessels *apparently intended*
for the Confederate service, will, it is . . . hoped, allay the
strong feelings which have been raised in Northern America
by the escape from justice of the *Oreto* and *Alabama*." Russell
realized that "a kind of neutral hostility should not be allowed to go on without some attempt to stop it."[36]

That attempt failed. The *Alexandra* case demonstrated
that the Enlistment Act could not cope with the issues raised
by Southern naval construction in British yards. In the summer of 1863, by judicial decree, English shipbuilders received
legal sanction to sell to the South, as long as the vessels received no warlike equipment in British territory. The South
asked nothing more because equipping ships beyond the
Queen's jurisdiction was proving a satisfactory course.

The moment was not right for the obvious solution to the
problem, a change in the British rules. Many Englishmen
recognized shortcomings in the Enlistment Act, but because
of the precarious parliamentary balance felt themselves power-
less. Any appearance of truckling to Yankee pressure would
have had immediate and serious political repercussions.[37]
Many also recognized that if the South took advantage of the

doctrine enunciated in the *Alexandra* decision, consequences for Great Britain might be serious. This rigidly legalistic situation was not satisfactory. When the United States, after the victories of Vicksburg and Gettysburg and with some two million men under arms, petitioned for detention of the Laird rams, Lord Russell, in opposition to his legal advisers, felt compelled to go beyond the law to accede to that request.

NINE | LAIRD RAMS: PART ONE

*I*N THE SPRING of 1862, when the major ironclad program—that of the Laird rams—began, Bulloch's capable
hands directed it. James North originally had responsibility
for securing rams in Europe, but because of dissatisfaction
with his work, Mallory transferred most of that burden to his
chief agent, though North retained supervision of the Clyde
ironclad.[1] In the spring of 1862 Bulloch surveyed facilities
and reported that several firms were willing to undertake
work on the new rams. He sent this information to Richmond,
but cautioned against over-optimism, sensing an unfavorable
shift in British opinion. He expected trouble, fearing that the
cabinet might resort to an order in council (which he thought
would "override ordinary rules of law") to proscribe his work.
Any incautious step might lead to a forfeiture of the ships.
Later, he complained that the foreign secretary was saying
that Number 290 had in effect evaded the law and was hinting
that no repetition of the offense would be tolerated.[2] Bulloch
could find no consistency in the actions of British officials.
Naturally, he did not know that Russell's advisers were themselves unsure of government responsibility and were in fact
seeking new interpretations of neutrality.

In April, 1862, he warned that Union pressure might result
in more stringent regulations for shipbuilders. To circumvent
such danger he suggested—years in advance of its time—an

ingenious system of prefabrication, by which hulls, frames, and woodwork might be constructed at home while the armor plate was made in England, with components later assembled in the South.[3] The plan, which might have given President Davis a navy—for it by-passed legal restrictions and surmounted Southern industrial deficiencies—was another demonstration of Bulloch's talent for improvisation. It would have eliminated the factor which doomed the naval program, seizure, without any valid legal reason, of ships *apparently* intended for the South. The plan never received support. Mallory, having few illusions about foreign aid and little expectation of European intervention, pressed for an ironclad fleet, and finally ordered Bulloch to proceed with the original plans. In the summer of 1862, after receipt of this authorization the agent ordered work to begin. At Birkenhead his contractor commenced ships Number 294 and 295, the famous Laird rams.[4]

* * * * *

Geography and Union strategy helped determine the design of the rams. The Confederate naval secretary had given his agent discretion but insisted that he keep in mind the formula for Southern success. Mallory needed vessels which could vanquish Union squadrons, not merely match them. He needed a flotilla with a decided advantage over enemy blockaders—one that would also be able to inspire fear in Northern coastal cities. In all planning the secretary tried to keep in view the qualities of enemy ships, while at the same time seeking to give his own fleet the equipment which would enable it to even up the numerical odds.[5]

The rivers and harbors of the South required vessels of shallow draft and narrow turning radius. To build in such features without decreasing fire-power and protective plate, the Laird engineers had to solve some difficult problems in weight distribution. Happily they found that turret batteries, a recent innovation, permitted heavier weight concentration

ONE OF THE LAIRD RAMS

The ship was bought by the British and commissioned into the British Navy as the *Wivern*.

THE *SCORPION*

Confederate ram under construction in the purchased by the British and commissioned
Laird's shipbuilding yard. This ship was into the British Navy as the *Scorpion*.

at midship with no decrease in maneuverability: the rams would be able to turn like ducks in the water.

As has been said, these vessels took their name from their most distinguishing feature, the ram, an iron piercer of great strength which protruded some six or seven feet beyond the prow. While the vessel was in motion this spur remained three or four feet below the water line, the idea being that it would then strike an adversary below its protective plate. The introduction of steam power had revived this ancient device by converting ships into powerful mobile battering rams "highly dangerous to wooden ships maintaining a close blockade at some Southern port." Fascination for the device and veneration of its supposed power became something of a mania in naval circles during the 1860's, especially after the Austrians at Lissa (1866) demonstrated that ramming might be used effectively at sea.[6]

The Laird rams were not large: they displaced about 1,800 tons on an average draft of only fifteen feet. Measuring 230 feet with a beam of forty feet, propelled by engines of 350 horsepower, able to reach a speed of 10 knots, these vessels had the qualities the South required and were ideally suited for operations against Union blockaders.

As the program got underway, money was not an immediate problem, for Mallory had made available a million-dollar credit with Fraser-Trenholm. By building both ships at the same yard Bulloch hoped to decrease both cost and Union interest in his activity and to take advantage of increased production speed. Both ships were promised for delivery in the spring of 1863, one in March, the other in April. Fully equipped, except for magazines, and armaments, they were to cost £93,750 each. Bulloch was pleased with the transaction, regarding it as a step toward victory and a European expression of confidence in his cause. [7]

Contract arrangements paralleled those used for the *Alabama*, with Bulloch acting as a private citizen and not as an official agent of the Confederacy. The Laird firm agreed to

deliver the ships in Liverpool with only the equipment ordi-
narily required on a commercial ship. There was no mention
of munitions or armament; the Laird officials asked no awkward questions about turrets (an unusual addition for a "commercial" vessel). Bulloch supposed that the Lairds knew of
his connection with the Confederacy, but at no time, he later
insisted, did either side hint that the ships were for the South.
Officials of the Laird yard did not know the destination of
the vessels; if necessary, they could swear that, so far as they
knew, they were not for use against a power with which Her
Majesty was at peace. The Lairds merely agreed to build two
ships "in obedience to an order, and in compliance with a
contract, leaving to those who bought them to make what use
they thought fit of them." To the best of their belief such
procedure provided no ground for government complaint.
In this view of maritime law and neutral obligation, the
Lairds were seconded by the lord of the Exchequer Court, and
Baron Pollock in 1863 provided a legal precedent for this
interpretation.[8]

Before making the contract Bulloch consulted his lawyer
on whether armor plating could be construed as "equipment"
under the Enlistment Act. According to the reasoning in the
Alabama affair, his lawyer told him, "the statute did not for-
bid the building of any description of ship . . . [and] the pro-
hibitory clause referred to arming or furnishing a vessel with
ammunition and ordnance stores for warlike purposes." Reassured, Bulloch continued his activity, and later learned that
the Lairds also had investigated this point before accepting
the contract and had received a similar reply. According to
Bulloch, "every possible effort was made to get at the meaning
and application of the Foreign Enlistment Act, so that there
might be no intentional or heedless violation of municipal
law and reckless indifference to the Queen's neutrality."[9]

During the early stages of construction Bulloch hoped that
the ships might leave Liverpool if unarmed. He wrote Mallory that if the war lasted until the spring of 1863, "these

vessels may yet have important and perhaps conclusive work in the question of the blockade."[10] But before long Bulloch began to doubt his ability to get the rams out of Britain; he saw signs of Union interest everywhere. Indeed, Northern counter-moves increased in intensity at about this time; in the spring of 1863, two prominent American citizens, John Murray Forbes and William H. Aspinwall, had arrived in Liverpool on a secret government mission to buy up British ships to keep them out of Confederate hands. When adverse publicity negated the plan, part of the liberal funds which Forbes and Aspinwall had brought with them were diverted to Consul Dudley for his counter-espionage work. Bulloch noticed that spies and informers for the Americans were swarming over the Laird yard, asking questions, bothering workmen, and shadowing him; and when work on the turrets began, he was sure that his adversaries would bring this fact to the attention of the authorities who, in turn, might use it as a pretext for seizure.

Then, in addition to the Northern detectives, Bulloch had to contend with a plethora of Southern agents, most of whom did little to aid his work or the cause of the Confederacy. Richmond authorities had the unpleasant habit of multiplying their overseas agents, and were not always as careful in their selection as they might have been. At one point, Mallory had contracted for six ironclads with some private persons who were subsequently captured by a Northern gunboat. When news of this venture was published in the British press, it had an adverse effect on Bulloch's work and may have "served to influence the course adopted by Her Majesty's Government in respect to the Liverpool rams, and other vessels alleged to be building for the Confederate States."[11]

While struggling with these problems, Bulloch also had to contend with the deficiencies of Confederate credit. Though the congress in Richmond had little trouble in appropriating money, it was not always successful in making funds available to overseas agents. Promised funds arrived late, if at all, and often were inadequate to the needs of the moment. What the South badly needed was a financial overseer, aware of the general objectives and resources of the Confederacy and invested with broad powers to coordinate expenditures and assign priorities in accordance with those objectives; but by the time Davis' government got around to coordinating its overseas activity—this was not accomplished until the autumn of 1863, after two-and-one-half years of war!—much irreparable damage had been done and many projects had been fatally handicapped.[12] By the nature of its organization and the administrative techniques of its president, the Confederacy was ill-equipped for independent, top-level decision-making in the field.

Meanwhile, the contractors for the rams were doing their best to comply with the terms of their contract with Bulloch. They built sheds to permit work in bad weather and installed gaslights to lengthen the work day. Their yard was one of the most advanced in the country, with working conditions superior to those of most competitors. Some four-thousand workers in the yard had a sort of vested interest in the success of this Confederate venture. After inspecting the Birkenhead facilities, a reporter for the Liverpool *Mercury* told his readers that the Laird plant was a model that the Admiralty and other shipbuilders of the country ought to emulate without delay.[13]

*   *   *   *   *

It was at this point, with the rams moving toward completion, thousands of able workers speeding construction under sheds and by gaslight, that a new move occurred in the complicated maneuvers of Northern and Southern diplomats which was to have a repercussion of importance in regard to the Laird rams. The move was made by the South, and its purpose was to turn construction of the hoped-for navy from England to France.[14] The idea was growing that the Queen's government, if going slowly, was, nonetheless, on its way toward making naval construction or departure of finished or virtually finished ships almost impossible, and that it would be better to turn to the realm of Louis Napoleon across the Channel, where, supposedly, in aristocratic circles, there was much sympathy for Southern aims. The phantasy of French aid held a fascination for men of the South. Why had they delayed so long in approaching the emperor? Like its neighbor, France had reacted to the war with a proclamation of neutrality, one more stringent and specific in its prohibitions. The third clause forbade Frenchmen from taking any part whatsoever in equipping or arming vessels of war or privateers for either belligerent, while enjoining them from acts "against the laws of the empire or the law of nations," hostile to either side or contrary to neutrality. As Bulloch put it: "There was no question here of the probable interpretation of a somewhat ambiguous statute, no dependence upon a Government pledged by constitutional requirement, as well as by habitual usage, to submit questions involving the rights of individuals to the legal tribunals." The proclamation and the autocratic nature of Napoleon's reign where so much depended on royal whim, together with the difficulty of appraising France's response to the war, led Confederates to concentrate their early activity in Britain where they thought they could expect "more liberty of action, a freer as well as a cheaper market, and surer means of discovering what might be safely attempted." Only after the British attitude began to stiffen, only after the Confederate commissioner in Paris had opportunity to size up Napoleonic aspirations—only when necessity dictated—did the South turn across the Channel.[15]

Long before the summer of 1863 the able and astute minister at Paris, John Slidell, had set to work. The French proclamation, for all its precision, contained sufficient ambiguity for a man of his adroitness to devise evasions; all he needed was a little cooperation and some looking-the-other-way from official quarters. He saw the difference between the governmental structures of Britain and France and knew that the latter, by virtue of its autocratic arrangement, might not get

trapped in legal proceedings, whereas in Britain, by custom
and parliamentary requirement, all questions involving definitions of neutrality might have to be submitted to public
and legal scrutiny. No one knew the limits of French neutrality, except Napoleon, who had not decided what they were!

Slidell did all he could to help arrange a favorable decision.
When he questioned French friends about the chances of
lifting the blockade, he found initial reluctance. He was informed that Britain's larger interest in "affaires Américanes"
gave her the honor of instituting action. A reliable but anonymous source summarized French sentiment by noting that it
was not proper "to draw the chestnuts from the fire for the
benefit of England; she must take the initiative; we will
promptly follow her lead, and we know that she can not much
longer defer the action which her industrial and commercial
interests so imperatively demand."[16] Slidell was led to believe
that France stood ready to declare the Union blockade inef-
fective—and might even grant recognition to the Confederate
States—"provided that Great Britain will consent to act simultaneously with her." He thought that Lord Russell was the
chief obstacle to European intervention in America and that
France could not move without his sanction.[17]

Early in the war it did seem as if the French were following
the British. On February 15, 1862, Russell announced a loose
interpretation of Article Four of the 1856 Declaration of Paris
by informing Lord Lyons in Washington that in order for
Her Majesty's government to consider a blockade effective, it
was only necessary to make entrance to the interdicted ports
"dangerous." It did not matter how many vessels eluded the
blockaders (compiling lists of ships which had evaded blockading squadrons was a favorite Southern pastime) ; now
"danger of capture" sufficed to assure British recognition of
the blockade. Soon thereafter a spokesman for the emperor
announced his assent to Russell's interpretation.[18] French
concurrence did not surprise Slidell because he thought that
the two nations had agreed that neither would take any action

in regard to the conflict without consulting with the other.[19]

In subsequent efforts to bring about French intervention, the minister met an unexpected ally in William S. Lindsay, an Englishman who was almost like an unofficial Confederate representative at Napoleon's court. As a member of Parliament, Lindsay had access to French officials. He visited the emperor in April of 1862 to urge intervention. Louis Napoleon seemed interested, agreed that the blockade did not meet the standards envisioned at Paris in 1856, and intimated that he favored declaring the Union blockade inoperative, but claimed he could not secure English assent.[20] Lindsay conferred with the British ambassador at Paris, but that gentleman saw no need to alter Russell's definition of blockade. After a second interview with the emperor, Lindsay, at Louis Napoleon's request, tried to stimulate British interest in bilateral action to open the Southern ports. Russell refused to see Lindsay, pointing out that all communication from the French government must come via diplomatic channels.[21] But a leader of the opposition, Benjamin Disraeli, told Lindsay that many Conservatives thought Russell too willing to do America's bidding, and that a part of Parliament believed a secret agreement existed between Washington and Whitehall. Disraeli thought that if Louis Napoleon initiated action vis-à-vis America, Russell might be forced to acquiesce for fear of bringing on a political crisis and a possible change of ministry.[22]

The emperor vacillated. He told Lindsay that he could not permit the people of France to suffer from Northern policy. Napoleon favored a general European appeal for open ports backed by "proper demonstration of force." If such a move failed, the emperor hinted that he might go it alone, might unilaterally declare the blockade inoperative. It was a vague promise, the kind at which the wily emperor was a master. He did not commit himself too far and hinted that the decision would depend on events at New Orleans. The fall of that city to the North, he hinted to Lindsay, "might render it inexpedient to act." That city fell to Federal forces, so Louis Napoleon remained safely on the fence. Conversations between Slidell and French officials continued through the summer of 1862, with no change; so skillfully did the French play the minister that even in late July he still thought Louis Napoleon might act without Russell or Palmerston.[23]

Nothing disturbed the aloofness of the French court until autumn, when Louis Napoleon again broached the subject of a navy. On October 28, 1862, he asked Slidell why the South had not created one. Caught off guard, the minister replied that in the war's early months it had seemed wiser to rely on European pressure to prevent the South's enemies from abusing their superiority at sea. But because that hope had proved illusory, President Davis instituted a naval construction program in Britain; if, however, the emperor could assure him that neutrality regulations permitted such a course in France, the South would gladly avail itself of such an opportunity. Louis Napoleon seemed interested, even suggesting that to lessen suspicion the ships might be built ostensibly for the Italian government. The emperor soon changed his mind, however, and after consultation with his advisers notified Slidell that the "Italian plan" was too hazardous.[24]

Slidell, by now wise to Napoleonic whim, waited for the next move: when it came, it was indeed interesting. In early 1863, one of the largest shipbuilders in France, M. Arman, a member of the Chamber of Deputies and confidant of the emperor, visited the Confederate commissioner to ask whether the South would be interested in a shipbuilding program. Arman hinted that there would be little difficulty in arranging one and went so far as to suggest that the ships might even be armed. Slidell suspected that such a proposition could not have been set in motion without official sanction. Alas, he told Arman, he had no funds for such a project. But, my friend, the Frenchman answered, that is nothing! Arman understood such problems. Then, after several conferences (and some professional advice from Bulloch) the negotiators came to terms. The contractor agreed to accept cotton bonds, if the emperor would allow their sale in France.[25]

In the autumn of 1862, at about the time Slidell had his interview with the emperor at St. Cloud, the shakeup at the Quai d'Orsay had replaced Baron de Thouvenel with Edouard Drouyn de Lhuys. The new secretary of foreign affairs, believing that these plots and projects were the responsibility of the minister of commerce or marine, assured Slidell that "he was quite willing to close his eyes . . . until some direct appeal was made to him."[26]

Slidell and J. Voruz (shipbuilder at Nantes and subcontractor for part of the Confederate order) then visited the minister of commerce, Eugene Rouher, to ascertain his reaction to the shipbuilding program. His reply was encouraging. Slidell reported to his superior on March 4, 1863, that Rouher had assured him that the French ministry would offer no objection to the plan. If financial details could be ironed out, success seemed certain.* The Confederate commissioner invited Matthew Maury and Bulloch to Paris for assistance with contracts and specifications.

The agents had discussed such a program earlier, but lack of funds, poor planning, and inefficient operations had stymied efforts to get it underway. Slidell's maneuvers revived hope. When Bulloch visited Arman in March, 1863, the Frenchman assured him that Louis Napoleon's government looked with favor on the plan, and that Minister Rouher had "unofficially" sanctioned the operation, requiring only that the ships depart under neutral flags. Because Arman's story tallied with Slidell's, conditions looked right. While financial matters were being arranged, designs and specifications for four clipper corvettes of 1,500 tons and 400 horsepower were prepared, and contract terms arranged. Arman agreed to build two of the ships and to subcontract two of them to Voruz. In this atmosphere Bulloch and Arman began a Con-

*The reader will remember that this was on the eve of the Erlanger bond issue, which was expected to ease financial difficulties.

federate construction program "undertaken at the instigation
of the Imperial Government itself." During negotiations "a
draft of the proposed contract was shown to the highest person
in the Empire, and it received his sanction." So, at least, was
the story told to Bulloch.[27]

*   *   *   *   *

Richmond officials had little reason to doubt French intent,
having convinced themselves that iron-plated warships could
be built in France and delivered to the Confederacy ready for
service. Lured by this inducement, the Confederate Congress
appropriated by secret act two-million pounds for an ironclad
construction program in "Southern Europe," and Mallory
designated Bulloch as agent-in-chief to carry out this new
mission, subject only to the Navy Department's requirement
that the ships be able to cross the ocean, navigate the Mississippi River, and withstand and outshoot the enemy's eleven-
inch and fifteen-inch guns. Swift dispatch of the ships was
essential. For many reasons Bulloch would have preferred
building the ironclads in Britain, but by the time this project
matured (in the summer of 1863), it appeared that Her
Majesty's government would allow no vessel suitable for war
to leave the kingdom. Moreover, the authorities in Richmond
were enthralled by the prospects of French hospitality. Hence,
Bulloch decided to buy French. Because of financial uncertainty, he had to limit the original contract to only two ironclads. These ships were almost 172 feet long between perpendiculars, with a breadth of nearly 33 feet and draft ("with
220 tons of coal, battery, and all stores on board") of 14 feet
4 inches. They were to be driven by two engines of 300
horsepower and independent twin screws ("working sepa-
rately, so as to be capable of a counter motion at the same
time"). The armor was 4 and ¾ inches thick at midship and
tapered to 3 and ½ inches at bow and stern, and the speed
was a guaranteed 12 knots in smooth seas, fully loaded. Specifications provided that the ships would conform to the stan-

dards of the French navy. Bulloch was pleased with these arrangements and cheered by signs of French encouragement.[28]

Meanwhile, Bulloch was having trouble with the Laird rams, then nearing completion. Could he transfer them to French registry to assure their escape from Britain? He went to work. During a visit to Arman in Paris he met one Bravay, the owner of a small business willing to undertake risky ventures with few questions asked. If not the oldest and most reputable of firms (one member had failed to sustain a slander suit against someone who had accused him of "having kept a house of ill fame at Paris"), Bravay and Company was nevertheless willing to take on the commission. Bulloch would have preferred better associates, but there was an element of danger, and he had to work with what was available. The shady Bravay, by coincidence, had just contracted—or said he had (one never knew when he was telling the truth)—to build two rams for the Pasha of Egypt. Well, then: what better plan than to transfer the Laird rams to French registry as vessels ostensibly going to protect the pyramids?[29]

British officials suspected the terminus; any move might precipitate seizure and judicial delay, the *Alexandra* verdict notwithstanding. Seizure might be arbitrary, even illegal, subjecting the Crown to damages—but lawyers warned Bulloch that the rams "were liable to the same proceedings, and if they should be seized we could not expect to release them from the Court of Exchequer during the war, if at all." It was worth any risk to avoid that calamity. Bulloch laid his plans with care, insisting that "all papers and letters relating to the sale must be such as would bear judicial scrutiny and tend to prove the *bona-fide* character of the transfer."[30] Officials of the Laird company remained in the dark about most of the transaction; they knew what Bulloch wished them to know. He instructed them to dispose of the rams to Bravay at a reasonable profit and terminate the contract, giving as the reason that government interference made it appear unlikely that the vessels would be allowed to leave the country. As he told the contractors, Bulloch hoped to avoid expensive litigation by selling the ships before Russell instituted proceedings against them.

Several European powers desirous of increasing their naval power had expressed interest in the rams. The Russians made a most attractive offer, which the Lairds wished to accept, but Bulloch reminded the pro-South contractors that Czar Alexander was the most pro-North monarch in Europe and that his agent might be an intermediary in a clever arrangement to augment the Northern navy. This word to the wise was sufficient to eliminate Russia's bid, allowing Bravay and Company to take title to the rams—in the name of His Serene Highness the Pasha of Egypt.[31]

Confederate legal advisers drew the transfer papers with extreme care, wishing to give Russell no pretext for seizure. If, by mischance, the British did confiscate the ships, an alternate course remained: Louis Napoleon might request their release as the property of a French subject. Bulloch thought that Russell could not refuse such a request and that Her Majesty's government might welcome a clear statement of French responsibility for the inconvenient vessels. Then, when the ships were safely out of Britain, it would be a simple matter, with French connivance, to return them to the Confederate navy.[32] All that could be done had been done, and Bulloch was hopeful.

As mentioned, the destruction of merchant shipping by the cruisers had driven many Northern vessels to foreign registry, and had put considerable pressure on Washington officials, especially on the secretaries of state and navy, to do something about the depredations. Convinced that Britain was a breeding ground for pirates, angered by steadily increasing tonnage losses, and determined to put an end to British procrastination and pseudo-neutrality, the Union moved to convince the British that it would not be in their interests to allow the Laird rams out of the country. In these circumstances, Lord John Russell and Charles Francis Adams began an important correspondence over neutrality rights and obligations which raised basic questions about international law not answered until the Geneva arbitration of 1871–72—and answered imperfectly even then. While the rams prepared for sea in the late summer of 1863, American notes of great pungency and pugnacity bombarded the Foreign Office, reminding Russell of past carelessness and warning of future danger if the rams escaped. Russell held his own, replying in kind.

This memorable exchange of notes was a crucial point in Civil War diplomacy. As a recent student of this chapter of Anglo-American relations has said, "The incidents involving the Laird rams are not merely the denouement of the shipbuilding story. They are the climax, the crisis which caused the British Government to attach itself irrevocably to the policy of legal obstructionism."[33] September at Birkenhead, no less than July at Gettysburg, doomed the Confederacy.

TEN | LAIRD RAMS: PART TWO

A MULTITUDE of pressures forced Her Majesty's government to reappraise Britain's obligations as a neutral. Among the more important were first, the escape of the *Alabama* and the furor caused by that vessel's deadly·efficiency, repeatedly bringing to mind some of the unpleasant consequences of such activity and reminding officials that continued construction of such ships might not be in the long-range interest of the nation; second, the restive state of Continental politics, especially in the Danish duchies and in Poland; third, the growing conviction, as 1863 wore on (particularly after Vicksburg and Gettysburg), that the Southern military position was not likely to improve; fourth, dissatisfaction among substantial portions of the business community with Whitehall's negligent attitude toward Confederate construction; and fifth, growing dismay at the losses suffered by London underwriters who carried the insurance on ships destroyed by the cruisers. The tolling of the dismal bell at Lloyd's reminded many merchants of the dangers of passive neutrality. Claims against English insurance companies disturbed Russell, as did a rising sentiment within the shipping industry for closer supervision of maritime policy. Philip Henry Rathbone, a man of influence in the maritime and mercantile community, vigorously criticized Palmerston's policy, asserting that the government's loose neutrality alarmed many Liverpool shipowners. Economic pressure had far more importance than memorials from emancipation societies, though as the meaning of Lincoln's proclamation percolated through England, it generated some little pro-Union sentiment that was not lost on the Queen's ministers.* In Parliament, opponents of the ministry taunted Russell that England would be "more vulnerable" than other nations if in future wars neutrals permitted privateers to be outfitted in their ports. An impressive array of journals, religious periodicals, and provincial newspapers stimulated interest in the Northern cause, especially among the middle classes, while reminding readers of the connection of the South with slavery. The press, particularly outside London, expressed growing concern over the consequences of the recent *Alexandra* decision. Ministers felt a deepening awareness of the problem; they were coming to see that issues raised by Southern shipbuilding were not merely legal. To compound confusion, the search for an accommodation had to be carried out under a veritable barrage of reminders from the American ministers about the "shortcomings" of British policy.[1]

* * * *

To Charles Francis Adams prevention of the departure of the rams was, of course, a matter of paramount importance. Several days after the Southern disasters at Vicksburg and Gettysburg, American agents approached the Foreign Office regarding seizure of the Laird rams. At Liverpool, Consul Dudley on July 7, 1863, applied to customs officials for a detention order because the vessels were being equipped, armed, and fitted out for the Confederate States with "intent to cruise against the Government and citizens of the United States, with which Government Her Majesty the Queen is not now at war."[2] So apprehensive was he about the impend-

*One must be careful, however, not to overestimate the impact of the Emancipation Proclamation in generating sentiment for the North. Indeed, current research suggests that it actually had little effect on public opinion.

ing escape of the vessels that he took the evidence to London. Moran suggested to his diary an adjudication by war: "If these ships go nothing will prevent a war between the two countries. . . . We had better be in open hostilities at once, for then we will know what to expect, and who are our friends and foes, as well as end this bastard neutrality." Adams adopted a tone suited to the occasion and forwarded Dudley's depositions to Russell on July 11 with a résumé of the case against the rams and a critique of the British position.[3]

The minister protested that in England all the sinews of war—men and money, ships and shells—were readily available. Construction of the most formidable kind of steam warships, incorporating "all the appliances of British skill to the arts of destruction," was the "gravest act of international hostility yet committed." Such ships clearly intended injury to American lives and property. There was evidence of a plot by which rebels could wage war from Liverpool to break a blockade "legitimately established" and "fully recognized" by the Queen. There was ample reason to investigate construction of the rams because they were being built at a yard which had supplied the Confederacy with one cruiser and whose owner was a known Southern partisan. The notorious Confederate agent, J. D. Bulloch, spent much time at the Laird yard in technical conversation with personnel. Americans felt themselves victims of "active malevolence" on the part of Britain; they had no choice but to regard British policy as "tantamount to a participation in the war by the people of Great Britain to a degree which . . . cannot fail to endanger the peace and welfare of both countries." Adams tactlessly asserted that British reluctance to take action against the rams stemmed not from want of will but from "absence of power in . . . existing laws to reach a remedy."[4]

Russell replied that the complaint had gone to the proper authority "in order that such steps may be taken in the matter as can be legally and properly carried out."[5]

The solicitor of customs, Felix Hamel, told the foreign

secretary that in light of the court's repudiation of government contentions in the *Alexandra* case, Dudley's evidence was not strong enough to support a seizure in court. The recent verdict was binding, unless reversed by a higher court; even an ad interim detention might be a costly blunder: "I presume that the vessels are of great value," Hamel cautioned, "and failure in obtaining a seizure and forfeiture would be attended with serious consequences in the shape of damages and costs."[6] Crown advisers also conducted an investigation of the ships at the end of July, reporting insufficient grounds to proceed under existing statutes—"there being no legal evidence whatever." They thought the French claim to ownership valid and advised that the government "ought not to detain or in any way interfere with the steam vessels in question."[7]

From the preliminary exchange on the rams one fact emerges: in spite of the *Alexandra* rebuke to the government (and the trial demonstrated British willingness to test the Union view of neutrality), Americans were never willing to admit that notoriety was not proof. Everyone in Liverpool "knew" that the rams were for the Confederates, but no one with first-hand legally acceptable proof of this connection would come forward with the affidavits necessary to sustain it in court. Even Minister Adams, for all his superb legal training, was reluctant to acknowledge that British courts could not "admit assertions for proof nor conjecture for certainty." His son and secretary thought the law officers correct in refusing to sanction seizure, and he told his brother that the evidence against the ships "was certainly not strong enough to condemn them," though he perceptively put a finger on one key to the affair when he said it "was no longer a case for the Courts."[8]

Henry Adams was not alone in recognizing the multidimensional aspects of the affair. Her Majesty's government had also come to see that the case had become something more than a legal matter, that it impinged on other areas of policy: economic, political, even moral. There was, for one thing, the problem of finding out who owned the rams—and, thanks to clever covering tactics on the part of the Confederates, this was no easy task. Russell instructed his ambassador at Paris, Lord Cowley, to sound out the French to determine whether Napoleon's navy had any interest in the rams. The telegraphed reply was emphatic: "Ironclad vessels are not for the French government."[9] Later, after Bravay's title became known, further inquiries at Paris compounded confusion, for Cowley could find no information about that illustrious house; he thought it did not exist. Then, too, Russell, though not fully satisfied with the advice of his legal advisers on this problem, was reluctant to override it, especially if by so doing he appeared to be responsive to foreign pressure.

In such an atmosphere rumors thrived. There was, seemingly, a story for every taste. The South suspected seizure; the North expected escape. From his post in Brussels, Henry Sanford reported that the "King of Belgium had written to the Queen of England urging detention."[10] In mid-August, treasury agents of the Crown in Liverpool noted the arrival of a Confederate naval officer and incorrectly assumed that he had come to take the rams out of Britain. In London, Benjamin Moran thought the *Florida* (reported cruising off the coast of the British Isles) had come "to convey her more formidable sister pirates."[11] Reliable persons and informed sources thought the government had decided to confiscate the ships, though the Americans remained skeptical. Investigations proceeded apace as customs officers paid frequent visits to the Birkenhead yard.

Then the movement of events slowed almost to a standstill, for it was the vacation month of August. There were no cabinet meetings on either side of the Atlantic; there were no signs of impending disaster, no hints of imminent war. Lord Russell went on holiday; Lord Palmerston ignored the rams; Minister Adams, to the horror of his diary-keeping secretary, predated dispatches 481–84 and took a night train to Scotland.

Finally, on September 1, Russell announced his decision on the rams—the government had no ground for action against them. Pointing out that much of the American information was hearsay, he informed Adams that Crown lawyers could find no flaw in Bravay's title nor detect any illegal intent in his action. Port officials insisted that they could find no evidence of Southern ownership. Regretfully, therefore, the Foreign Office could not interfere.[12] Sent from Scotland, this note did not reach the American legation until 4:00 P.M. on September 4.

On the following day, a public exposition of the government's position on the rams appeared in the Liverpool *Mercury,* which published Russell's reply to a local emancipation society request for intervention at Birkenhead. The secretary told the antislavery group that "prosecutions cannot be set on foot" for violations of the law without "affidavits of credible witnesses," and inferred that the absence of such evidence tied the government's hands.[13]

During the first week of September, 1863, the ram affair reached a climax. On his thirty-fourth wedding anniversary, September 3, Adams returned from a ten-day vacation to face perhaps the most important problem of his diplomatic career. It seemed to him that British inaction might bring war. He could leave nothing undone to avert it. He sent a mild note reminding the Foreign Office that there could hardly be a doubt of the purpose of the rams. The next day, September 4, after Dudley again had warned that one of the vessels was nearly ready, Adams sent a somewhat stronger note, "a last solemn protest against the commission of such an act of hostility against a friendly nation."[14]

He then received Russell's note of September 1.

Depressed by months of diplomatic drudgery and the "moral pettiness" of British statesmanship, he predicted that a "collision must now come of it." After a night of anxiety he resolved to send a stronger appeal, the "superfluous" note of September 5, 1863:

At this moment, when one of the ironclad war vessels is on the point of departure . . . on its hostile errand against the United States I am honored with the reply of your Lordship Russell's note of September 1 . . . I trust I need not express how profound is my regret at the conclusion to which Her Majesty's Government have arrived. I can regard it no other wise than as practically opening to the insurgents full liberty in this kingdom. . . . It would be superfluous in me to point out to your Lordship that this is war.

For once, almost the only time, Adams allowed frayed nerves to overcome courtesy and tact. In his anxiety to impress upon the British the seriousness of events he had overstepped the bounds of diplomatic propriety. The note displayed, understandably but regretably, all the attributes of American pressure that the British found most obnoxious. The message stated that Washington could not tamely submit to relations which were so "utterly deficient in reciprocity," and that further correspondence on the rams was "inexpedient." Adams rebuked the British for procrastination, that "fatal objection of impotency which paralyzes Her Majesty's Government" and which raised such barriers to "further reasoning." The next move, he said, was up to his superiors.[15]

It is well to note that, contrary to popular opinion, while this note came close to threatening a breach of diplomatic relations, it did not threaten war. When read in its entirety, "by its four corners," as the lawyers say, the note indicates that Adams did not intend his remarks as a threat. Had he substituted "unneutral act" in place of "war" the note would have attracted much less attention from historians. As his diary makes abundantly clear, he was playing for time, though genuinely frightened by the prospect of war. His task as a diplomat—and he was extremely good at the trade —was to prevent, not precipitate that calamity.

Before the Foreign Office received his note, the British already had set in motion the cumbersome machinery of detention. The undersecretary of state for foreign affairs, on September 1, informed Home Office officials, who had jurisdiction at Birkenhead, that so much suspicion surrounded the ships "that if sufficient evidence can be obtained to lead to the belief that they are intended for the Confederate States," they ought to be held for investigation.[16] Two days later, September 3, Russell telegraphed his assistant, Austin H. Layard, to stop the rams "as soon as there is reason to believe that they are actually about to put to sea, and to detain them until further orders."[17] Shortly after noon on September 4, Russell sent another telegram to Layard assuming full responsibility for the detention, whatever the consequence might be. Thus, on his own initiative, independently of American pressure, without law office or cabinet concurrence —and at considerable risk of "both a legal rebuff and political embarrassment"—Russell stopped the rams. Adams had indeed written a superfluous note.[18]

*   *   *   *   *

Russell's move was a mere holding action until the government could prepare a case against the inconvenient vessels.[19] He wrote to Palmerston of the decision, informing him of the solicitor general's approval "as one of policy, though not of strict law." The motive was simply to test the Enlistment Act again, for one might reasonably argue that ships plated with iron and equipped with turrets and a ram provided prima-facie evidence of warlike intent. There was also some desire to convince the domestic and American public that a "kind of neutral hostility should not be allowed to go on without some attempt to stop it."[20] The British chargé in Washington told the State Department that Her Majesty's government was determined to do everything "proper and justifiable" to enforce neutrality, and he reminded Frederick Seward, son of and secretary to the secretary of state, that the Queen's ministers had ordered detention at some risk.[21]

The Russell decision set off an extensive debate among royal officials. Waddington of the Home Office wrote to Layard at the Foreign Office on September 4 that the rams probably *ought* to be detained, but that in the opinion of legal advisers of the Crown the facts did not "afford sufficient legal evidence that these vessels are intended for the Confederate States." The prime minister, equipped for accurate analysis by a lifetime of crisis diplomacy, recognized a flaw in the maneuver but supported his colleague. Pam did not spend much time worrying about rams, being more concerned with Continental politics, but his mind pared the Birkenhead business to essentials. "I think you are right in detaining the Ironclads now building in the Mersey," he told Russell, "although the result may be that we shall be obliged to set them free. There can be no doubt that ships plated with Iron must be intended for warlike purposes, but to justify seizure we must . . . prove that they are intended for . . . the Confederates and to be employed against the Federal Government." He wryly reminded the foreign secretary that securing such proof might not be as easy as ordering a seizure.[22] Other members of the official family expressed approval. Sir George Grey and the Duke of Argyll, while supporting detention as necessary, fixed on the difficulty of proving Confederate connection as the defect in the government's case. Argyll supported detention because he believed their departure would give rise to "irremedial mischief."[23]

Not all members of the government were convinced of the wisdom of the act. However enthusiastic the cabinet, law officers could not share the relief. They realized how expensive the step might be, both financially and in decreasing the protection for private property. They warned on September 12 that the government had exceeded its authority because there was no legal sanction for stopping "the exportation of ships of war or ships which Her Majesty shall judge capable of being converted into ships of war."[24]

An acrimonious exchange continued between the foreign secretary and the American minister. Adams' tactlessness had stirred the latent anti-Americanism of Whitehall, and the riposte on the rams caused lapses from the usually correct prose of these two men. If Adams' note of the fifth had been rude, Russell's reply of the eleventh skirted discourtesy. Britain was a country governed by law and not will, he told Adams; and her courts could not "admit assertions for proof, nor conjecture for certainty." Secretary of State Seward "with his knowledge and perspicuity of judgment [the inference was plain that the London representative of the United States lacked both] cannot fail to acknowledge that it was necessary to show, not only that these vessels were built and equipped for . . . war but also that they were intended for the so-called Confederate States." The note hinted that Adams had failed to provide proof of either. Russell scored another hit by telling his adversary that "these matters will no doubt be duly and dispassionately considered . . . at Washington however they may have been understood in London." The president and secretary of state might view the affair more calmly. And regardless of what the American minister thought or said, the Queen wished above all "faithfully to perform the duties of neutrality." Her Majesty's government could not allow the laws of the realm or the rules of international comity to be interpreted by a foreign minister.[25]

Adams lashed back. British neutrality was "nothing more than a shadow under which war may be conducted," and the attitude of the ministry indicated that international obligations were scarcely "worth the paper on which they are written." He ticked off the charges against Victoria's government: specifications, allowing insurgents "persistently to transgress the limits of neutrality," permitting ships to be built in the ports of Britain "with intent to make war on the United States," arming rebel ships with connivance of

British subjects, making no serious remonstrance against use of the British flag by cruisers. Adams quoted Russell on neutral responsibility. Because unneutral acts might imply indirect participation in hostile acts, and because they tended to involve neutral states in war, the foreign secretary had said on one occasion that all lapses from neutral conduct ought to be treated by neutrals as offenses against "public policy and safety." The foreign secretary, Adams tartly hinted, should take cognizance of the discrepancy between his practice and his preaching. The minister noted that Russell had turned down an American offer of a reciprocal revision of neutrality statutes on the ground that the law was "fully effective" in its present form. The British note of September 1, Adams argued, had admitted of no inference but that of surrender of all power "to prevent the violation of these admitted obligations of neutrality." Peace was endangered by mischief-makers who were permitted free rein in the realm for "want of a scruple of technical evidence to prove a gross and flagrant fraud." Adams respectfully submitted that "the interests of two nations are of too much magnitude to be measured by the infinitesimal scale of the testimony permissible before a jury in a Common Law Court." Would the noble Lord please consider what security the United States had "when all the barriers are virtually removed out of the way of an effective levying of war against them from this kingdom of the most formidable scale." If the Enlistment Act was adequate, why was it not enforced? This surely was a "most fitting and urgent occasion upon which all the majesty of the law may be invoked to the end of establishing justice and maintaining peace." Adams warned that the Confederates would stop at nothing, "however audacious or dishonest."[26]

Russell replied in a blistering note on September 25, the last of the series. Stressing his desire that the duties of neutrality be carried out impartially and strictly, he told Adams that there were passages in his note which "so plainly and repeatedly imply an intimation of hostile proceeding toward Great Britain on the part of . . . the United States, unless steps are taken by Her Majesty's government which the law does not authorize, or unless the law which you consider as insufficient is altered," that the ministry could not allow the statements to go unchallenged. Russell made clear that Her Majesty's government would "not be induced by any such consideration, either to overstep the limits of the law or to propose to Parliament any new law." Nor would Britain "shrink from any consequences of such a decision." The foreign secretary did not mention that this note had the approval of Queen Victoria and Prime Minister Palmerston.[27]

In cabinet meetings Palmerston had advocated a strong line, and his influence was very apparent in the last two notes (both written by Russell) to Adams. There was little love between Britain's first lord and America's representative. Pam spoke for a sizeable portion of opinion when he lashed at the American's tendency toward insolence. He once told Russell that the proper tone for answers to Adams' more bellicose notes was to say in civil terms "you be damned." Some such comment seemed necessary, Pam said, "because we are going to take the Iron Clads away from the Confederates and we might, if we said nothing, have the appearance of humble submission to Yankee Bullying." While Pam was reasonably sure that iron-plated ships with rams could not be peaceful, he was certain he had no proof that the ships were for the Confederates. Above all, he resented dictation from the Yankees and wanted whatever was done to be done according to British estimates of responsibility.[28]

Parliamentary revision of legislation would have cleared up most of the problems connected with Confederate activity, but no action along that line could be taken for fear of bringing on a political crisis and possibly a new election. At this time the cabinet was sensitive because of its tenuous control of the House of Commons. A simple alteration of the customs act could have allowed the government to prevent the departure of suspected ships of war "to certain countries without license."[29] Touchiness to outside pressure teamed with the unstable party alignments to prevent this. Palmerston recognized that the cabinet could not propose any substantial change in the Enlistment Act.[30]

The principle of neutrality was simple, its application more complex. Russell told his colleagues that the statute laid down a clear admonition, "You shall not fit out any vessel as a cruiser . . . in the service of any state. . . . If you do, you will commit a misdemeanor and . . . such vessel fitted out . . . and armed with the intent mentioned will be forefeited." But the line between constructing a merchant vessel and "building a vessel with the intent that she should be employed in the service of a known belligerent" was difficult to trace. The rams were warships and probably for use against blockading squadrons. But "suspicion and surmise" could not replace fact. One might fairly assume that these were vessels of war and built for the South, but he wondered whether "moral certainty [was] sufficient ground for legal forfeiture of the vessels." If two ships might go to the South, why not twenty or two hundred? Was that not war? Was it not "contrary to the whole spirit" of the Foreign Enlistment Act?"[31]

Undersecretary Hammond of the Foreign Office on September 21 reviewed Russell's position. The vessels were "clearly warships of a most formidable kind;" France "had nothing to do with them;" Bravay's title was "probably a blind;" and the frenzied pace of construction, even after the Egyptian ruler had renounced his claim, indicated a mission other than cruises on the Nile. Still, the facts did not prove much, although in an ordinary case of felony or misdemeanor, similar circumstances would probably justify holding an accused person, at least until a thorough investigation could be made. The Foreign Office thought the detention warranted.[32]

Notes to Paris, St. Petersburg, Constantinople, and Copenhagen did little to clear the mystery. Southern sailors in Liverpool and rumors of ram-napping pushed Russell toward the next step. Detention no longer served government purposes, and a new step, seizure, became necessary.[33]

*   *   *   *   *

On October 8, Undersecretary Hammond told treasury officials of Russell's decision to take the rams into custody. A copy of this order went out to customs men at Liverpool, authorizing them to seize the ships at once; then the Admiralty ordered Captain E. A. Inglefield of H.M.S. *Majestic* to aid port officials in so doing.[34] The order exposed the government to legal counterattack. If the Crown had to record a legal basis for its action, as now seemed likely, a question of evidence would be raised. Treasury officials were unhappy in the position of "instruments for carrying out the views of the foreign office," and fearful of their own heavy responsibility in the affair. They suspected that the government had gone too far, that the government's role had changed from defensive to obstructive, with consequent financial liabilities for which treasury officials would be accountable. The government would have to state the point of law by which they justified the seizure. Treasury Secretary Hamilton was not convinced that this step was warranted. "I have only to remind you," he remarked to Hammond, "that so far as the facts have been before the Law Officers, their opinion is that evidence does not justify the interference of Government." Hammond agreed, but pointed out that in the case of the first ram the alternatives were "either to seize her at once or to stand by and see her run away with."[35]

Russell elected to take both rams. The Duke of Argyll approved the move, chiding the Queen's legal lights for dilatory tactics. "They would never have advised you to do what you have so rightly done: they will find reasons why it should have been done—now that it is done. Wherefore I say, three cheers for the House of Russell."[36] The commander of the royal forces in Canada, General Monck, expressed a widely held view that the Lairds had come close to violating the spirit of the Enlistment Act, "if they have not actually overstepped the line." He was glad that the government had decided to investigate the rams before they left the Mersey.[37]

Adams recorded deep appreciation in his diary, equating his satisfaction to that which followed the resolution of the *Trent* affair.[38] Some days later, Henry Adams wrote his brother Charles in America, expressing gratification. The new move indicated to Henry that "the gale that has blown so long is beginning to veer about. If our armies march on; if Charleston is taken and North Carolina freed; above all if emancipation is made effective; Europe will blow gentle gales upon us and will again bow to our dollars." British willingness to take the first step, despite the opposition of legal advisers, was to young Adams "reasonable ground for confidence" that they would take others as the need arose. The British would not like it, would groan and grumble, but "in some stupid and bungling way" the necessary things would be done. He admitted that the law officers were probably correct in their interpretation, but correctly reasoned that the ram affair had spilled over the boundaries of legal technicalities.[39]

Russell received numerous reports of the effect of his act on American opinion. Minister Adams conveyed official thanks, promised cooperation, and expressed a hope that the war would leave no friction between the two governments.[40] From Washington, Chargé Stuart reported that Secretary Seward had no further apprehension about Anglo-American relations now that the ram business was being resolved. Some days later, Lord Lyons informed superiors that the seizure had produced "the best effect" on American public opinion and had elicited a more friendly regard for Britain.[41]

The course of events at Birkenhead had one consequence of special poignancy: seizure marked the final failure of

Bulloch's efforts to redress the naval balance in America. Largely through no fault of his own and partly because his advice had not been followed, he found himself checkmated —a result that caused him great personal pain and much professional disappointment. Under the circumstances, he saw no alternative but to salvage the remnants of British operations and turn to the Continent for what succor might be available there. Russell's decision effectively checked the Confederate attempt to build a navy in British yards.[42]

To lessen economic unrest at Liverpool, the government allowed work on the ships to continue, but on October 26, with the approval of the Law Office, Russell took "full possession" of them, moored them in the Mersey under the *Majestic*'s guns, and placed armed guards on board. The next day customs officials informed the builders that the vessels had passed into government custody, and informed Bravay, via the Lairds, of the change in status, pointing out that the move did not prejudice any questions of legal title.[43]

Attempts to recover the vessels failed. Russell refused to let go of them, telling Hammond to inform the owners that the "well-considered" seizure order could neither be altered nor revoked.[44] Months passed with no sign of legal action, no hint as to when court proceedings might begin. Bulloch, sure that the government's case was legally indefensible, wished to hurry it to court but his lawyers warned that any move would complicate matters still more. There was nothing to do, they said, except wait: British justice would not be hurried. In a final effort to free the ships, Bulloch tried to bring about French intervention, and for a time it seemed as if Louis Napoleon might take a hand in the business. But he thought better of it, informing Bravay and Company that under the circumstances he could not request the British government to free the vessels.[45] At this time, it will be remembered, exposure of extensive Confederate naval activity in France had embarrassed the emperor. Northern representatives kept insisting throughout 1864 that French hospitality to Southern cruisers ought to cease. Louis Napoleon had troubles enough at home; he didn't need to import ram trouble, too.[46]

Purchase of the rams by the Royal Navy provided a way out of an embarrassing predicament. That solution had been suggested by Palmerston soon after the detention, when he told Admiralty officials that Britain was behind France in ironclads and that the rams might prove useful as "peace keepers" in the Channel. He thought it unwise to permit them to fall into the hands of either the French or Americans, predicting that if they went on the open market a "diplomatic wrangle" would ensue. Better to keep them at home. By the end of the year Russell also had come around to this view, and opponents in the cabinet were won over to it.[47] Though Secretary Somerset did not want to buy the rams at any price, thinking them "not good for much," Admiralty officers appraised them and "with scrupulous regard to their intrinsic worth" set their combined value at £220,000 (of which £188,000 reverted to the Confederates). Terms, more or less satisfactory to all concerned, were finally worked out, and in May, 1864—"with a law suit in one hand and the valuation in the other"—the Admiralty made an offer which Bravay felt compelled to accept. Her Majesty's government then took possession of the Laird rams, renaming them *Scorpion* and *Wivern* when they were commissioned into the Royal Navy.[48]

It probably relieved Crown officials that the case did not go to court, for it seems unlikely that the seizure could have been sustained by judicial decree. The Crown's contention that the ship's physical structure was prima-facie evidence of warlike intent was vulnerable, and the unreversed *Alexandra* decision stood as a potentially damaging precedent against the government's case.[49] By purchasing the rams, the Admiralty accomplished the government's purpose with a minimum of embarrassment to Russell and his colleagues.

Naturally, the melancholy turn of events did not please the South. Bulloch, who was deeply affected by the seizure, de-

scribed the loss as a severe setback to Southern aspirations—
a state of affairs in which regret for the public loss was mixed
with private frustation. The failure of this mission, he told
Mallory, reduced him to the "condition of a disabled ship
taken possession of by a current she has no power to stem."[50]

Conversely, the Northern camp received the news with
jubilation. "Undoubtedly to us this is a second Vicksburg,"
Henry Adams told his brother; it was, "the crowning stroke
of our diplomacy." He then offered an explanation for the
change in Palmerstonian policy: "We have a clear and convincing position before the British public, for we come with
victories on our standards and the most powerful military and
naval engines that ever the earth saw."[51]

For Lord Russell the affair had produced too many head-
aches. And for us, with the acid-etched portrait of the foreign
secretary in Henry Adams' *Education* echoing in our minds,
it is easy to condemn his vacillation and indecision, and with
the wisdom of hindsight to describe as fumbling his honest
efforts to extricate Britain from a situation legally correct
but morally questionable. Against his better judgment he
had to take a course that legal advisers assured him was indefensible, and he himself gave the best rationale for British
action by pointing out the need for occasionally going behind
and beyond the law. One should perhaps commend the foreign secretary for a sincere and sustained attempt to act in a
manner "morally right and politically expedient," without
at the same time making a mockery of cherished British constitutional guarantees. He did better than one might have
expected. His handling of the incident—"a complex, in-
finitely intricate legal problem"—was at least as good as that
of his American adversary. One might go further and suggest
that at many points it was better.[52]

*   *   *   *   *

After innumerable conferences, labyrinthine discussions—and
with much reluctance—Her Majesty's government, as noted,

moved to detain, seize, and purchase the acutely-embarrassing
Laird rams because the cabinet had decided that it would
not be in the British interest to allow the vessels to depart.
But suppose the decision had been otherwise. What result
would the rams have had on the Northern blockade? Would
they have been able to disperse the Union squadrons, as
Bulloch hoped? Would they have proved powerful enough to
open Southern ports to the commerce of the world? Or were
they, as Minister Adams contended shortly after the war,
merely "little mean things" scarcely worth the apprehension
they had caused?[53]

Is there any evidence by which one may evaluate the potential performance of these vessels? Fortunately, there is.
While it is not in any degree conclusive—for the rams were
never tested in battle—this material permits at least a tenta-
tive assessment of their capabilities. Three facets of performance need evaluation: general seaworthiness, the condition
of the crew after an extended voyage, and the value of the ram
principle itself.

Because only one Confederate ironclad got to sea during
the war (the French-built *Sphinx-Olinde-Stonewall-et al.*),
part of the evidence for performance must come from its
experience. After Napoleon III had changed his mind about
allowing Confederate construction in his realm, one of Bulloch's French ironclads was sold to Denmark, but by a complicated and comic-opera operation the South recovered
possession of the vessel. Part of the plot was to sabotage its
trials so the Danes would reject it. As things turned out,
sabotage, if such there was, was hardly necessary. A Confederate naval officer, Captain Thomas Jefferson Page, was
sent to Copenhagen to return the ship to France, and during
the voyage in wintry, gale-lashed seas, the ship behaved, as
Van Doren Stern points out, "as if she were as unseaworthy
as the enormous block of stone that had given her her original
name."[54] Page reported that the ship leaked badly around
the rudder post (possibly as a result of some last-minute

alterations made in Denmark) and that the "formidable" vessel had serious structural shortcomings. Moreover, the supposedly fast *Stonewall* (equipped with a double screw) took eighteen days to reach its rendezvous at Belle Ile.[55] By the time it reached the southern coast of Brittany, Captain Page knew that his ship had dangerous defects and its performance would not come up to expectations. "I fear that the power and effect of this vessel have been too much exaggerated," he told Flag Officer Samuel Barron, warning him of over-optimism.[56] In defense of the ship, however, one ought to note that it weathered a "frightful storm" before putting in at El Ferrol, Spain, in early 1865, and, though it was too late to do the Confederacy any good, that the ship did cross the Atlantic, providing thereby some evidence of seaworthiness, if telling nothing about its fighting potential.

More to the point for present purposes, there is evidence of the performance of the Laird rams after their commission into royal service. The Admiralty tested them and found that the *Wivern* performed "indifferently": it "rolled 18 to 20 degrees, often had her decks awash, and in heavy swells her hull was almost completely hidden from observers in other ships." It was also "extremely wet and uncomfortable," emphatically "not safe as an ocean cruiser."[57] The sister ship proved somewhat better. In one maneuver the *Scorpion* "was laid broadside on with the sea on her quarter and proved buoyant and steady."[58] Another point in favor of the rams was that their turrets could operate in heavy seas. Accordingly, one might conclude that the rams would have had a mixed record for ordinary battles at sea.* On the basis of extensive examination and testing, the Admiralty did in fact conclude that the rams "would be well-adapted to lake defence in Canada, or for harbour defence at home."[59] It seems safe to assume, therefore, that they would have proven adequate

*It should be remembered, however, that these ships were designed for a different purpose.

to the "harbor duty" for which the Confederacy intended them.

When they arrived off the American coast would their crews have been in fighting trim? On this point there is interesting evidence from a variety of sources. The French ironclad *Normandie* crossed the Atlantic in late 1862, and the captain's report of that pioneer voyage stressed the debilitating effect of life below deck where a constant humid heat turned quarters and work areas into veritable steamrooms.[60] Just after the war an American ironclad on a goodwill voyage visited Britain, where a Royal Navy captain inspected it soon after its arrival and left this impression of his visit:

I never saw such a wretched, pale, listless set of officers and men. They seemed to have no go left in them and crawled about the decks in a state of debility, one and all. I was shocked and immensely struck by their inactive appearance which remained vividly impressed on my mind's eye. More than one officer declared he would not for any consideration, of his own free will, go through the same experience. . . . The vessel was compared to a dungeon under water filled with a stifling atmosphere by a steam engine; the crew had no place to go in bad weather, all the openings being battened down in a very light breeze, and the foremost cowls . . . through which the engines and fans . . . drew the fresh air, were turned aft to keep the water out, so that for days and nights the crew were kept below, living on and breathing over and over again their own breath.[61]

In this report there may have been some residue of the period's anti-Americanism, perhaps even some professional jealousy, but it seems probable that the early ironclad warships were uncomfortable enough to hamper efficient operation; life aboard them may even have precluded going into action after an extended voyage, as Oscar Parkes suggests in his study of British battleships. Such a view receives corroboration from a later experience of the *Scorpion* in the North

Atlantic. Some years after the war, in late 1869, the vessel was en route to the British West Indies and ran into some really ugly weather which drove it into Queenstown, Ireland, for safety. From there, the crew, much frightened by their narrow escape, petitioned the Admiralty to excuse them from going to sea in a vessel so unsafe. Any ship would be preferable to the ram. By odd coincidence, another Confederate ironclad, Lt. North's frigate (then the *Danmark*), ran into the same storm, and the crew experienced a similar loss of faith in the vessel's seaworthiness. Had the Laird rams escaped during the war, they probably would have arrived for their work in American waters with crews in less than fighting trim.

How valid was the ram principle, the revival of an ancient technique of naval war? Could the mobile battering rams have done sufficient damage to Northern blockade ships to cause a loosening of the stranglehold they exercised on the South? The records of the Royal Navy provide "one of the few solid bases for speculation about the destructive power of the two British-built ironclads," for on May 9, 1864, one of the rams was involved in an accident. The report to the comptroller general stated:

I beg to report that on Monday last . . . a Vessel laded with ore in attempting to cross the bow of the Iron Clad Ram 'El Toussson' [*Scorpion*] in charge of Lieutenant Brodrick . . . drifted across her projecting bow & with no other impetus than that of the tide & her own weight smashed in her side & in a few minutes was in a sinking condition. . . . As this is the first occasion as far as I am aware, that the formidable nature of these Vessels has been tested, it has occurred to me the information might be interesting to the Lds. Commrs. of the Admiralty.[62]

This seems an adequate demonstration of the destructive power of the rams. On the basis of it one might conclude with a recent writer that "these floating fortresses could have smashed the wooden ships of the Union blockading squadrons like egg shells; and then, with their powerful 9-inch guns, they could have laid the northern seaport cities under tribute and caused the North to cry for mercy. In short, if the rams had put to sea, the South would probably have won its independence, and the North, already angry over the *Alabama* affair, would almost certainly have declared war on Britain."[63] Perhaps so. That at least is the traditional view.

But there is conflicting evidence which suggests another conclusion. In 1865, Britain's chief Admiralty designer, Edward J. Reed, told a meeting of naval architects about an experience with the same ram. One night while en route from Liverpool to another British port, the *Scorpion* accidentally ran into another ship:

She tried the ram principle, and what happened? The other ship did not seem to know anything about it, just went on and took no notice. The ram, on the contrary, had her forecastle ripped open to a very considerable extent. The captain tried to steam after the other ship, but found he could not do it without risking the swamping of his ship, and had the other ship been an enemy, he [the captain of the ram] would have been obliged to turn tail and run away.[64]

Who, then, would have been "obliged to turn tail and run away" if the rams had appeared off the southern coast of America? There is, of course, no fully satisfactory answer to this intriguing question, but on the basis of what is now known about the performance of Confederate ironclads, one might, with some justification, raise a question about the ability (long taken for granted) of these ships to raise the blockade.

ELEVEN | STUDY IN CONTRASTS

*M*ATTHEW Fontaine Maury's second ship had a
checkered career under three names: originally the
Victor, it was purchased in the autumn of 1863 as a Royal
Navy reject, barely escaped confiscation, fled to France, and
floated out the remainder of the war far from action in the
quiet of Calais harbor. Its story demonstrates the increasing
desperation of the South and the growing hostility that Mallory's men encountered in the dockyards of Britain and
France as the military fortunes of the Confederacy waned. No
self-respecting navy would have considered putting this ugly
hulk into service—even the Chinese, who at the time were
desperately in need of ships, balked at buying the relic.
For all his considerable talent in the realm of oceanography,
Maury left much to be desired as a purchasing agent. By late
1863, when this sad story opens, the South's never-strong
international position had deteriorated to the point where
some agents felt they had to take whatever was available. So
it was with Maury.

Even a cursory investigation should have uncovered the
obvious inadequacies of the vessel—for they were widely
known. The naval survey of 1863 had condemned it, and the
London *Times* ascribed its release from royal service to
general unseaworthiness. A competent mechanic could have

established that the engines had outlived their usefulness and were capable of delivering only a fraction of their rated 350 horsepower. The Admiralty had reported the vessel as "rotten and unserviceable," too defective even to warrant repairs for harbor duty. When a British firm offered to pay the £9,375 sale price for this nearly worthless vessel, Admiralty officials gladly accepted, as well they might. Using funds made available by Bulloch and operating through Coleman and Company, Maury bought the vessel on September 14, 1863, just a week after the detention of the Laird rams. According to custom, the government reserved sale of the masts and rigging, but the ship with all other machinery and fixtures passed Coleman and the Confederates.[1]

Renamed *Scylla,* it remained at Sheerness dockyard in London for a major and badly needed overhaul. Its presence and the upsurge of activity surrounding it soon aroused Northern curiosity. From the consul in London, Freeman H. Morse, Adams learned of its probable Southern connection but concluded that the evidence about it was as yet too skimpy to warrant a formal request for detention. Then, surprisingly, in a unique move, British officials took the initiative, and without waiting for American complaint, ordered the ship detained. Once again the order came too late. Suspicious of continued interest in the ship and seemingly well informed about government intentions, the owners sent their ship to France without completing preparations for its cruise.

Partly for reasons that have been set forth elsewhere, and partly because the Continent again had become restive as a result of the intensification of the dispute over the Danish duchies following the death of Denmark's king in November, the British were doing their best to seek an accommodation with the North in the late months of 1863. Moreover, in the present case there was added reason for official concern over activity at Sheerness. Coleman and his associates were outfitting their ship close to vessels of the Royal Navy, and a rumor spread that the *Scylla* was being equipped with government material.

But when harbor police searched the vessel—on the very day of its flight to France—they found no government property, no guns, no warlike equipment of any kind, and no violations of the rules. Accordingly, they gave the ship a clean bill of health. Charles Bernard, who later investigated its escape for the Treasury, reported that it had left port either late on the twenty-fourth or early on the twenty-fifth of November without clearance, and that there was no evidence of neglect of duty by yard officials.[2]

Soon after the ship's escape, Consul Morse furnished Adams with evidence which seemed to call for vigorous Union complaint. According to Morse's information, government workers had aided the ship's escape. On the basis of this information Adams declared in his complaint to Russell that the vessel had in fact been prepared as a Confederate cruiser, "with the connivance and direct aid of many of Her Majesty's officers stationed within the royal dockyard at Sheerness." According to the American informants, a rumor that Admiralty inspectors planned a search for government property had prompted the hasty departure. Adams forwarded depositions which, he said, supported the charge that government workers had outfitted a ship for use against a friendly power. This, as he pointed out to Russell in uncharacteristically vapid prose, involved "a case of hostile equipment" attempted by British subjects.[3]

Again the American case was weak. In the opinion of Russell's legal advisors, Adams' contention and the supporting evidence would not stand up in court. The hostile equipping of which he complained proved to be nothing more than innocent hospitality. The captain of H.M.S. *Cumberland,* acting on his own initiative and without permission of the yard commandant, had assisted in putting a new mast on the *Scylla* to test a new derrick. That red-faced young officer did not know that he had violated international rules by his kindness. While investigating the American complaint, the Foreign Office turned up evidence that "men belonging to the dockyard have been induced to assist in fitting out this vessel and that some of them had assisted in taking her to Calais." Because British wages were not high, some workers had taken leaves of absence to work for better pay outfitting the *Scylla* at Calais. When this was brought to the attention of Admiralty officials, they dismissed one worker—for giving information to the Yankees![4]

Later, in mid-December, Adams supplied proof that a British citizen, Robert Gordon Coleman, owned the vessel, and that an inspector at Sheerness, William Rumble, and other yard employees had recruited part of the crew. Lord Russell considered the charge serious enough to warrant paying seamen their usual wages to assure their presence as witnesses in court. The court fined some of the defendants and acquitted others. The Admiralty placed Rumble on half pay, for though technically not guilty of any violation of neutrality according to a verdict in the Court of Queen's Bench, his activity after the identity of the ship became known seemed to provide grounds "for the accusation that an officer employed in Her Majesty's service had aided and abetted those parties, who, in violation of Her Majesty's proclamation, were concerned in fitting out the 'Scylla' as a vessel of war."[5]

The ship had gone to France where it received a new captain, a new flag, and a new name, *Rappahannock*. Its presence there soon aroused the interest of American representatives, who complained to the French Foreign Office, which promised an investigation. French officialdom proved no more efficient than the English. The American minister, William L. Dayton, procured evidence that the ship was intended to be used against Union commerce and insisted that it be detained, warning that if it escaped, the United States would hold France to strict accountability for any damage to American commerce and property. Seward backed his minister in these remonstrances and urged a stronger tone. The secretary insisted that Dayton spare no effort to prevent the departure of hostile expeditions from French ports. He instructed Dayton to impress upon officials that toleration of Confederate activity would be a serious threat to the friendship between the two countries and that France would bear full responsibility.[6]

Unaware of growing American pressure on the French, Confederates struggled to get the *Rappahannock* ready. By mid-December, Barron thought she might be ready in two weeks, but at the year's end it still was in harbor. Agents had secured a gun battery in England, but despaired of getting it across the Channel.

Tightening English regulations in fact reflected the decline in Southern military fortunes following the disastrous summer of 1863. Affairs in Europe were approaching a crisis, Barron reported, and by the end of the year he believed that Russell was no longer neutral but a partisan of the North.[7] Bulloch held the same view. Believing that friendly cooperation animated Washington and Whitehall, he told Mallory that the combined efforts of Russell and Adams had proved "irresistible" and that they had checkmated attempts to get ships out of England. With some exaggeration he charged that all the machinery of the Queen's government had been placed at the disposal of the American minister, to be worked on orders from Washington.[8] This dispatch was written shortly after Bulloch learned of Napoleon's decision not to involve himself in the attempt to get the Laird rams out of England. Loss of the rams, he said, caused "greater pain and regret than I ever conceived it possible to feel."[9] In late 1863 and early 1864 there was much reason for pessimism; and a review of British action might convince the most ·dent Southern patriot that all was not well abroad. Un-.vorable activity of one sort or another involved the Laird .ams, the *Alexandra,* and the *Canton;* there was also a mounting list of Admiralty regulations which, ostensibly impartial, operated against the South. Bulloch, before learning of the Emperor's decision regarding the rams, thought that France was extending benefits denied in England. Barron also thought so as he struggled to get the reluctant rebel ready for sea. He told Mallory in early January, 1864, that three cruisers enjoyed the "hospitality and national courtesies of this Empire." Such behavior, he said, was in contrast to the "determined hostility" of Her Majesty's government. Convinced of the friendship of a monarch who would not allow Yankee bluster to intimidate him, Barron asserted that "Louis Napoleon is not Lord John Russell!"[10] He did not add—perhaps he did not know—that the emperor of the French, that dictator of plebiscites and bayonets, did not lack vision where his interests were concerned, and that he was as skillful at reading handwriting on the wall as his neighbor across the Channel. In his own peculiar way he was as shrewd as the diminutive British foreign secretary, and the Confederates would have been well advised to keep that fact in mind. Nothing illustrates the Southern capacity for self-delusion so well as their naive insistence that Napoleon III was an active partisan of their cause.

After repeated warnings from American representatives regarding the danger of unneutral acts, the imperial government was having second thoughts about its Confederate connections. The sinuous emperor had reappraised his position, and by February, 1864, he had decided that aiding the South was not in the French interest. On the fourth of that month Lt. Campbell of the *Rappahannock* received permission—almost an order—to leave Calais. The commissioner of maritime registry who brought the clearance told Campbell that failure to follow instructions might lead to a long detention, perhaps until the end of hostilities. Campbell ignored the hint. The next day the minister of marine issued a "clarification" of French neutrality, which virtually eliminated Confederate use of French facilities. Some days later, officers of the ministry ordered the *Rappahannock* held indefinitely.[11]

This move puzzled the Southerners because they had, so they thought, been careful. Campbell informed Barron that the ship had entered port with permission and had received no war equipment. Barron told Slidell that he and his men had refrained from all activity that might jeopardize neutrality.[12] When Slidell inquired about the ship's fate, the French foreign minister apologetically told him that detention resulted from infringement of the neutrality proclamation of 1861. Slidell gently pointed out that in view of the recently granted permission to leave, the infraction must have taken place in the very recent past. He asked for release of the vessel. He received a shrug, a spread of the hands, a smile. In an appeal to the emperor in mid-March he pointed out that detention of the ship appeared inconsistent with "friendly feelings" toward the South and with French neutrality.[13] Napoleon did nothing. Some insight into the French attitude toward the vessel was provided by a conversation between the legal adviser to the British legation at Paris and Victoria's ambassador at the French court. The lawyer indicated that French law on neutrality was imprecise, that much depended on the personal whim of the emperor, and that the government only could act on general principles, deciding every case as circumstances dictated: "Everyone knows," he told the ambassador, *"les circonstances spéciales."* The vessel at Calais was, he affirmed with Gallic logic, a special case.[14]

By the spring of 1864, just as the Southerners had about given up hope of freeing the ship and had announced their intention of selling it, a new element entered the case. The French appointed a special committee of lawyers to examine the seizure. After weeks of review, the *Comité Consultatif du Contentieux* ruled that the vessel might go free—*dans les conditions où il est entré*—if its crew equalled the number of men who arrived in it (thirty-five, by decision of the committee). Because they believed that operating with so small a crew was unwise, and seeing little possibility of altering the ruling, the Confederates paid off the crew and with French permission allowed the ship to remain at Calais as a sort of floating depot and rendezvous for naval agents. To strengthen Southern resolution to keep it there, four Federal warships kept watch over the harbor.[15]

Confederates came to the agonizing reappraisal of French policy demanded by circumstances. Chief Flag Officer Samuel Barron complained of the emperor's "perfidious conduct," and informed Mallory in August, 1864, that "the friendly disposition" shown during the early months of his mission in France had turned "decidedly adverse," and that restrictions were now as rigid and as vigorously enforced as ever they had been across the Channel. At about the same time, Bulloch characterized French action as even more unfriendly than Britain's: "Every pledge has been violated, and we have encountered nothing but deception and duplicity," and he went on to say that he was at the mercy of French whim.[16] The Confederate secretary of state, Judah P. Benjamin, fulminated against French apostasy in an angry dispatch to Slidell but cautioned that "we are compelled by present circumstances to submit in silence to these aggressions." Therefore, no matter how strong the provocation, the Confederate commissioner must give no excuse for a rupture of diplomatic relations between Paris and Richmond, for such a break could only augment difficulties, while having no impact on French action. Complaints must be deferred and insults borne with patience, Benjamin advised, until such time as the South would be able "to impress on all nations the conviction of her ability to repel outrages, from whatever quarter they may be offered."[17] Slidell put the case accurately and succinctly: "The weak have no rights; the strong no obligations."[18] With no victories on their standards, the Southerners found their international position more and more precarious. Secretary of State Benjamin reported President Davis indignant at the "evasions and injustice" of the French in regard to the *Rappahannock*; nor could he himself resist the conclusion that there was "bad faith and deception" in the policy pursued by the emperor, and he was convinced that the cabinets of Washington and Paris had worked out a complete "entente." Slidell wondered to his French friends whether the sentiments of the emperor had become "less kindly" toward the South because of the ships that had been built in France as a result of official suggestions. Slidell noted that the Confederacy "had been treated with extreme harshness" and said that it was difficult "to account for such a sudden change of policy, if there were no corresponding change of feeling." As before, he received an evasive answer and a significant smile.

The idle cruiser continued to float at anchor, a drain on Southern resources until a British ship broker received permission from the Foreign Office to purchase and register the vessel—with a warning that such a procedure would not protect him against American claims. And once again, Slidell provided the proper comment: "The affair of the *Rappahannock*," he told Benjamin, "has been a series of blunders from the very commencement." Surely, the sad affair of the reluctant rebel reflects little credit on anyone connected with it. Poorly conceived, badly managed, a comedy of errors from start to finish, the project showed Southern naval procurement at its worst.[19]

While it is, of course, true that conditions in the waning weeks of 1863 and the early months of 1864 certainly did not favor the overseas activity of the Confederates, that fact does not tell the whole story. For despite the declining fortunes of the South and the stiffening of European attitudes, it was still possible to achieve great things—as Bulloch demonstrated by the artfulness of his arrangements for procuring the last Confederate cruiser.

*   *   *   *   *

Destruction of the *Alabama* in June, 1864, crippled Confederate naval forces, created a crisis in the overseas chain of command, and confronted Mallory's chief agent with a new challenge and a magnificent opportunity. In the summer of 1864 the Southern navy was a cipher. Captain Winslow had eliminated the most serious threat to Union shipping by sinking Semmes's ship off Cherbourg; only one British-built cruiser, the *Florida*, then on its last voyage, remained to harass the remnants of Northern commerce; the nearly worthless *Georgia* had been sold; and French authorities at Calais were detaining the *Rappahannock*. Naturally, the South wanted to revive its navy.

The Confederates faced a difficult task in trying to replace the *Alabama*, for much of the raider's effect had been psychological: fear had kept the Yankees off the oceans. News of the "ship-eater's" fate would embolden timid merchants, while the improved position of the London underwriters and the possibility of increased employment among Union seamen might prompt a resurgence of Union maritime activity that could only augment Southern woe. Only a raider of similar reputation could keep American vessels in port. Finding such a ship would not be easy; escaping with it might prove impossible. With time at a premium, Bulloch needed to find a ready-made raider, get it out of Britain, and prepare it for action—all this while under near-constant surveillance by a network of Northern agents honed to efficiency and effectiveness by long practice in the art of uncovering the South's subtlest subterfuges. He accepted the challenge. The story of the last Confederate cruiser is the story of Bulloch at his best.

Naturally, he needed no orders from Richmond to start his work. Contact with maritime circles familiarized him with most of Britain's merchant marine, enabled him to identify many ships on sight, acquainted him with their specifications and their defects. No ship seemed adequate. Then he remembered one that possessed all the qualities he wanted, a lovely vessel he had seen a year earlier floating on the chocolate Clyde in Glasgow. Where was that ship?

While in Scotland looking for blockade runners in August, 1863, he and his trusted and very able assistant, Lt. Robert R. Carter, had discovered a majestic ship, the *Sea King*, anchored on the Clyde. To their experienced eyes her beauty came from that careful combination of design, material, and craft which is art. They learned that the "beautifully modelled" and "excellently finished ship" bore the trademark of Alexander Stephen and Sons, the justly-famous Clydebank shipbuilders, whose name was a guarantee of quality and craftsmanship. They would have been more impressed had they seen the diary in which the builder tabulated test results. But even without statistics it was an impressive sight: full-rigged to run before the wind, teak planking to resist the ravages of wind and wave, composite construction for strength and space, auxiliary engines with retractable screw, spacious quarters for captain and crew. The ship would make a fine addition to the Confederate navy, and they resolved to buy it. At that time, however, the ship was preparing for its maiden voyage, an eight-to-ten-month trip to the Far East, and so was not for sale.[20]

Mallory's men were not the only ones aware of this vessel's potential as a ship of war. From Glasgow in the autumn of 1863 Dudley also had reported the presence of a ship which might easily be converted into a cruiser, and he relayed to Washington rumors of an impending sale to the Confederates. Minister Adams informed Russell that British subjects were actively engaged in fitting out a vessel to resume the *Alabama's* dirty work; and Secretary Seward warned that Britain "may be held justly responsible" for losses that Americans sustained as a result of the new cruiser's depredations.[21]

The vessel fully deserved the attention it received from North and South, and soon acquired a sinister reputation. Becoming the C.S.S. *Shenandoah*, it roamed the far reaches of the North Pacific and Arctic oceans destroying Union vessels long after the war ended. Then, following a thrilling voyage halfway around the world, it surrendered to British

C. S. S. *SHENANDOAH*

officials at Liverpool seven months after Appomattox, the last cruiser to lower the Confederate flag.

After learning of the *Alabama's* destruction, Mallory instructed Bulloch to find a replacement for that raider. Forced sale of the Laird rams in the spring of 1864 had temporarily increased Southern resources, so even before the secretary's order arrived, Bulloch had started a search. Meanwhile, Carter had returned to Richmond, had told Mallory about the *Sea King*, and had convinced him of its suitability for service. Mallory ordered its purchase, primarily for use against Union whaling fleets in the northern Pacific and Arctic oceans.[22]

While Carter and Mallory were discussing the ship in Richmond, Bulloch's agents were completing purchase of the vessel, just returned from its maiden voyage with a fair claim to the title of "sea king," having logged over three hundred miles in twenty-four hours. After inspection by Lloyd's of London, it became the property of Richard Wright (father-in-law of Charles Prioleau of Fraser-Trenholm). To convince consuls and customs men of its peaceful purposes and to confuse Union spies, Wright moved his ship from Liverpool to London by a roundabout route, making many stops along the way to give it every appearance of being a sedate trading vessel engaged in legitimate commercial ventures.

Even in London so stately a ship could not escape comment. Measuring 222 feet with a beam of 32 feet, it displaced about 1,152 tons on a draft of nearly 16 feet. With engines of 47-inch bore and 33-inch stroke developing over 200 horsepower, it could steam faster than many Federal warships. In port it carried only the equipment of an East Indian merchantman, which it purported to be.[23]

Despite American efforts to forestall departure until its status could be determined, the ship escaped. Union agents knew that Bulloch had a ship in London, but could not identify it. Before investigation turned up Wright's Confederate connection, the ship went to sea, eluding Federal cruisers sent to intercept it. Southern agents had learned their lessons well. Bulloch refused to go anywhere near the ship and forbade the use of his name in connection with it. In the best cloak-and-dagger tradition, Lt. William Whittle (designated second officer on the new raider) was instructed by Bulloch to take a room at Wood's Hotel in High Holborn under the name of W. C. Brown, sit in the coffee room there with "a white pocket handkerchief rove through a button-hole of your coat, and a newspaper in your hand," and await the appearance of an agent who would identify himself with an intricate array of signs and countersigns, and then arrange to spirit the officer aboard ship "without attracting notice." Melodramatic though they were, these precautions worked.[24]

Meanwhile other agents had purchased a tender for the cruiser and made the usual arrangements for a rendezvous. Known as the *Laurel*, the tender was also expected to recoup its purchase price and make a profit as a blockade runner. Before long, Union agents were again asking probing questions about it. Dudley told Adams that officers from the *Georgia* planned to sail on the tender and that the little ship had signed an unusually large crew. The activity surrounding the vessel aroused his suspicion, though he admitted that he did not have sufficient evidence to warrant seizure. Undisturbed by Union attention, the vessel's owners advertised for passengers and freight to Cuba, but, as a result of carefully-planned secret maneuvers, the freight "consisted of stores and armaments for the cruisers" and the passengers were "the officers and a few choice men for her." The tender carried guns designed for the *Canton*, as well as other equipment originally intended for the refitting of the *Alabama*, including four 55-hundredweight, 8-inch, smoothbore guns, and two Whitworth 32-pounders, two 12-pounders, and a collection of small arms, ammunition, clothing, and coal. Because customs officials could uncover no violation of municipal law, they allowed the *Laurel* to leave Liverpool on October 8, 1864—the same day that the *Sea King* left London.

The two ships then headed for their rendezvous off the African coast.[25]

The component parts of this expedition meshed perfectly; both ships arrived without mishap at Funchal, Madeira, the tender on the sixteenth and the raider two days later. On October 19, in a frantic and backbreaking thirteen hours, the supplies and war equipment were transferred—dumped would perhaps be a more appropriate word—on to the decks of the newly-christened *Shenandoah,* which unfurled the Confederate flag; and an attempt was made to enlist a crew from the personnel of the supply ship. But something— perhaps the memory of the *Alabama's* fate and a growing awareness of augmented Union naval resources—dissuaded enlistment on so perilous a cruise. Needing about a hundred men for efficient operation, the captain could lure less than a quarter of that number by his promise of bounty and well- paid adventure. As time went on, however, the crew filled out with "volunteers" from captured vessels.[26]

When news of the commissioning of yet another raider reached Minister Adams, he predicted that it would be a danger to the remaining commerce of his country.

Orders to the commander of the new raider were simple and to the point: do the enemy's seaborne commerce "the greatest injury in the shortest time."[27] Because there were hardly any American ships to capture on the major trade routes of the world, a new hunting ground was assigned to the commanding officer, Lieutenant James I. Waddell. Using Matthew F. Maury's *Physical Geography of the Sea* to locate whaling grounds and fleet routes, the Confederate Navy De- partment outlined the raider's area of operations—the far reaches of the North Pacific and Arctic oceans. Using this plan, Waddell achieved spectacular results. In the icy lone- liness of the northern seas the *Shenandoah* continued prey- ing on helpless whaling vessels long after Lee surrendered. Its capture of a dozen such ships on June 28, 1865, was per- haps the final hostile act of the Confederacy. Not until August

C. S. S. SHENANDOAH

2 did the "Rip Van Winkle" of the seas meet the British *Baracuta* and learn of the war's end. Waddell immediately had all guns dismantled and ordered all offensive actions to cease.[28] The last Confederate cruiser had travelled nearly 40,000 miles, captured thirty-eight ships, destroyed thirty-two of them (worth approximately $1,172,223), and taken some 1,053 prisoners.[29] Then, determined not to fall into Yankee hands and despite danger and near-mutiny, Waddell, in true cavalier tradition, started the last leg of that lonely 17,000-mile voyage back to Liverpool.[30]

The arrival of the *Shenandoah* in Britain nearly seven months after the war had ended was, to say the least, greatly embarrassing to all concerned. The London *Times* impolitely condemned its arrival as an "unwelcome event." Customs officers requested instructions from the Foreign Office when the ship appeared on November 6, 1865.[31] What did His Lordship wish to do with the vessel and crew? Some days later the Admiralty reported that no British subjects had been found on board and that the crew therefore had been released. So meager were the possessions of the departing officers that Captain Paynter of the Royal Navy remarked that a lieutenant in Her Majesty's service would have considered himself poorly paid if so perilous a voyage had resulted in so little profit. The American consul then took possession of the ship.[32]

Thus ended a memorable cruise, grand in conception, grand in execution, and awesomely grand in the sad futility of its finale.[33] The story of the *Shenandoah,* so different from the disappointing tale of the *Rappahannock,* nonetheless has within it many of the leitmotifs of the larger, more sombre theme of the Confederacy's defeat.

TWELVE | BLOCKADE RUNNERS

*O*NE CHAPTER remains in the history of Confederate attempts to build naval craft in Great Britain. In 1864–65 an effort was made to construct and operate a fleet of government-owned blockade runners. Attempts to raise the blockade by using the coercive power of cotton had failed; Confederate cruisers had demonstrated their inability to decrease the strength of blockading squadrons; and the debacle of the Laird rams had illustrated some unfortunate consequences of openly challenging British neutrality. Bulloch and his associates reacted to these failures by turning to a program for the construction of government-owned vessels that might be expected to penetrate the Union blockade of Southern ports. This was a last-ditch endeavor to stave off military defeat; if it failed the government at Richmond, lacking supplies for the hard-pressed forces of General Lee, would fall. There had been some desultory activity in this direction throughout the war, but much of the equipment that reached Southern armies passed through the hands of 'middlemen at exorbitant cost to the treasury. The profits of individual enterprise and the success of a small-scale venture under the supervision of the ordnance department indicated the value of a publicly-owned transport system.[1]

* * * * *

Confederate efforts to circumvent the blockade fall conveniently into two phases, each with slightly differing goals and methods. The first phase, a stage which might be described as the triumph of private enterprise, began haphazardly shortly after the attack on Fort Sumter and, like Topsy, "just growed." With refined techniques and highly specialized equipment, private entrepreneurs carried in the bulk of Southern supplies. Such operations continued to the end of the war, for financial rewards remained high, sometimes reaching a phenomenal return of 700 percent. All sorts of people—women, Yankees, and especially Englishmen, many of whom were either naval officers "on leave" or deserters from Her Majesty's North American squadron—tried their hands at the trade.[2]

Soon after the Union announced its blockade, the lucrative business of evading it began, and as Northern security tightened around the Southern ports, both danger and profit multiplied. On April 19, 1861, President Lincoln declared his intent to set up a blockade of the insurrectionary states, and some days later he extended its limits so that, on paper at least, he had sealed off nearly four thousand miles of the American coast from Cape Henry, Virginia, to the border of Mexico, a distance greater than that from New York to Liverpool. At first this could be nothing more than a declaration of intent, a wish, a paper blockade; but in time Federal forces began to put bite in the decree, establishing squadrons off the major Southern ports and setting up roving patrols outside the territorial waters of the British islands in the Caribbean. As the hazards of the business increased, amateur runners ceased operation, and the bulk of the trade passed to professionals, with only courageous captains continuing to participate in it.[3]

Blockade running now required nerve, cunning, and special ships: fast, low, camouflaged vessels with plenty of cargo space. New ships incorporated the successful innovations of predecessors. The sleek, raked lines of these turtleback transports resembled in silhouette the destroyers of the first and

MODEL OF THE *COLONEL LAMB*
Confederate blockade runner built in Liverpool, England

second World Wars. Built for speed, they often sacrificed safety to get it. The noted naval historian James Russell Soley described the typical runner as a "long, low sidewheeler of from four to six hundred tons, with a slight frame, sharp and narrow, its length perhaps nine times its beam. It had feathering paddles, and one or two raking telescopic funnels, which might be lowered close to the deck. The hull rose only a few feet out of the water, and was painted a dull grey or lead color, so that it could hardly be seen by daylight at two hundred yards."[4] To decrease chances of attracting attention these ships used anthracite or "Cardiff coal" that burned with little of the black smoke so characteristic of nineteenth-century steamers. In the war's early months, on a moonless night, the runner stood a good chance of success, though in time the Union navy perfected counter-measures and caught many of the runners. But with the elements of surprise and speed on his side, the runner continued to have a slight edge. Certain professionals, "the impudent ones"— men such as Captains Carlin, Wyllie, Wilkinson, "notorious" Tom Lockwood, Pasha Hobart, John Newland Maffitt (the prince of runners), and, of course, the incomparable Rhett Butler—continued to outwit Federal squadrons with insolent ease, writing thereby one of the most romantic and perennially popular chapters in Civil War history.[5]

Many motives lured men to this wartime business: love of adventure, sympathy for the South, dislike for Yankees. Most came for money. They saw the ports of the South as "an Eldorado of wealth to the man who could go in and come out in safety."[6] The hinterland of the Confederacy seemed a cornucopia of white gold. Successful captains cleared £1,000 for a round trip from Nassau to Wilmington; chief engineers earned half as much; crew members received extraordinarily high wages; and pilots often could name their own price for a week or ten days of work.[7] In addition, there were opportunities for private speculation. Sailors might bring in cigars, liquor, perfume, corset stays; captains filled their cabins with cotton on return voyages. "When half crowns could be turned into sovereigns at a single venture, capitalists could afford to run almost any risk."[8] One ship reportedly earned some £85,000 for twenty days of work, and a profit of £30,000 on each leg of a journey was not uncommon.[9] One runner, the Clyde-built *Robert E. Lee,* under the command of John Wilkinson, ran to the South some twenty times in a ten-month period.[10] Another, the *A. D. Vance,* made over thirty trips, while Captain Carlin got past Federal squadrons about twenty-four times.[11] Profits remained high throughout the war, and the Charleston firm of Fraser-Trenholm and Company made tremendous profits, some say as much as four million pounds! Even in late 1864 the blockade was still porous enough to allow an average of two out of three ships to elude its vigilance.

How much danger was there? It is difficult to say. Of course, it required some courage to take a frail, unarmed craft through the Federal gauntlet, just as it took caution, nerve, and resourcefulness to escape detection. On the other hand, the danger, especially when compared to the carnage at Shiloh or in the Wilderness campaign, must have been slight. If ships of the blockading squadrons were widely dispersed, it was neither difficult nor dangerous to slip through gaps in the line; if closely bunched, the danger of hitting each other with shell fire made the Federal gunners overcautious and decreased the possibility of hitting a small, fast-moving target. Captain Wilkinson of the Confederate navy, a man of experience in the trade, regarded the open sea as more dangerous than the most vigilant blockader. To the professionals, men who knew their business and did not take chances, exploding boilers, leaking ships, rough weather, hidden rocks, and shallow reefs presented more of a threat than Federal gunners. Many runners were captured; some estimate the number as high as 1,500, though it is well to remember that only about 300 of these were steamers, some of them ill-equipped for the business. For a fast, well-equipped, steam-driven vessel, with an alert crew and smoothly functioning machinery, operating according to the rules worked out by experience and favored by fog, mist, rain, and luck, the risk could not have been great; perhaps one vessel in six was captured. And once in a while an indignant British citizen would languish in a Northern prison or a captured pilot might enjoy Fort Warren's vaunted hospitality. It was not, all in all, a bad life and sometimes it was a pleasantly exciting and most rewarding one.[12]

* * * * *

Throughout the war there were parallel efforts at blockade running under official or quasi-official sponsorship. In the first years of the war these attempts at a government-directed transport system comprised uncoordinated, *ad hoc* trips from Britain to the South, but gradually, as the benefits became evident, they evolved into a full-scale program of blockade running under the auspices of the Confederate Navy Department.

One of the earliest officially sponsored blockade runners was the *Bermuda*. In the summer of 1861 the Confederacy's fiscal agents in Liverpool, Fraser-Trenholm, decided to test the effectiveness of the blockade by sending this ship to a Southern port with a cargo of war material. For this enterprise Bulloch acted as technical adviser, having no official connection with the voyage. Under command of Captain Eugene Tessier, the *Bermuda* reached the South in mid-September. It was then loaded with cotton and returned to England. According to her owner Edwin Haigh, at no time during the entire voyage did Federal ships interfere with the passage; they did not warn her away from the American coast, nor molest her in any way. The vessel entered a Southern port without being able to ascertain whether the blockade was in effect. Haigh and other interested shippers therefore decided that the North had only a "paper" blockade, one not binding under international law.[13]

The *Bermuda*'s second trip to the new world—in 1862—
came to grief. Haigh had planned to duplicate his feat of
the previous year, but news of increased Northern vigilance
apparently prompted second thoughts, and the owner re-
routed his vessel. On this second voyage it would not enter
any blockaded port. Rather, it would touch only at some
Caribbean islands, pick up cargo, and return home. The
nicely planned schedule was disrupted on April 27, 1862,
when a Union cruiser stopped the *Bermuda* some four hundred miles off the American coast, and took it to Philadelphia,
where after much delay it was tried for running the blockade. That trial furnished a definition of Northern views
regarding the responsibilities of neutrals to the blockade.

The able defense attorney for the *Bermuda*, George Whar-
ton, pointed out the ambiguity in the charge and assailed the
loose interpretation of international law on which it was
based. Here, he argued, was the case of a British ship, owned
and loaded by British merchants, traveling to a British
colony, which "while navigating in the direct line from
Bermuda to Nassau, and at the distance of about 415 miles
from that portion of the American coast the blockade of
which she is alleged to have violated, while sailing among
these British islands in a direct line toward her place of destination, . . . [was] overhauled by a cruiser of the United
States Government, captured, and brought here for trial
and consequent condemnation."[14] The prosecutor viewed
the facts differently. The cargo, he charged, was either enemy-
owned or intended for enemy use. Even if the ship had stopped
at a neutral port, she was liable to capture if the owner's
intent was to send her to a Southern port. According to the
prosecutor's reasoning, a ship en route from England to the
South could not evade capture merely by having her captain
signify an intent to stop at a neutral port during the voyage.
If Nassau was a way station, the doctrine of continuous
voyage, that convenient and pliable rule (decked with whatever embellishments would meet current exigencies) applied,

and the vessel became fair game the moment it left British jurisdiction, that is, at any point beyond the three-mile territorial limits of the Queen's dominions, including the British Isles.[15] The United States was arguing in effect that it had the right to determine the ultimate destination of a cargo, and if in the view of an America prize court that cargo was destined for the South, it might be "confiscable." The argument boiled down to this: even though the final destination of a ship might be a bona-fide neutral port, the possibility that its cargo might be transshipped to the South would justify capture of the ship and condemnation of the cargo.[16]

Because it hinged upon an evaluation of the owner's intention of entering a blockaded port, the Union case appeared weak. Intent, as every lawyer knows, is difficult to pin down. Liverpool's commercial community believed that the ship had sailed for neutral ports because its cargo had been consigned to British islands in the Caribbean, and because a return cargo had been consigned to Britain.[17] Britons argued that the American officer had acted upon a vague and dangerous interpretation of international law—as indeed he had—by capturing a neutral vessel far from the blockaded coast of America. Still, the United States government had reason for not releasing the ship. Its former voyage through the blockade had tainted it—made it guilty by reputation, condemned by public opinion, in the North. It simply would not do to allow it to go free "pour encourager les autres." So some seven months after the trial began, on March 5, 1863, the United States Prize Court ruled the ship lawful prize, and that same day confiscated the *Bermuda,* despite appeal proceedings instituted by the defendant.

The decision made a mockery of the old rule that "free ships make free goods," long one of the major premises of the American interpretation of neutral rights. Bulloch complained, with some justice, that the North was encroaching upon neutrals not by legal principles or justice but by a policy of self-interest, in a word, by expediency. But as one British runner philosophically decided, "If the Americans were stretching the theory of blockade, it was only because we were extending its practice."[18]

Soon after the *Bermuda*'s first voyage, the Confederates in Liverpool under Bulloch's capable direction organized and undertook another transatlantic trip to the South. At first the chief agent was apprehensive about his authority to allocate funds to such a venture, but in the autumn of 1861, after obtaining the approval of the Confederate envoys, he bought a small steamer, the *Fingal,* for a return trip to Richmond. To lessen the suspicions of Northern spies, who were already in operation, he arranged to board the ship several miles down the coast from Liverpool. En route to this rendezvous with Bulloch, the *Fingal* had a freakish accident; it rammed and sank a coal carrier. Bulloch had no wish to become involved in a lengthy investigation of the accident, so he left instructions for Fraser-Trenholm to make full restitution and ordered his ship away.[19] After some days at sea it was discovered that the ship had an inadequate supply of water and no condensing apparatus; it was necessary to make an emergency stop at the Azores, during which Bulloch discovered, at Terceira Island, the perfect place for outfitting his cruisers after their departure from British jurisdiction. That discovery, as we have seen, had an important effect on subsequent Confederate naval activity.

After a slow voyage, the *Fingal* reached Bermuda, picked up a pilot, and headed for the American coast. To this point the crew had not been informed of the ship's mission. At a deck conference, Bulloch took them into his confidence, explained the purpose and danger of the enterprise, and received enthusiastic assent. Chief Engineer McNair, a reliable and silent Scot, had foreseen the course of events, set aside a supply of smokeless coal, and cleaned the flues and fireboxes so that the boilers would be at peak efficiency for the final spurt home.

The last night out, soon after midnight, "as nice a fog as any reasonable blockade runner could have wanted" enveloped the ship, and under its protection the *Fingal* edged toward land, so as to be inshore of patrol boats. With engines silent, nerves taut, the crew waited for daybreak. Suddenly an errie wail shattered the silence, and a sound like an "unearthly steam whistle" threatened to disclose their presence to every Federal vessel for miles around. Then it came again. The offending chanticleer, that bird of morning, did not greet another sun, for it met quick and violent death at the hands of a frightened sailor. The ship was again favored with a profound stillness.

At daybreak all was in readiness for the dash into the harbor, but mists obscured the channel markers, without which even skilled pilots might run aground or be blown up by an explosive cargo in the tricky, protected entrance at Wassaw Sound. The pilot, therefore, suggested running to the more navigable entrance at Savannah, some seventeen miles up the coast. The engineer's preparations now proved their worth as the ship pushed northward at a steady eleven knots. Even the elements helped. The fog moved out to sea, stopping in time to form a curtain between any lurking patrol boats and the shore. With such conditions, and with skill and luck, the *Fingal* arrived safely at its destination on November 12, 1861, after a thrilling transoceanic voyage, much of it through blockaded waters. She carried a cargo including over 14,000 Enfield rifles, 400 barrels of gun powder, and substantial quantities of war equipment, perhaps the largest shipment of exclusively military and naval supplies brought into the Confederacy during the war—and brought in without the middleman's expensive profit.[20]

Bulloch returned to England, as noted, but the press of other work prevented exploitation of the procedures introduced by this successful innovation. It was many, many months before that technique again was put to the test. It was successful once more. In the autumn of 1863, about the time Her Majesty's government was taking custody of the Laird rams, Bulloch had another problem of supply requiring an imaginative solution. The Navy Department had ordered a special set of marine engines for a vessel under construction in the South, and from fear of having some of the intricate parts go astray Bulloch was hesitant to trust delivery to regular commercial carriers. To solve the problem he bought another steamer for delivering them directly to the South under supervision of a naval officer. For the task he needed a particular ship, larger, and more seaworthy than a conventional runner, yet fast enough to outrace Union guard ships if necessary. Once again acquaintance with British maritime resources paid a handsome dividend. He and the officer selected to make the voyage, Lt. Robert Carter, found a suitable vessel in Glasgow, and, having assured themselves that it fitted Southern requirements, bought it. It was tested "in every possible way in which it occurred to us that she might be tried in an attempt to run the blockade," and as Bulloch said, this preliminary care was amply repaid by subsequent performance.[21] Under a British flag, with Carter unofficially in charge, the *Coquette* cleared for the Caribbean Islands in October, 1863, and reached them safely. Engine failure foiled a first attempt to run past blockaders, but the second attempt succeeded. In the months that followed this vessel shuttled between the South and the British islands, until defective engines slowed its speed, exposing it to capture. The ship was sold at a good price. More important, savings on inbound freight and profit from the cotton which it carried out paid for the ship many times. Purchase of a ship merely to transport a pair of marine engines across the Atlantic seemed at first extravagant, a violation of prudent business practices, but the times did not call for conventional solutions. Bulloch's willingness to undertake the unorthodox served the South well on this occasion, as on many others.[22]

* * * * *

Profit on the *Coquette* investment, the success of similar
efforts in officially-controlled blockade running by the ordnance department, frequent entreaties by overseas naval
agents, and the loss of the Laird rams—all these eventually
combined to convince Confederate officials at Richmond that
a program of government-owned-and-operated transport
might be a wise and profitable innovation.[23] Bulloch and
Mallory had been advocating such a plan for many months,
pointing out its advantages—economic as well as military—
and emphasizing that British officials probably would not
molest small, unarmed steamers, and that contraband sent to
the Caribbean islands on bona-fide neutral ships might then
be transferred to government vessels captained by naval officers for the short, dangerous runs in and out of the blockaded
ports.[24] It was, however, a long time before these arguments
took effect. Not until early 1864 did the Confederate government pass laws which attempted to limit the importation of
luxury goods and to reserve part of the cargo space of each
runner for government use. However necessary for the common good, the laws were difficult to enforce, and they gave rise
to great resentment and considerable smuggling.

Late in the war, when the naval program seemed finished,
the Confederacy turned to a fleet of small, fast blockade-run-
ners. By that time, blockade-running on a transatlantic scale
(in the style of the *Fingal*) was impractical because ships
suitable for the long ocean voyage did not lend themselves to
the last-minute, full-pressure dash into port. By 1864 Federal
squadrons had refined their measures to the point where the
runners needed every possible advantage. Several seizures and
condemnations had convinced Mallory that the South required very special ships. The Bulloch-Mallory-McRae plan
offered some chance of getting supplies to Southern armies.
Also, such an arrangement as Bulloch proposed presented
little threat to the Queen's neutrality because it provided few

opportunities for countermeasures. Crown legal advisers believed that a neutral nation had no lawful authority to prevent merchant vessels from sailing to blockaded ports.[25] Agents carefully refrained from attempts to arm the vessels, though that idea was talked about.[26] Even though the foreign secretary had threatened to seize any ship with a proven Confederate connection, British registry easily averted that danger. "With due respect to the pain of Her Majesty's displeasure," one veteran runner later explained, "we all knew that to run a foreign blockade could never be an offence against the laws of the realm, nor were we pursuaded that . . . attempts to enter the proclaimed ports could ever constitute a breach of neutrality."[27]

If, as has been suggested, President Davis sometimes saw himself as a commander-in-chief on horseback, he certainly never envisaged himself as a commander on the quarterdeck. He was largely ignorant of the importance of seapower and hence tended to underrate the precarious nature of the new nation's overseas supply line. As is well known, he at first based his foreign policy on the fallacious assumption of the power of cotton to precipitate foreign intervention. Having made that miscalculation, Davis compounded it by a series of bad decisions the cumulative effect of which was to hasten disaster for the South.[28] Anxious for European recognition, he pursued the wrong tactics to achieve it. As one student of the South's foreign policy has well said: "The Confederates realized too late that the primary objective of their foreign policy should . . . have been to get the implements necessary for victory rather than recognition which would have followed it."[29]

A few of the president's advisers had recognized the crucial importance of government control of transportation. As early as 1862 a group of naval officers had suggested that the Navy Department be given responsibility for such a program. To finance that plan would have required that large amounts of cotton be exported to the credit of overseas agents. But the

Confederate Congress, with little sense of urgency, delayed authorization of treasury agents to buy up cotton for export to Europe on government account. When James Spence's ideological deviance from the South's party line on slavery became embarrassing,[30] overall supervision of Confederate financial and purchasing operations in Europe became the responsibility of Colin McRae. Originally sent to Europe as overseer for the disbursement of funds from the Erlanger loan, McRae, in time, assumed the functions of a credit czar. A major part of his work was to coordinate the plans for purchase of the fast, light-draft steamers needed to get the cotton to British islands in the Caribbean for trans-shipment to Europe. Unfortunately, it was well into 1864 before McRae and his co-workers could set seriously to work, and not until the summer of that year was the decision made to implement a full-scale program of government runners.[31]

Again, a good plan was delayed by financial uncertainty. As one student of Confederate purchasing operations has nicely put it, the "lack of credit rather than the dangers of the blockade" finally cut the South's supply line.[32] Bulloch and McRae required extensive credit at a time when British contractors had become wary of Southern investments and skeptical of Confederate ability to redeem pledges with cotton run through the blockade. Ship builders expressed interest in the plan but demanded security. Contracts for the ships had to be written in such a way that a part (usually fifty percent) of the cotton carried on these ships had to be allocated to the builders, the arrangement to continue until the ship was paid for. At a time when the South needed to export every available pound of cotton to finance the war, Davis had to share the freighting capacity of his government transports with private investors.[33]

Months went by before McRae could report progress, and on June 2, 1864, he told Bulloch that the above terms were the best available. For his part, Bulloch had found several ships, but, because they were in advanced stages of construction, they could not be modified for the South's particular purposes. He took them, hoping that future contracts might permit the necessary refinements. These four ships were much alike: length 230 feet, beam 26 feet, horsepower about 180, freight capacity nearly 800 bales. To expedite the program, Bulloch and McRae divided responsibility, the latter assuming financial burdens, the former taking up technical ones. They planned a full flotilla of ten runners of approximately the same specifications, with the last six incorporating the requirements of the trade. Two of the ships were to be designed to carry 350 bales on five feet of water or 700 bales on a draft of six feet (these for use in the shallow waters of Texas and Florida). Bulloch hoped that these ships would reduce Richmond's dependence upon expensive speculation in shipbuilding ventures.[34]

Though McRae's contracts had stipulated that British officers must command the ships until they were paid for, Bulloch wanted Southern officers in command as soon as possible, so that the government could reap the full benefit of the plan. He recognized that it would be advantageous for the ships to retain their neutral registry.[35]

The South had high hopes for this fleet of runners. Bulloch thought that they might constitute an Atlantic bridge by which the Confederacy could sustain itself. Early in the war he had advocated government control of cotton export to Europe for financing the overseas construction program, but Richmond officials did not then recognize the wisdom of the plan. When President Davis finally got around to putting this scheme (which Samuel Thompson has called "one of the most intelligent bits of strategy ever formulated by the Confederacy") into operation, money was scarce, the blockaders more efficient, and British contractors more watchful. "The whole that could be accomplished," Bulloch sadly concluded, "was not sufficient to turn the scale or to greatly delay the final result of the war."[36]

THIRTEEN | CONCLUSION

*W*HAT CONCLUSIONS, then, may one draw from a study of the response of Her Majesty's government towards Southern efforts to build naval craft in British shipyards? What consequences followed from the mid-nineteenth century confrontation of Crown and Confederacy?

At the outset we may note that strong hands guided the South's naval affairs. Talented and resourceful, completely dedicated to their cause, Mallory and Bulloch imaginatively worked to devise and nearly carry out a bold strategy which would compensate for naval inferiority and circumvent industrial deficiencies. Forward-looking and flexible, they approached their respective tasks with a flair for improvisation and a willingness to gamble. It would, in fact, be difficult to imagine more ingenious and faithful public servants.

The history of Southern naval procurement, largely and rightly the monument of James Dunwoody Bulloch, still compels admiration: it remains an impressive achievement, one too long neglected by historians. Bulloch's contribution to the Confederate cause deserves greater recognition than the present unkempt tombstone which marks his burial place in Liverpool's Toxeth cemetery. His service to the South fully justifies ranking him, as one recent commentator has done, with the greatest of Southern heroes.

But how good was the Southern plan? Given the conditions

of the early 1860s, few students of the Civil War dispute that the South did surprisingly well; most would agree with Allan Nevins that the "most remarkable fact" about the war was "that it lasted so long before the end came." Yet a natural sympathy for the underdog, the always fascinating story of a struggle against impossible odds, ought not to prevent an objective appraisal of the South's naval strategy. While perhaps only the trained sea strategist and engineer can speak with authority on that facet of the war, a historian may point to certain shortcomings in the Confederate view of naval war.

The spectacular cruises of the *Alabama, Florida,* and *Shenandoah* epitomize one major defect of naval operations. Cruisers, however effective (and by all accounts the Confederate cruisers were extraordinarily effective), could neither alter the course of the war nor affect its outcome. Even if these corsairs had driven Union shipping completely from the seas (as they very nearly did) and had lured many more blockaders away from their stations, would the result have differed? Probably not, for foreign shippers stood ready and eager to take up the slack in American trade. And in view of the continued importance of international good will, to what extent could the South have risked interference with neutral trade? At best, then, the cruisers could inflict only nuisance damage on Northern shipping and embarrassment on the Union navy, while their ability to cause war weariness in the North remains problematical. The blockade continued to be the important factor, and Southern hopes that the raiders might separate Union vessels from the blockading squadrons proved largely illusory. For in spite of the brilliant diversionary tactics of the British-built cruisers, Lincoln was able to maintain and strengthen his stranglehold on the South because the North possessed the financial and industrial resources to compensate for whatever losses the cruisers inflicted.

The second phase of Mallory's strategy, his plan to use vessels equipped with rams, seemed to promise better results. But here, too, a word of caution seems in order. There is some evidence (admittedly hypothetical in nature) that the rams might not have performed up to expectations, and it is no longer permissible to accept a century of historiography which has, a priori, assumed the blockade-breaking power of the rams. Technical difficulties aside, the South's reliance on this weapon was unwise, primarily because the North could produce ironclads more quickly and in greater numbers than Mallory could procure them in Europe. Granting that the rams might have had some initial success and opened a port or two, how long would it have been before Union ironclads began to bottle up the South's small fleet of blockade-breakers? The commander of the *Stonewall* (the only Southern ram to get to sea) recognized his danger as he sought to escape from Federal warships: "If this vessel is thus to be pursued in every port into which she may find it necessary to enter, you see at once what her condition must inevitably become. She cannot run to sea and there remain, as could the *Alabama* and *Florida,* and this the enemy must be as well aware of as we are."[1] Bottled-up rams could break no blockade. Hence the second part of the naval plan, like the first, failed to provide adequate remedies for the larger problems facing Davis: naval strategy, however brilliant, could not by itself save the South. That strategy, since it was just one means to a greater end, could succeed only to the extent that it contributed to popular Northern dissatisfaction with the war or to Southern military invulnerability or to British convictions about the wisdom and justice and rightness of intervention.

Aside from strategic shortcomings, the Confederacy, as we see now after a century of study, blundered in other ways as well. Having little industry, the South had to seek ships abroad, bringing on the problem of international credit. Richmond authorities did not have and could not easily get export capital, certainly not in the amounts needed for a full-scale, multi-million-dollar program—unless they were willing to capitalize their chief economic asset, cotton; and this, for a variety of reasons, they declined to do. Clement Eaton has

THE *DANMARK*

(See also illustrations on pp. 139 and 140)

spoken of the Maginot mentality of the South, of the "illusion that cotton was king," and has noted that the "fundamental assumption of Confederate diplomacy—the theory of the invincibility of King Cotton—proved to be a fallacy."[2] Frank L. Owsley has analyzed in detail the defects of cotton diplomacy; here we need only extend that analysis to the naval effort. As noted, poor fiscal policy continually hampered the work of Mallory's men. To worsen a bad situation, funds were not always allocated properly because too many ágents of too many departments competed with each other, in effect working at cross purposes. The South waited until late 1863 to put its overseas financial affairs in order and to appoint a capable czar of fiscal operations, but by then it was too late.

An inadequate and inefficient bureaucratic organization hampered the embryonic nation. Poor communication, overlapping responsibility, well-meaning but inept personnel, kinks in the chain of command—all these plagued naval procurement. A new state may naturally expect some difficulty in arranging its administrative machinery, but the South took an undue amount of time to coordinate its foreign construction program; one might almost say that such operations never received the attention they deserved. Much of Bulloch's trouble stemmed from lack of centralized control, whether at home or abroad. (The contretemps over the command of the *Florida* is apropos here, as is the imprecise delegation of responsibility to the navy and treasury departments for the payment of the costs of building warships—to say nothing of the confusion, ineptness, and folly of the Erlanger loan deal.)

Another serious problem that handicapped overseas naval agents was the "landmindedness" of high-ranking Confederate officials, especially Jefferson Davis. "One of the ironies of Southern history," in the view of Professor Eaton, "was the contrast between the boast that the slave-based society of the old South produced superior statesmen and the reality of feeble or mediocre conduct of civil administrátion of the Confederacy."[3] As David M. Potter has pointed out in his critique of the Confederate president, Davis made many mistakes. None was more fraught with danger than failure to support his naval assistants. Davis apparently did not understand—and made little effort to understand—the significance of seapower for the South. The fatal mistake of the Confederacy, according to one postwar account, was neglect of the navy.[4]

If the Confederacy had had a coordinated program under Bulloch's personal control, adequate financial resources, and the full support of President Davis, would the outcome have differed? Here one must consider the British response to Southern activity. That response, as seen, was a complex mix of legal uncertainty, economic self-interest, and political expediency, heavily laced with indifference and inefficiency. Under changed conditions a more subtle confrontation between Southern shipbuilding and British neutrality might have yielded other results, though that too remains doubtful, given the attitude of Her Majesty's ministers—neither pro-North nor pro-South. Britain's response to the Civil War may perhaps best be described as one of indifferent neutrality. At the peak of intervention sentiment in the autumn of 1862 the *Times* cautioned that a war with the North, even with European backing, would be a blunder of the first magnitude. "In a good cause, and as a necessity forced upon us in defence of our honour, or of our rightful interests," the "Thunderer" affirmed, "we are as ready to fight as we ever were; but we do not see our duty or our interest in going blindfold[ed] into such an adventure as this."[5] Britain preferred to stand aloof, to let the raging parties settle their differences in their own way. Russell, described with some exaggeration and much inaccuracy as a "daring pilot in neutrality," was used by *Punch* to express a common sentiment: the nation wished to remain "sternly neutral."[6] The moderate *Illustrated London News* expressed similar sentiments with clarity and precision. The primary objective of British policy was "neutrality pure and simple," that paper told its readers in November, 1863:

"This is no question of sympathy or sentiment; it is no question of the rights or wrongs of the belligerent parties; but it is one of solemn national duty on the part of this country."[7]

The middle position is never popular in times of stress, and it should not be too surprising that during the war representatives of both the Union and Confederacy frequently railed against the same British injustice and partiality toward the enemy.

But if Her Majesty's government was indifferent, it did not fail to seek its own advantage. Though the prime minister had little real interest in American affairs, his response to them was nonetheless based on a realistic appraisal of immediate and long-term objectives. Pam followed a line—not always, to be sure, a straight line, but one he thought reasonably well calculated to advance the welfare of the Queen's subjects. In the long run, national self-interest certainly was a better guide for British action during the war than the confused, difficult-to-interpret, and inadequate body of misunderstanding that then passed for international law. Early in the war, the *Florida* trial demonstrated the impossibility of keeping Confederate construction within the antiquated frame of the Foreign Enlistment Act, and the *Alexandra* decision in June, 1863, reinforced that same point, as did any number of opinions from the legal advisers of the Crown. But given the fragile political alignments of the period, the general disposition to drift—and in the absence of any alternative that looked appealing to the incumbent ministry—it proved impractical or impossible or inexpedient to modify the law, especially in view of Northern pressure for such a move. (Palmerston, it must be remembered, had a deep-seated and long-standing horror of any seeming subservience to foreign influence.) When, however, it became reasonably clear what the military verdict in America would be, Her Majesty's government went behind and beyond the law to halt Confederate construction. Because she could not dispute the logic of history, Britain did what was necessary rather than what was legal.

From 1861 to 1865, Great Britain had no good definition of neutrality: she had instead a series of neutralities—each one flexible, expedient, and designed for the moment. All were stopgap measures subject to misunderstanding, pregnant with mischief. Historians have frequently overlooked this key factor in Anglo-American Civil War diplomacy. To find unity in the Palmerstonian response to Southern shipbuilding is impossible; to generalize about the British "attitude" to the war is unwise because the Queen's ministers decided each detention, every seizure, on an *ad hoc* basis. No yardstick existed by which officials could measure violations; no good precedents set limits to lawful commercial activity; no judicial decisions defined the rules of the war game. Britain sometimes changed the rules during the game—but they needed revision when the old ones no longer applied. Techniques applicable to wooden sailing ships proved most inadequate in the new era of steam and iron. The task of Her Majesty's law officers was neither enviable nor easy; it was not pleasant for them to balance principle against expediency, or to stretch the law to fit situations for which it was not designed. These men worked under trying circumstances to protect private property, to foster commercial enterprise, and to uphold cherished constitutional guarantees, while at the same time they attempted to hold the government to compliance with the responsibilities of strict, impartial neutrality.

Throughout the war, with but one notable exception—the mediation maneuver of 1862—the likelihood of British intervention in American affairs was slight, and probably would have remained so regardless of Davis' naval and diplomatic strategy. The move toward mediation in the fall of 1862 came perilously close to success. It was frustrated mainly by Lee's failure at Antietam, which gave rise to suspicion, especially in the prime minister's mind, that the time was not yet, that the military verdict was not in. Before Gladstone spoke at Newcastle, Palmerston, who had once been described as "half hornet and half butterfly," demonstrated the aptness of that description by refusing "to take up arms" as a solution for the American problem.[8] Moreover, a growing awareness that Lincoln's government would almost certainly reject any mediation or armistice proposal aimed at Southern independence helped kill enthusiasm for Russell's proposal. Northern refusal meant, of course, a real possibility of British military involvement in the war, and for that, even the most ardent advocates of mediation recognized, there was little support. As modifications of the plan came under discussion, it became clear that Britain's true interests required a prudent approach to transatlantic affairs. Conditions in Europe concerned Victoria's ministers far more than the epic clash of the blue and the gray. Palmerston, who was convinced of Napoleonic duplicity and whose attitude toward the emperor was shared by the Queen and a good many of her countrymen, preferred not to turn his back on the Tuileries. Nonintervention seemed the proper policy for maintaining peace and providing prosperity. However bad conditions in the cotton districts might become, many people recognized, as the *Times* stated on November 13, 1862, "that it would be cheaper to keep all Lancashire on turtle and venison than to plunge into a desperate war with the Northern States of America."[9]

Fortunately for the North, and perhaps for the world, the move toward mediation did not touch any sensitive nerve in the British body politic; it could therefore be debated objectively and unemotionally within the government. So viewed, intervention promised no advantage at great risk. Palmerston, who, as Cobden once said, liked to drive his chariot close to the brink of a precipice, again showed that his grasp of the realities of foreign policy was as firm and clear-sighted as ever it had been. For the last time in his life, the man whom Talleyrand regarded as perhaps his cleverest adversary demonstrated some of the finesse that had made him famous. Understanding the ways of international power politics much better than they were understood in Richmond, he had few illusions, glittering or otherwise, about the South.

Once he had made up his mind that interference in America could be neither decisive nor effective without military support, he lost interest in it, and only a resounding Southern military victory could have revived that interest. Great Britain, Lord Palmerston once remarked in a rhetorical way, had neither eternal friendships nor eternal enmities. She had only eternal interests. And those interests — as he interpreted them — surely did not dictate involvement in the American Civil War.

Desire for recognition blinded Southern leaders to the self-interest of European statesmen. "It was tragically naive," one student of the war has written, "to think that the maritime powers would lightly risk conferring international respectability on a rebellion whose lasting success remained yet to be demonstrated."[10] The South realized too late that the rhetoric of rebellion fell on deaf ears. It refused to acknowledge that it would be impossible by logic or speeches or propaganda to persuade British statesmen to pull Confederate chestnuts out of the fire. Neither brag nor bluff, nor even the coercion of cotton, could move Palmerston. Only the fortune of arms could do that. Britain did not intervene because she could never quite forget the connection between slavery and the South, because she was never fully convinced that the South could maintain itself, because she saw no real advantage in doing so, and because Palmerston preferred peace to war.[11] At the one time he might have been moved to a more aggressive response to the war, success did not crown Confederate arms. The stalemate at Antietam proved a disaster for the South, for Lee's failure in Maryland deprived Jefferson Davis of a prime ingredient—some say *the* essential ingredient—in victory, British intervention.

ABBREVIATIONS

*Abbreviations most commonly used in the Bibliographical Essay
and Notes are listed below:*

BM	British Museum
CFA, Diary	Charles Francis Adams, Diary (widely available on microfilm)
C & E Library	Customs and Excise Library
DU	Dudley Papers, Huntington Library, San Marino, California
FO	Foreign Office
FR (date)	U.S., State Department, comp., *Papers Relating to the Foreign Affairs of the United States, 1861–68* (Washington, 1862–69)
HMC	Historical Manuscripts Commission
HO	Home Office
LC	Library of Congress
LO	Law Office
NA	National Archives
ORN	U.S., Navy Department, comp., *Official Records of the Union and Confederate Navies in the War of the Rebellion,* 3 vols. and index (Washington, 1894–1927)
PRO	Public Record Office
RA	Royal Archives
WC	Windsor Castle

Bibliographical Essay

Few phases of American history have attracted the attention lavished on the Civil War. There seems to be no end to the literature on that subject. Hence, the problem of selection assumes importance: the student must necessarily limit himself to the more important manuscript materials and secondary works. To aid him, the profession is rapidly filling the gaps which exist in bibliographical aids.

BIBLIOGRAPHICAL AIDS

The student may wish to start work by consulting Roy. B. Basler *et al., A Guide to the Study of the United States of America* (Washington, 1960). In this convenient compilation the editors have brought together a reference to "standard" works in diplomatic history and foreign relations, in which the annotations are models of compression. There are in addition helpful sections on Civil War history in Oscar Handlin *et al., Harvard Guide to American History* (Cambridge, Mass., 1954). Still useful is Samuel Flagg Bemis and Grace Gardiner Griffin, eds., *Guide to the Diplomatic History of the United States, 1775–1921* (Washington, 1935), which may be supplemented by the American Historical Association's *Writings on American History* and the *Index to the Writings on American History* (Washington, 1956). There are short but useful lists of manuscript material in Harry J. Carman and Arthur W. Thompson, eds., *A Guide to the Principal Sources for American Civilization, 1800–1900, in the City of New York* (New York, 1960). Philip M. Hamer, *Guide to the Records in the National Archives* (Washington, 1948),

provides exactly what its title promises. Another valuable research tool for the student of Confederate affairs is Henry P.
Beers, ed., *Guide to the Archives of the Government of the Confederate States of America* (Washington, DC, 1968). This volume,
sponsored by the National Archives and Records Service, has
a good chapter on the naval records of the South. Filling a long-
felt need is Philip M. Hamer, ed., *A Guide to Archives and
Manuscripts in the United States* (New Haven, Conn., 1961).
A handy introduction to international manuscript sources is
Lynn M. Case and Daniel H. Thomas, eds., *Guide to the Diplomatic Archives of Western Europe* (Philadelphia, 1959). The
reader may wish to consult the useful Grace Gardiner Griffin,
*A Guide to Manuscripts Relating to American History in British
Depositories Reproduced for the Division of Manuscripts of the
Library of Congress* (Washington, 1946). The Public Record
Office will, for a small fee, provide photographic reproductions
of the index of their FO 5 file, Anglo-American correspondence,
part of which deals with the Civil War period. Recent publications on the war must be searched out in the indexes of such
periodicals as the *American Historical Review,* the *Mississippi
Valley Historical Review* (now the *Journal of American History*),
the *Journal of Southern History,* and *Civil War History;* the
editors of *Civil War History* periodically publish lists of doctoral
theses in progress. A valuable index to doctoral dissertations completed in United States and Canadian universities is Warren F.
Kuehl, *Dissertations in History* (Lexington, Kentucky, 1965).
Arnold H. Trotier and Marion Harman, eds., *Doctoral Dissertations Accepted by American Universities* (New York, 1964),
is another useful index. The series known as *Dissertation Ab-
stracts* (various titles and sponsors) provides a convenient check-
list of current research in American universities. Many of the
major American and foreign universities publish—with varying
frequency—lists of theses and dissertations accepted. The Institute of Historical Research, University of London, publishes
an annual list of *Historical Research for University Degrees in
the United Kingdom.* (List No. 30, May, 1969, is in two parts:
Part I, Theses Completed 1968, Part II, Theses in Progress 1969.)
British graduate students are turning out a number of very fine
studies of the American Civil War.

GENERAL WORKS

For a study of Anglo-American diplomacy during the Civil War one should start with the near-classic account of Ephraim Douglass Adams, *Great Britain and the American Civil War*, 2 vols. (New York and London, 1925). This well-documented work has a British orientation, being as its author stated, "primarily a study in British history." Though one may question some of the author's conclusions, point out a number of minor mistakes, and disagree with its emphasis, the work nonetheless retains high rank in its genre. The other major work on the subject of Civil War diplomacy is Frank Lawrence Owsley, *King Cotton Diplomacy: Foreign Relations of the Confederate States of America*, 2nd rev. ed. (Chicago, 1959). Despite its obvious Southern bias, this work continues to be useful, though few will accept its conclusions without reservations. (For example, one recent study of the economic impact of the war in one British city has concluded that Owsley's "picture of industrial England as 'politically apathetic, sodden, ignorant and docile' is mere caricature." D. G. Wright, "Bradford and the American Civil War," *Journal of British Studies*, VIII [May, 1969], 69–85, quote on p. 84.) Both of these works slight naval affairs, and there is no satisfactory treatment of Confederate procurement. The best source for that story remains James D. Bulloch, *The Secret Service of the Confederate States in Europe or How the Confederate Cruisers Were Equipped*, 2 vols. (New York, 1883; new edition, 1959). (The new edition was done photographically, so the pagination is the same as in the original.) This first-hand account of Southern shipbuilding in England and France is well-told, lively, judicious, and accurate—that is, it stands up well when tested against other sources; it is the major and indispensable work for any evaluation of Confederate naval affairs. Bulloch makes a fine witness. For a distinguished history of all phases of Southern life in the war years consult E. Merton Coulter, *The Confederate States of America* (vol. VII of *A History of the South*, edited by Wendell H. Stephenson and E. Merton Coulter [Baton Rouge, La., 1950]). Covering much the

same ground in much less detail is the more sprightly Clement
Eaton, *A History of the Southern Confederacy* (New York, 1954;
paperback edition, New York, 1961). To see the war in different
perspective one may view it from the eyes of an objective Englishman in Alan Barker, *The Civil War in America* (London,
1961; paperback edition, New York, 1961). Jefferson Davis, *The
Rise and Fall of the Confederate Government* (2 vols., New
York, 1881; paperback edition, New York, 1961), has written
the Southern apologia, setting forth the right of secession and
providing varied insights into the virtues and defects of the
Confederacy.

A highly regarded account of Southern foreign policy is James
M. Callahan, *Diplomatic History of the Southern Confederacy*
(Baltimore, 1901); this work is especially useful for its account
of the acquisition of the Pickett Papers, a major collection of
documents on diplomatic and naval affairs in the South. There
is much sprightly (and acid) comment in Burton J. Hendrick,
Statesmen of the Lost Cause (Boston, 1939). In concluding this
brief résumé of general works one need only direct the reader
to the monumental study by James Ford Rhodes, *History of the
United States from the Compromise of 1850 to 1877,* 7 vols.
(New York, 1893–1907). Allan Nevins has a brilliant chapter on
Civil War foreign relations in his *The War for the Union: War
Becomes Revolution, 1862–1863,* II (New York, 1960). This is,
of course, part of Nevins' multi-volume restudy of the war. If
the reader wishes to put the incidents of the war into the overall
pattern of diplomacy, he may consult one or more of the follow-
ing excellent texts on that subject: Robert H. Ferrell, *American
Diplomacy: A History,* 2nd ed. (New York, 1969); Samuel Flagg
Bemis, *A Diplomatic History of the United States* (New York,
1937), and subsequent editions; Thomas A. Bailey, *A Diplomatic
History of the American People,* 5th ed. (New York, 1955);
Julius W. Pratt, *A History of United States Foreign Policy*
(Englewood Cliffs, New Jersey, 1955).

SPECIAL WORKS: MONOGRAPHS

Confederate naval affairs have been subjected to piecemeal examination in a number of works, but there is no satisfactory

treatment of that subject, either in its technical or diplomatic aspects. The pertinent facts must be culled from many sources. An excellent starting place for such a search is an unpublished dissertation at Vanderbilt University, Herbert H. Todd, "The Building of the Confederate States Navy in Europe," 1940. Though limited in scope and documentation this early sketch of this important subject remains a useful jumping-off spot. A more up-to-date treatment for the general reader is Philip Van Doren Stern, *The Confederate Navy: A Pictorial History* (New York, 1962). Mr. Stern spent several years scouring the archives of the United States and Europe for the well-chosen illustrations, and the narrative is many cuts above the usual picture history. Mr. Stern also has published a study of the world aspects of the Civil War, *When the Guns Roared* (New York, 1965), though the student may find it a bit kaleidoscopic in approach. The Confederate Publishing Company of Tuscaloosa, Alabama, has put out a number of fine studies dealing with various aspects of Confederate naval activity. Here we may cite two short but good treatments: Wilbur D. Jones, *The Confederate Rams at Birkenhead: A Chapter in Anglo-American Relations* (Tuscaloosa, 1961), and Charles S. Davis, *Colin J. McRae: Confederate Financial Agent* (Tuscaloosa, 1961). Another important recent contribution to the literature of Civil War naval activity is Stanley Hoole's edition of *Four Years in the Confederate Navy* (Athens, Ga., 1964), an account of Lt. Low's experiences with several of the Confederate cruisers.

Useful for their detailed treatment of complex subjects are Samuel B. Thompson, *Confederate Purchasing Operations Abroad* (Chapel Hill, N. C., 1935), and William M. Robinson, *The Confederate Privateers* (New Haven, Conn., 1928). The former work may be supplemented by Richard Lester, "Confederate Finance and Purchasing in Great Britain During the American Civil War," Ph. D. thesis at the University of Manchester, England, 1962. For an extended but haphazard treatment of Southern naval affairs the patient reader may wish to consult the ponderous J. T. Scharf, *History of the Confederate States Navy from Its Organization to the Surrender of Its Last Vessel* (New York, 1887). Covering much the same material (and much easier to read) is James Russell Soley, *The Blockade and the*

Cruisers (New York, 1883; paperback edition, New York, n.d). These two works exhibit all the virtues and vices of late-nineteenth-century naval historiography. Virgil Carrington Jones has, in three volumes, summarized *The Civil War at Sea* (New York, 1960–62); although not primarily a diplomatic study, this work details many of the international ramifications of Southern naval activity. The work is, of course, slanted toward the general reader and not the specialist. One may examine the Federal side of naval operations conveniently in Richard S. West, Jr., *Mr. Lincoln's Navy* (New York, 1957). Still the best work on its subject is Thomas L. Harris, *The Trent Affair* (Indianapolis, 1896). With different intent and technique an English writer has made this incident yield its full quota of drama and humor: Evan John [Simpson], *Atlantic Impact, 1861* (New York, 1952). This most famous of all Civil War diplomatic incidents is well-handled in a number of articles, including Arnold Whitridge, "The Trent Affair, 1861: An Anglo-American Crisis that Almost Led to War," *History Today*, IV (1954); Charles Francis Adams, "The Trent Affair," *Massachusetts Historical Society Proceedings*, XLV (1911); R. H. Dana, "The Trent Affair: An Aftermath," ibid., (1912); V. H. Cohen, "Charles Sumner and the *Trent* Affair," *Journal of Southern History*, XXII (1956); an important article on a little-understood phase of the incident is Lynn Case, "La France et l'affaire du'Trent,'" *Revue Historique*, CCXXVI (1961); W. W. Jeffries, "The Civil War Career of Charles Wilkes," ibid., XI (1945). The only biography of the impetuous and not always understood Wilkes is Daniel Henderson, *The Hidden Coasts* (New York, 1953), but this work is marred by factual errors and poor style. Wilkes is still awaiting his biographer.

The Confederate raiders have attracted a disproportionate amount of attention, much of it of limited use. The accounts tend to be journalistic, inaccurate, and based on secondary sources, many of which are themselves suspect. An interesting exception—though not free entirely from error—is the delightful vignette, Edna and Frank Bradlow, *Here Comes the Alabama* (Cape Town, S. Africa, 1958), which is an engaging small study of that raider's visit to Cape Town in 1863 and of the origin of a South African folk tune based on the ship's name. Another treatment of the most famous cruiser, again in somewhat popular style, is Kenneth Poolman, *The Alabama Incident* (London, 1958). More scholarly treatment is to be found in two fine articles which Douglas Maynard has prepared: "Union Efforts to Prevent the Escape of the Alabama," *Mississippi Valley Historical Review*, XLI (1954), and "Plotting the Escape of the Alabama," *Journal of Southern History*, XX (1954). Still another facet of that ship's career is examined in Frenise A. Logan, "Activities of the Alabama in Asian Water," *Pacific Historical Review*, XXXI (1962). An article somewhat different from any of the above appeared in a small English periodical. The author was librarian in Her Majesty's Customs and Excise Library, and from the port records and official English sources has put together a provocative estimate of the Crown's legal responsibilities in regard to that famous raider. Rupert C. Jarvis, "The Alabama and the Law," *Transactions of the Historic Society of Lancashire and Cheshire*, CXI (1959). Perhaps the best way to follow the exploits of this famous ship is through the eyes of her captain; for those so inclined, Philip Van Doren Stern has edited and abridged Semmes's famous journal: *The Confederate Raider Alabama* (selections from *Memoirs of Service Afloat During the War Between the States* [Bloomington, Ind., 1962]). Still another near-contemporary account is Frederick Edge, *The Alabama and the Kearsarge* (Philadelphia, 1868). Alan R. Booth has expertly analyzed one complex phase of the cruiser's career in his "Alabama at the Cape, 1863," *American Neptune*, XXVI (1966). For a well-written account of the exploits of the *Shenandoah* see George W. Groh, "Last of the Rebel Raiders," *American Heritage*, X, (Dec., 1958), 48–51, 126–127.

The naval personnel of the Confederacy have been much neglected by historians. A brief and not altogether satisfactory estimate of one of them is Philip Melvin, "Stephen Russell Mallory, Southern Naval Statesman," *Journal of Southern History*, X (1944); though the title is an apt characterization, the article does little to convince the reader that it is deserved. Mallory deserves much better and receives it in the only biography extant, Joseph T. Durkin, *Stephen R. Mallory: Confederate Navy Chief* (Chapel Hill, N. C., 1954). Bulloch receives somewhat better treatment in the competent review of his work by William P. Roberts, "James Dunwoody Bulloch and the Confederate Navy," in the *North Carolina Historical Review,* XXIV (1947). A less scholarly review of this same subject without the personal point of view is David Woodward, "Launching the Confederate Navy," *History Today,* XII (1962), but here again the reader is warned of the superficial examination of sources, the lack of analysis, and the selective nature of the commentary. A brief summary of Bulloch's career may be found in Virginia Bulloch-Willis, "James Dunwoody Bulloch," *Sewanee Review,* XXXIV (October-December, 1926), 386–401. A series of biographical sketches of key naval personnel—Union and Confederate—appears in Jim Dan Hill, *Sea Dogs of the Sixties* (Minneapolis, 1935). The chapters on Bulloch and Waddell proved most useful in this study.

There are two fine articles on the activities of the American consul at Liverpool, whose job it was to prevent the departure of raiders from that British port. In the first, Thomas H. Dudley himself reviews the highlights of his mission. "Three Critical Periods in our Relations with England during the Late War: Personal Recollections of Thomas H. Dudley, the Late United States Consul at Liverpool," *Pennsylvania Magazine of History and Biography,* XVII (1893); the consul was no man to hide his talents or play down the importance of his role in thwarting Confederate activities. In truth his was a most important post, and he filled it well as Brainerd Dyer points out in a more recent evaluation of the consul's work: "Thomas H. Dudley," *Civil War History,* I (1955). Douglas Maynard has expertly explored two facets of overseas activity, one Northern and one Southern. "The Forbes-Aspinwall Mission," *Mississippi Valley Historical Review,* XLV (1958), in which the attempt to buy up foreign ships to prevent them from falling into the hands of the Confederates is well summarized. And in another fine bit of historical detective work and extensive research, this same author put together "The Confederacy's Super-"Alabama," *Civil War History,* V (1959). An interesting sidelight on the cruise of the *Alabama* is provided by A.M.G., "The Pride of Mr. Laird," *Blackwood's Magazine,* CCXCIV (1963), 213–23. This charming vignette is based on the letters of a sailor on the famous raider.

Elliot A. P. Evans, "Napoleon III and the American Civil

War," Ph. D. thesis at Stanford University, 1940, confirms a long-standing assumption "that Mexico was indeed Napoleon's primary concern." Though it treats the Civil War years in two short chapters, Henry Blumenthal's *A Reappraisal of Franco-American Relations 1830–1871* (Chapel Hill, N. C., 1959), is a fine summary of Confederate activity in France. Knowledgable about French sources, calm and incisive in appraisal, and wise in conclusion, this book deserves a wide audience; and its bibliography provides helpful clues to sources in France. The most thorough and up-to-date evaluation of the French response to the war is Lynn M. Case and Warren F. Spencer, *The United States and France: Civil War Diplomacy* (Philadelphia, 1970), a book based on extensive archival research and one which brings the story of Confederate naval construction in that country to a high level of sophistication and one which skillfully evaluates the work of Slidell and raises some important questions about his competence. The authors have included a summary chapter, "Men and Issues," which will be required reading for all students of the war. This model study is a welcome addition to the literature of the international dimensions of the Civil War. Another "standard" monograph, virtually the only thing on its special subject, is George W. Dalzell, *The Flight from the Flag* (Chapel Hill, N. C., 1940). Nicely written though it is, this work is not footnoted, so many a valuable clue has no source. For example, Dalzell identifies Bulloch's informant in the Foreign Office, but gives no evidence supporting the choice. History wishes to know more of the mysterious Mr. Buckley.

The complicated story of Britain's neutral obligations may be followed out in Mountague Bernard, *A Historical Account of the Neutrality of Great Britain* (London, 1870). Of greater utility are the articles by James P. Baxter on this important subject: "Some British Opinion as to Neutral Rights, 1861–1865," *American Journal of International Law*, XXIII (1929) and "Papers Relating to Belligerent and Neutral Rights, 1861–1865," *American Historical Review*, XXXIV (1928). For a more narrowly focussed evaluation of Britain's legal response in 1863 see F. J. Merli, "Crown versus Cruiser: The Curious Affair of the *Alexandra*," *Civil War History*, IX (1963). In the first major study of the Civil War prize cases, a young historian has bril-

liantly related them to the larger context of diplomacy and
Anglo-American animosity; the work, which contains a fine
bibliographic essay (and many other virtues, as well), points up
the intricate relationship between national self-interest and international law— in both Britain and the United States. The author
of this fine study deserves high praise for his sophisticated approach to a complex and long-neglected phase of the international dimension of the war: Stuart L. Bernath, *Squall Across
the Atlantic: American Civil War Prize Cases and Diplomacy*
(Berkeley, Calif., 1970.) For a different perspective on some of the
legal issues involved in the war consult Stuart Bernath, "Squall
Across the Atlantic: The *Peterhoff* Episode," *Journal of Southern
History*, XXXIV (1968), 382–401.

The Confederate raider *Florida* has attracted attention in
books and articles, the former usually being journalistic in approach. Edward Boykin's *Sea Devil of the Confederacy* (New
York, 1959) is a sort of companion volume to the same author's
treatment of the *Alabama* in *Ghost Ship of the Confederacy*
(New York, 1959). More scholarly, hence more limited in appeal,
are the following: Donald Higginbotham, "A Raider Refuels:
Diplomatic Repercussions," *Civil War History*, IV (1958), and
Frank L. Owsley, Jr., "The Capture of the C.S.S. *Florida*," *American Neptune*, XXII (1962). In this same journal John E. Wood-
man has thoroughly explored a fascinating "tempest-in-a-teapot"
incident: "The Stone Fleet," *American Neptune*, XXI (1961);
this piece of work is a model of thorough research presented with
literary verve showing that "a failure and complete was your old
stone fleet," as Melville summarized the plan. Less satisfactory
than some of his other articles on naval activity in Europe is
Douglas Maynard, "The Escape of the *Florida*," *The Pennsylvania
Magazine of History and Biography*, LXXVII (1953). The most
detailed scholarly study of this vessel's career has been provided by
Frank L. Owsley, Jr., in *The C.S.S. Florida: Her Building and
Operation* (Philadelphia, 1965).

For the always fascinating topic of "public opinion" one may
consult Belle Becker Sideman and Lillian Friedman, eds., *Europe
Looks at the Civil War* (New York, 1960; paperback edition, New
York, 1962); Donaldson Jordon and Edwin Pratt, *Europe and the
American Civil War* (New York, 1931). A pioneer work which

retains its usefulness, this book incorporates the research of two independent studies, and Samuel E. Morison suggested their inclusion in one work. W. R. West has explored *Contemporary French Opinion of the Civil War* (Baltimore, 1924).

The technical and economic aspects of Confederate ship-building are tangentally examined in "official" company histories of the firms engaged in the lucrative task of constructing Southern ships. For the present study the following were useful: Horace White, *'Fossets': A Record of Two Centuries of Engineering* (Bromborough, Cheshire, England, 1958 [Fawcett, Preston and Company, Ltd.—the *Florida*])*; The Fairfield Shipbuilding and Engineering Works: History of the Company; Review of Its Productions; and Description of the Works* (London, 1909); John Carvel, *Stephen of Linthouse*: A Record of Two Hundred Years of Shipbuilding* (Glasgow, 1950).

Confederate blockade running has attracted possibly more attention than any other phase of Civil War naval history. But again, most of the accounts are popularizations, centering on the "romance of the rebel reefers." All the glamour and adventure, the danger and the profit, lure the reader and writer away from the more mundane (but important) aspects of procurement in European yards. Hamilton Cochran, *Blockade Runners of the Confederacy* (Indianapolis, 1958), is one such journalistic account; another is Robert Carse, *Blockade: The Civil War at Sea* (New York, 1958). There are excellent chapters on this topic in the already-cited Van Doren Stern, *Confederate Navy*. More useful and somewhat different in approach—being a first-hand account of numerous trips through the Federal squadrons—is Thomas E. Taylor, *Running the Blockade: A Personal Narrative of Adventures, Risks, and Escapes During the American Civil War*, 2nd ed. (London, 1896). Another interesting—almost unbelievable—account of blockade running adventures is that provided by Augustus Charles Hobart-Hampden [Pasha], *Sketches From My Life* (New York, 1882). Thus far the most authoritative source of information on this part of the war is the series of well-researched articles which Marcus W. Price has prepared for the *American Neptune*, (see, for

*This company built the magnificent C. S. S. *Shenandoah*.

example, XXI, 1961, 81–106). Mr. Price hopes to collect his information in book form before long. Bern Anderson in his *By Land and By River: The Naval History of the Civil War* (New York, 1962), suggests that work of the runners has been exaggerated, but has little evidence for this "revision" of historiography. To pursue the matter further the interested reader may consult Frank E. Vandiver, ed., *Confederate Blockade Running Through Bermuda* (Austin, Texas, 1947); Francis Bradlee, *Blockade Running During the Civil War and the Effect of Land and Water Transportation on the Confederacy* (Salem, Mass., 1925); James Merrill, "Notes on the Yankee Blockade of the South Atlantic Sea Board," *Civil War History*, IV (1958); Kathryn A. Hanna, "Incidents of the Confederate Blockade," *Journal of Southern History*, XI (1945), 214–29.

Charles Francis Adams, Jr., has published a number of articles on Civil War diplomacy in the *Massachusetts Historical Society Proceedings:* "A Crisis in Downing Street," XLVII (1914); "Seward and the Declaration of Paris," XLVI (1913); "The Crisis of Foreign Intervention in the War of Secession," XLVII (1914); "The British Proclamation of May, 1861," XLVIII (1915). Also useful is the same author's *Studies Military and Diplomatic, 1775–1865,* (New York, 1911).

Another important item in the Adams' family bibliography of Civil War writings is Brooks Adams, "The Seizure of the Laird Rams," *Massachusetts Historical Society Proceedings,* XLV (1911). For reasons set out in the text of this present work (see pp. 213–17), this study is overdone, though it remains a useful starting place for its subject. Adam's note to Russell was not as effective as Brooks Adams contends.

The literature, book and periodical, on other aspects of the war takes up a good proportion of shelf space in any library. Few can hope to master all of it, but for help in special subjects one may browse lightly or delve deeply in the following works. James G. Randall, "Lincoln and John Bright," *Yale Review*, XXXIV (1944); Bray Hammond, "The North's Empty Purse, 1861–1862," *American Historical Review*, LXVII (1961); Robert Futrell, "Federal Trade with the Confederate States, 1861–65," Ph. D. thesis at Vanderbilt University, 1950; Martin P. Claussen, "The United States and Great Britain, 1861–1865; Peace

Factors in International Relations," Ph. D. thesis at University of Illinois, 1938; L. B. Schmitt, "Influence of Wheat and Cotton on Anglo-American Relations During the Civil War," *Iowa Journal of History*, XVI (1918); this may be supplemented with E. Ginzberg, "Economics of British Neutrality During the American Civil War," *Agricultural History*, X (1936). A more recent appraisal of the economic aspect of the war in its relation to diplomacy is Amos Khasigian, "Economic Factors and British Neutrality, 1861–1865," *Historian*, XXV (1963). For an appraisal of the economic impact of the war on one British city see D. G. Wright, "Bradford and the American Civil War," *Journal of British Studies*, VIII (1969). Another important re-study of the impact of the war on Britain is Mary Louise Ellison, "The Reaction of Lancashire to the American Civil War," Ph. D. thesis, University of London, 1968. This work calls into question the supposed passivity of the working class of the region studied and suggests that there was a fairly general desire for a more active response in favor of the South. The study is based on a wide and intensive investigation of the press of the region. Another aspect of the war has been studied in Charles P. Cullop, *Confederate Propaganda in Europe, 1861–1865* (Coral Gables, Fla., 1969).

Confederate difficulties in meeting the demands of war are examined in James Merrill, "Confederate Shipbuilding at New Orleans," *Journal of Southern History*, XXVIII (1962), and Winfred P. Minter, "Confederate Military Supply Policy," *Social Science*, XXXIV (1959). A new study of the domestic obstacles to a successful Southern shipbuilding program concludes that failure traces to military, geographic, and political factors, as well as to inability to appreciate the fundamental importance of seapower to the outcome of the war: William N. Still, Jr., *Confederate Shipbuilding* (Athens, Ga., 1970). James P. Baxter's *The Introduction of the Ironclad Warship* (Cambridge, Mass., 1933), is still useful and remains the "standard" work on its subject.

The historiography of the war has been subjected to reevaluation. See, for example, the fine analysis by Max Beloff, "Great Britain and the American Civil War," *History*, XXXVII (1952); a more recent and less detailed argument is Robert H. Jones, "Anglo-American Relations, 1861–1865, Reconsidered, "*Mid-*

America, XLV (1963); Jones bases his appraisal primarily on the British *Sessional Papers.* Joseph M. Hernon, "British Sympathies in the American Civil War: A Reconsideration," *Journal of Southern History,* XXXIII (1967); Wilbur D. Jones, "The British Conservatives and the American Civil War," *American Historical Review,* LVIII (1953); and C. Collyer, "Gladstone and the American Civil War," *Proceedings of the Leeds Philosophical Society,* VI (1951); also R. Harrison, "British Labour and the Confederacy: A Note on the Southern Sympathies of Some British Working Class Journals and Leaders During the American Civil War," *International Review of Social History,* II (1957), focuses on various phases of the British response to the war and points up the complexity of "attitudes" toward the war. Another provocative British view of the war has been provided by that most perceptive student of American history and politics, Sir Denis Brogan, in *American A-pects* (London, 1964), Chapter Three, "A Fresh Appraisal of the Civil War," pp. 22–51. This essay was originally published in *Harper's Magazine* (April, 1960). For a view from the British side that is heavily slanted in favor of the South see Sheldon Van Auken, "English Sympathy for the South: The Glittering Illusion," B. Litt. thesis, Oxford University, 1957. Though one may disagree strongly with both the assumptions and arguments of this work, it is a provocative analysis.

In concluding this section of a long but by no means exhaustive listing one may cite the interesting collection of essays on the war compiled and edited by David Donald under the title *Why the North Won the Civil War* (Baton Rouge, 1960; paperback ed., New York, 1962); for the present study the chapters by Norman Graebner, "Nothern Diplomacy and European Neutrality," (pp. 55–78) and David M. Potter, "Jefferson Davis and the Political Factors in Confederate Defeat," (pp. 91–112) proved most helpful, but all the essays here are of high calibre and will repay study. Distilled into this small volume are the results of many lifetimes of scholarship; each of the authors brings a special competence to his task. One can do no better in ending such a list than direct the reader to one volume that after many years remains head and shoulders above all the rest. If a person had to choose one book and one book only on the Civil War, he would be wise indeed if he selected James G. Randall, *The Civil War and*

Reconstruction (Boston, 1937). Though this work has been "modernized" in a new edition, many readers will stick by the older version, which, despite a stiff prose style, retains the imprint of the author's personality.

BIOGRAPHIES, AUTOBIOGRAPHIES, MEMOIRS, REMINISCENCES

English participants in the events of the Civil War are amply represented in historical literature; many of the key figures of that period have been treated in multi-volume works. H. C. F. Bell has written a fine two-volume study of *Lord Palmerston* (London, 1936). A more recent book on this great nineteenth-century diplomat and statesman is Brian Connell, *Regina v Palmerston* (London, 1962); this work consist mainly of excerpts from the correspondence of Queen Victoria and one of her many prime ministers. Connell's character sketches are delightful, though the volume is marred by many mistakes in transcription. Somewhat outdated but still useful for the documents it contains is Evelyn Ashley, *The Life and Correspondence of Henry John Temple, Viscount Palmerston*, 2 vols. (London, 1879). In smaller compass and more deftly written—overwritten may be a better description —is Philip Guedalla's *Palmerston* (London, 1926). One of the more important recent publications on the prime minister's career is Donald Southgate, *"The Most English Minister. . ."* (subtitled *The Policies and Politics of Palmerston* [New York, 1966]). This is a sensitive and sensible evaluation of the prime minister's work, primarily in foreign policy; it is a necessary adjunct to any appraisal of the still-misunderstood prime minister (a book published in 1965 calls him a "war monger") who so fully reflected his age, and whose work—and importance in keeping Britain out of war—is so little known to American students of the Civil War. Still another glimpse of this fascinating character is provided by Kingsley Martin, *The Triumph of Lord Palmerston: A Study of Public Opinion in England Before the Crimean War* (London, 1924; revised edition, London, 1963). A much less satisfactory view of Pam at work is provided by Benjamin Sacks, "Lord Palmerston's Diplomatic Partisanship During the American Civil War," MA thesis, McGill University, 1927. Details of the career of the foreign secretary may be followed in Spencer Walpole's two-volume *Life of Lord John Russell* (New York, 1891); this must be supplemented by the very fine biography by A. Wyatt Tilby, *Lord John Russell: A study in Civil and Religious Liberty* (New York, 1931). Also Donald Southgate, *The Passing of the Whigs* (New York, 1962), and G. P. Gooch, ed., *The Later Correspondence of Lord John Russell, 1840–1878* (New York, 1925), contain useful information on various phases of his career. The pro-North George Douglas Campbell, eighth Duke of Argyll, has left an interesting *Autobiography and Memoir*, ed. by the Dowager Duchess of Argyll (London, 1906).

The Southern commissioners to Europe have had their stories told in Louis M. Sears, *John Slidell* (Durham, N. C., 1925), and Virginia Mason, *The Public Life and Diplomatic Correspondence of James M. Mason with Some Personal History by His Daughter* (Roanoke, Virginia, 1903). The American minister to London, long overlooked by historians, is the subject of a recent study of his life and work. The young and able Martin B. Duberman has done a first-rate job on the complex and aloof Bostonian who represented the United States at Court of St. James's. *Charles Francis Adams, 1807–1886* (Boston, 1961), is the only satisfactory biography of this man. Duberman's work supersedes the brief biography written by Charles Francis Adams, Jr., of his father, *Charles Francis Adams* (Boston, 1900). A detailed study of Adams' London mission may be found in Norman B. Ferris, "Tempestuous Mission, 1861–1862," Ph.D. dissertation, Emory University, 1962. Another unsatisfactory biography of a Civil War figure is Brainerd Dyer, *The Public Career of William M. Evarts* (Berkeley, California, 1933). The Pulitzer Prize biography of Charles Summer by David Donald raises some interesting problems in historiography for the student. David Donald, *Charles Sumner and the Coming of the Civil War* (New York, 1960); for a critical evaluation of this work see Louis Ruchames, "The Pulitzer Prize Treatment of Charles Sumner," in the *Massachusetts Review*, Summer, 1961.

The biographies of Lincoln are legion, and there is no reason to list them here: one may find a "life" to suit any taste. For this study Jay Monaghan's sparkling diplomatic study of the president's handling of foreign affairs was invaluable: *Diplomat in*

Carpet Slippers (Indianapolis & New York, 1945; paperback edition, Indianapolis, 1962). Written with much the same attention to style, witty and informative, alive with sharp comment, is one of the classics of American letters, Henry Adams, *The Education of Henry Adams* (New York, 1918). The young Adams was secretary to his father during the latter's mission to England, and the son had a sharp eye and an even sharper pen.

The American consul (later minister) in Paris is the subject of another fine biography, Margaret Clapp, *Forgotten First Citizen: John Bigelow* (Boston, 1947). That fascinating person can also be studied in his own works: the ponderous five volumes of the *Retrospections of an Active Life* (New York, 1910), and the dainty-by-comparison *France and the Confederate Navy 1862–1868* (New York, 1888; recently reprinted by Bergman Publishers, N.Y., 1968). Though neither strict biography nor a first-hand account (recorded by "two friends" long after the war) Caleb Huse's *The Supplies for the Confederate Army How they were Obtained in Europe and How Paid For* (Boston, 1904), is a source of information on that topic, even if the book gives much less than its title promises. A fascinating portrait—though slightly embellished —is furnished by the much-edited *Diary of Gideon Welles* (New York, 1911). (But see the new three-volume edition [Boston, 1960] of this diary, edited by Howard K. Beale in accordance with the most rigorous canons of historical scholarship.) Another diary of considerable insight was kept by the perceptive English war correspondent, William H. Russell, *My Diary, North and South* (New York, 1863).

Roundell Palmer, one of the chief legal advisers to the Crown during the Civil War years, has left his recollections of those times; they shed much light on the English view of neutral obligations and responsibilities. Roundell Palmer, (1st Earl of Shelbourne), *Memorials Part I: Family and Personal, 1766–1865* (London, 1896). Palmer was the Queen's solicitor general and chief prosecutor for the Crown in the famous *Alexandra* trial in 1863; his name appears on most of the legal opinions submitted to the Foreign Office during the war.

Sarah F. Hughes has edited the letters of her father, John M. Forbes, and these shed some small light on English conditions. Forbes was a member of the special commission sent by the Union to buy up ships in Europe to keep them out of Confederate clutches. Sarah F. Hughes, ed., *Letters and Recollections of John Murray Forbes* (Boston, 1899). While this is not a major source, it has some information on the Laird rams and the *Alexandra*. Information about another unofficial minister to England may be found in Harriet A. Weed, ed., *Life of Thurlow Weed Including His Autobiography and a Memoir* (Boston, 1884). The son and secretary to the American wartime secretary of state has left a useful account of his own service. Frederick W. Seward, *Reminiscences of a War-Time Statesman and Diplomat, 1830–1915* (New York, 1916). The lack of a judicious, up-to-date study of the Civil War secretary of state has at last been overcome by the recent publication of Glyndon A. Van Deusen's first-rate biography, *William Henry Seward* (New York, 1967). An older, briefer, and still useful account of his stewardship may be found in Henry Temple, "William H. Seward," in *American Secretaries of State and Their Diplomacy*, edited by Samuel Flagg Bemis, Vol. VII (New York, 1927–29). There is also the long outdated Frederic Bancroft, *The Life of William H. Seward* (New York, 1900). Another source for information on the wartime activity of the secretary of state is Gideon Welles, *Lincoln and Seward* (New York, 1874). The sharp-penned naval secretary must be taken with a grain of salt, but his comments are interesting, nonetheless. We catch reflections of the American State Department, its operations and operators, in the old but informative Thomas Newton, *Lord Lyons: A Record of British Diplomacy* (London, 1913); the British minister was a firm friend of the North, though the tactics of Seward tried his patience on many occasions. We may follow the life of another friend of the North in John Morley's biography of Richard Cobden: *Life of Richard Cobden* (London, 1908). Few sources for wartime activity exceed the observations of the Adamses for insight, evaluation, and acid comment. A handy "Adams-eye" view of the war is the compilation of Worthington C. Ford, *A Cycle of Adams Letters, 1861–1865* (Boston, 1920), in which various members of the family speak with customary candor.

Biographies of the Confederate president are plentiful, though for one reason or another they all fall short of being in any sense of the word "definitive." Useful are: Dunbar Rowland, ed. and comp., *Jefferson Davis, Constitutionalist: His Letters, Papers, and*

Speeches (Jackson, Miss., 1923); Hudson Strode, *Jefferson Davis* (1955, New York). For a provocative estimate of the South's leader see Frank E. Vandiver, "Jefferson Davis and the Confederate State," An Inaugural Lecture Delivered before the University of Oxford on February 26, 1964, Oxford, 1964. Printed as a pamphlet, Oxford, 1964; also, his *Their Tattered Flags: The Epic of the Confederacy* (New York, 1970), which may challenge traditional views about the Confederacy and the reputation of its president.

NEWSPAPERS AND PERIODICALS

"Newspapers of the past," Robert E. Quirk has noted, "are the historian's staff of life." But just as man does not live by bread alone, so too must the historian be wary of too much dependence on this source. Used with caution and discretion the newspapers reveal information not available elsewhere. Nineteenth-century editors, like American olive packagers, were addicted to superlatives, so immediately one must make allowance for overstatement. Nevertheless, by omission and emphasis, almost as much as by statement, newspapers constitute a valuable historical source useful to illustrate rather than "prove." The *New York Tribune*, *Harpers Weekly, Leslie's Illustrated News,* the *Boston Commercial Advertiser, New York Times, Richmond Enquirer, Richmond Examiner, De Bow's Review, Atlantic Monthly,* all these, to name but a few, provide an interesting "climate of opinion," even when they supply no direct news.

If anything, British newspapers were more partisan than their Yankee and Rebel brethren. The influential London *Times* is a major source of information, both as to fact and opinion. It was practically a government organ, and its opinions were reprinted throughout the kingdom. While not an English paper, Hotze's *Index* had brief and limited influence, especially in pro-South circles. For its cartoons alone the English *Punch* is worth any student's time. It has no rival, no equal. It is a unique—and delightful—source for British views. For a glimpse into the charm of this journal, see Oscar Maurer, "Punch" on Slavery and Civil War in America, 1841–1865," *Victorian Studies,* I (1957).

There were, of course, many other London papers, *Morning Post* (pro-Palmerston throughout), *Morning Star* (Bright's paper, and pro-North, naturally), and London *Gazette.* Whenever possible, the provincial papers were used. There is much information in the Southampton *Times,* the Liverpool *Mercury,* the *North British Daily Mail,* and the Liverpool *Courier.* All have a fascination of their own, even if the searcher comes away from them with little material.

Useful periodicals are the *American Historical Review, the Mississippi Valley Historical Review* (now the *Journal of American History),* the *Journal of Southern History,* the *North Carolina Historical Review, Massachusetts Historical Society Proceedings, Civil War History,* and the constantly improving *Civil War Times Illustrated.* The various state historical journals, especially in the South, devote a good portion of their space to Civil War material.

An invaluable source of material on the war is the *Illustrated London News (1861–66),* for its illustrations as well as for its comment. The English journal, *History Today,* provides interesting and informative articles, for the English continue to take much interest in our Civil War.

PRINTED SOURCES

The present study is based largely on material available in the U. S., Navy Department, comp., *Official Records of the Union and Confederate Navies in the War of the Rebellion,* 31 vols. (Washington, 1894–1927). Volumes II and III of the Second Series contain the bulk of material on Confederate naval activity; most of the dispatches from Bulloch and his associates may be found in these volumes. Occasionally these must be supplemented by the extensive *War of the Rebellion: Official Records of the Union and Confederate Armies,* 130 vols. (Washington, 1880–1901).

The second major source for the present study is U. S., State Department, *Diplomatic Correspondence, Papers Relating to Foreign Affairs, 1861–1869,* 19 vols. (Washington, 1861–70). This valuable reference contains most of the official correspondence between the secretary of state and the American minister in London. It also contains numerous excerpts from the English press on matters of concern to Washington. (For example, *FR:1864,* pt. I, supplement, pp. lxiii–lxx, contains a number of depositions on the *Canton*.) A useful but unofficial compilation of Civil War information of varying worth is Frank Moore, ed., *The Rebellion Record: a Diary of American Events, with Documents, Narratives, Illustrative Incidents, Poetry, etc.*, 12 vols. (New York, 1862–71). Though not immediately related to the present focus of research, the *Congressional Globe* contains mountains of material relative to the Northern conduct of the war.

For the British side of the war one must consult *Hansard Parliamentary Debates*, 3d ser., London, 1830–91; see also Great Britain, Parliament, House of Commons, and House of Lords, *Sessional Papers*, 1861–65. Also consult the large body of material relating to the *Alabama* claims. See the U. S., State Department, *Correspondence Concerning Claims Against Great Britain*, 7 vols. (Washington, 1869–71). Somewhat easier to use for the American point of view is the one-volume Geneva Arbitration Tribunal, comp., *The Case of the United States to be Laid Before the Tribunal of Arbitration to be Convened at Geneva* (Washington, 1871). There is a British counterpart to this volume published in London, 1872, as a facsimile reprint of the official U. S. case, so printed as to be fully interchangeable with the American volume. The N. Y. Public Library has the London version, which is cited in the notes to Chapter Eleven. Other parts of the story of the British-built cruisers may be searched out in U. S., State Department, *Papers Relating to the Treaty of Washington*, 6 vols. (Washington, 1872–74).

Of some small utility is the handy compilation by James D. Richardson, *A Compilation of the Messages and Papers of the Confederacy, Including the Diplomatic Correspondence, 1861–1865* (Washington, 1905; new edition edited by Allan Nevins, New York, 1966). An invaluable printed source of information for activities at the London legation of the United States is Sarah A. Wallace and Frances E. Gillespie, eds., *The Journal of Benjamin Moran*, (Chicago, 1948). Although a diligent worker, Moran thought his services in the legation were not properly appreciated. He was a shrewd—albeit biting—commentator on those who passed through the legation. The *Journal* is a mine of information on London in the 1860s. The secretary was somewhat critical of his superior, the United States minister.

MS SOURCES: ARCHIVES

The most important archival source used in this study is the corpus of material designated FO 5 in the Public Record Office in London. Under this file one will find the volumes devoted to particular ships built for the Confederates, the action taken in each particular case, or, as often happened, the reason for declining to act. These files can then be cross-checked against the records of other branches of the government, as for example, Treasury, Home Office, Law Office, or Admiralty. Such research, though time-consuming, gives a well-balanced picture of official British reaction to Confederate construction. Many of the Foreign Office documents have, of course, been published, but most have not, and those published usually lack the often fascinating marginalia of the originals. These records may then be supplemented by Customs Office correspondence and manifests, most of which are carefully preserved at Her Majesty's Customs and Excise Library, London. In addition to the government documents, the author examined the records of Alexander Stephen and Company, Ltd., Glasgow, and these provided much information about the impact of Confederate activity in Clydeside shipyards; Professor Peter Payne and his colleagues at the University of Glasgow kindly made available to me the Denny MSS, which provided many nuggets of information about Southern activity.

On the American side there are the records of the Department of State in the National Archives, especially the instructions to the consuls in Great Britain and their dispatches to the State Department. Most important and extensive, of course, are the reports from Liverpool and London. Thomas H. Dudley and Freeman Morse were, as their reports show, competent men, who worked long and hard to foil the Confederates. Their reports show the difficulty of the task. There is much material in reports from the other consuls in the British Isles, all of which may be conveniently consulted in the National Archives Building in Washington.

In the same place one may also consult the Naval Records Collections of the Office of Naval Records and Library. This little-used source contains all sorts of information on naval affairs and courts martial, of which there were a great many during the war.

PERSONAL PAPERS: MS COLLECTIONS

The Papers of Lord John Russell are preserved in the Public Record Office in London, and constitute a valuable and useful collection. Much of Lord John's correspondence has been published, but there are many items in the PRO that have not. To assure complete coverage, the researcher must sift through large amounts of material, for these papers are not indexed but are arranged in rough chronological order. In this important source one finds many hints to the varied, constantly shifting, chameleon response of the British to the war in America. Perhaps the most important single source for this study—the value of which is difficult to exaggerate—is the collection of Palmerston Papers now being catalogued at the Historical Manuscripts Commission in London. These papers provide fascinating glimpses of the prime minister in action. Without thorough study of this source no account of the Civil War years in Britain can be considered complete. In the PRO one may also consult the private (as well as official) correspondence of Lord Cowley, the British ambassador in Paris. His papers provide much information not available elsewhere. At the same depository the papers of Edmund Hammond, who was an undersecretary of state during the war, are available. What one clerk was saying to another clerk—to paraphrase G. M. Young—provides some interesting sidelights on the British response. There are, of course, scattered references to the war in the notes from the foreign office to its ministers in the various capitals of Europe, and these are often more informative than the "official" messages to Washington. Of necessity such sampling must be highly selective for the mass of material is very great indeed.

In addition, the Royal Archives at Windsor Castle provide extensive hints on the British attitude toward the war though there are relatively few references to the Confederate navy. A perusal of these papers confirms the difficulty of arriving at a correct and reasonable assessment of the British attitude.

In comfortable, almost luxurious, surroundings in the British Museum, one may examine the papers of many prominent Englishmen. The papers of Austin H. Layard (undersecretary for foreign affairs) and William E. Gladstone show the difficulty that influential men had in arriving at an accurate appraisal of the war. Judging from the small number of references to the war, that event did not loom large in British eyes, even in the so-called critical periods.

A valuable source for the light it sheds on the always fascinating and crucial subject of British opinion toward America—though of limited utility for the present study—is the collection of Clarendon papers at the Bodleian Library, Oxford.

Widely-scattered American manuscript sources were consulted in the preparation of this study. By far the most valuable collection of private papers relating to the international aspect of the war is the Dudley Papers at the Huntington Library in San Marino, California. The wide-ranging correspondence of this dedicated Unionist provides valuable information on all phases of Confederate naval activity. Use of the collection is expedited by the index or guide to its contents prepared by Mr. Philip Van Doren Stern when he used the collection. In addition to the valuable commentary, the collection contains a number of useful photographs, including two of that mysterious ship, Frigate Number 61. The William H. Seward Papers in the Rhees Library of the University of Rochester proved disappointing, as did the Thurlow Weed Papers in the same depository, though both are important Civil War source collections which shed much light on the political and social history of the mid-nineteenth century. The model indexes for these papers make them easy to check.

The New York Public Library contains a number of useful collections, chief of which, for this study, is the John Bigelow material. Well indexed and easily used, this material shows Bigelow's varied activity in Europe to halt the French construction plans of the Confederates; here we find the secret copied letters from French builders to Bulloch and Slidell; we see the concerted efforts that Bigelow, Dayton, and Sanford made to frustrate Southern plans. Also at the New York Public Library one may consult the papers of Horace Greeley, but these have little, almost nothing, to say about naval matters, though they are more useful for domestic politics.

For the Gustavus V. Fox Papers one must visit the New York Historical Society Library. This is a valuable source, and though

much of it has been published, there are many items of importance which have not. The correspondence with John Erricson,
designer of the *Monitor,* is extensive and shows Fox's interest in
naval technology, and the description of conditions in the Union
navy at the outbreak of the war is especially useful. Here again
one must turn over many letters before finding items of particular
interest. The letters are bundled chronologically. The small body
of William L. Dayton Papers may be examined in the very attractive surroundings of the John Foster Dulles Library at Princeton
University. One wishes the collection were larger so more time
might be spent in these ideal working conditions. The efficient
index speeds one's work.

At the Houghton Library of Harvard University one may consult the Charles Sumner Papers, but it is a time-consuming task,
for they are not indexed. The most important parts of this material have been published; see, for example, Vol. XLVI of *Massachusetts Historical Society Proceedings,* 93–164.

Of course, the bulk of Civil War manuscript material is in the
Library of Congress. For Confederate affairs in general, and naval
affairs in particular, one must consult the Pickett Papers, compris-
ing a large segment of Confederate diplomatic correspondence.
Much of this material found its way into the published *Official
Records of the Union and Confederate Navies,* but much good
information remains hidden away in obscure parts of this interesting collection. Less useful for the present work were the Henry
Hotze Papers and the Matthew F. Maury Papers. The James M.
Mason Papers provided useful information, as did the Gideon
Welles Papers. Though he was no better as a recorder than as a
participant, the James Heywood North Diary and Papers in the
Southern Historical Collection of the University of North Carolina, Chapel Hill, provide a useful commentary on the reasons
for Southern failure. One could never tell the importance of the
agent's mission from the comments he made about it. In the
William Whittle Papers at the Norfolk Public Library, Norfolk,
Va., there is an important collection of J. D. Bulloch letters which
are not cited either in his *Secret Service* or in the *ORN.* Professor
Warren F. Spencer is preparing these letters for publication. The
author would like to thank Professor Spencer for bringing these
to his attention.

In conclusion one may note two rather unusual historical sources. The first is Paul DuBellet, "The Diplomacy of the Confederate Cabinet Abroad," typewritten MS, New York, 1865. The stated purpose of this little exposé was, according to its author, "to open the eyes of my co-citizens of the Southern States, as well as those of all unprejudiced minds in the North, upon the source of many of the misfortunes which befell the Southern cause. . . ." A most interesting document, this, but one which must be used with extreme caution. It has now been published in the Confederate Centennial Studies edited by. Wm. Stanley Hoole, *The Diplomacy of the Confederate Cabinet of Richmond and Its Agents Abroad: Being Memorandum Notes Taken in Paris During the Rebellion of the Southern States from 1861–1865* by Paul Pecquet DuBellet (Tuscaloosa, 1963). Also in the manuscript division of the Library of Congress is a typed copy of the diary and reminiscences of Stephen R. Mallory (the original is on file in the Southern Historical Collection in the Library of the University of North Carolina). No man was in a better position to observe the inner workings of the Confederate government, but this document, with a mere thirty or so pages devoted to the war years, is of little value to students of Southern naval affairs; one looks in vain for commentary on Richmond political affairs, the troubles of naval procurement, Mallory's reaction to the work and personalities of his overseas agents. This diary—had it been kept with the skill of an Adams or the acerbity of a Welles—would have been a major historical source. Fortunately Mallory's reputation does not rest on his talent as a recorder.

Lastly there is that model of a diary, the diary of Charles Francis Adams. Now widely available on microfilm, this intimate view of men and events gives much information about the Civil War. From his vantage point, Adams could observe and record at first-hand a large part of the diplomatic interchange between the United States and Great Britain. His diary contains invaluable material on many aspects of the war and records reactions to men and events. As Adams' biographer, Martin Duberman, has said, its judicious entries are "a perfect mirror of the man."

Notes

CHAPTER ONE

1. For an authoritative statement of Secretary Seward's response to the war, one must consult the excellent biography by Glyndon G. Van Deusen, *William Henry Seward* (New York, 1967). In appraising Seward's conduct of affairs, one has to keep in mind the Secretary's rash tendency to shoot from the hip and to seek foreign wars: "Seward performed great services; but his proposal that the North provoke a war with Spain and France to extricate itself from its difficulties, as criminal as it was stupid, must make Americans blush that they had a foreign minister capable of such an act." Allan Nevins, *The War for the Union,* I, *The Improvised War, 1861–1862* (New York, 1959), p. vi. For the role of Welles see Richard S. West, Jr., *Mr. Lincoln's Navy* (New York, 1957); and, of course, the superb edition of *The Diary of Gideon Welles,* ed. Howard K. Beale, 3 vols. (New York, 1960).

2. James P. Baxter, *The Introduction of the Ironclad Warship* (Cambridge, Mass., 1933), p. 115 and *passim.* This model study remains the best work on its subject. For a recent footnote to the naval revolution in France see Charles S. Williams and Frank J. Merli, eds. and trans., "The Normandie Shows the Way: Report of a Voyage from Cherbourg to Vera Cruz, 4 September 1862," *Mariner's Mirror,* LIV (May, 1968), 153–62. See *Moniteur de la Flotte,* March 5, 1863, for remarks of M. le contre-admiral on naval technology.

3. G. A. Ballard, "British Battleships of the 1870's: the *Warrior* and *Black Prince,*" *Mariner's Mirror,* XVI (April, 1930), 168–86; James D. Bulloch, *The Secret Service of the Confederate States in Europe: Or How the Confederate Cruisers Were Equipped,* 2 vols. (New York, 1884; new edition by Philip Van Doren Stern, New York, 1959), II, 2. (The reader may find it more convenient to consult the 1959 edition, which is identical, except for a few minor corrections.) Hereafter cited as Bulloch, *Secret Service.*

4. James R. Soley, *The Blockade and the Cruisers* (paperback ed., New York, n.d.), p. 232; the preceding quotation about substituting apathy for zeal is on p. 5, and for an extended treatment of the subject of naval preparedness see especially Chapters One and Eight. For an authoritative statement of conditions in the Union navy in early 1861 see U. S., Navy Department, comp., *Report of the Secretary of the Navy* (Washington, 1862), in which the secretary admits, with refreshing candor, that "the department was very indifferently prepared" for the crisis confronting the country. For additional comment on the state of the navy during and just before the war, consult Harold and Margaret Sprout, *The Rise of American Naval Power, 1776–1918* (Princeton, N. J., 1939), especially Chapters Nine and Ten.

5. Soley, *Blockade and Cruisers,* p. 232.

6. Quoted in Bruce Catton, *The Coming Fury,* I (New York, 1961), p. 24 citing the *Congressional Globe,* 36th Cong., 1st sess., 1860, pt. IV, 2847–49. This is the first volume of Catton's *Centennial History of the Civil War,* 3 vols, (New York, 1961–65).

7. Soley, *Blockade and Cruisers,* p. 235; West, *Lincoln's Navy,* pp. 99–129; Joseph T. Durkin, *Stephen R. Mallory: Confederate Navy Chief* (Chapel Hill, N. C., 1954), *passim,* especially pp. 153–56. In April, 1862, a petition for Welles' removal from office was circulating in Boston, Mass. See Vol. 50 of the Gideon Welles Papers in the Library of Congress, Washington, D. C.

8. Catton, *Centennial History of the Civil War,* II, *Terrible Swift Sword* (New York, 1963), pp. 211–12.

9. U. S., Navy Department, comp., *Official Records of the Union and Confederate Navies in the War of the Rebellion,* 30 vols. and index (Washington, 1894–1927), Series II, Volume II, 69, Mallory-Conrad, May 10, 1861. Hereafter cited as *ORN.* See also, Durkin, *Mallory, passim,* especially pp. 130–56 and p. 343.

10. Kenneth M. Stampp, *The Peculiar Institution* (New York, 1956); Wilbur J. Cash, *The Mind of the South* (New York, 1960); Clement Eaton, *A History of the Southern Confederacy* (New York, 1961), especially Chapter Seven, "The Logistics of the Gray Army," for the role of Gorgas. Nevins, *Improvised War,* Appendix I, pp. 424–26, for capsule comparison of resources of North and South.

11. Durkin, *Mallory,* pp. 149–50.

12. Bulloch, *Secret Service,* I, 22.

13. Raphael Semmes, *The Confederate Raider Alabama: Selections from Memoirs of Service Afloat During the War Between the States,* ed. Philip Van Doren Stern (Bloomington, Ind., 1962), pp. 27–28.

14. Durkin, *Mallory,* p. 150, note 96, citing J. T. Scharf, *History of*

the Confederate States Navy from Its Organization to the .Surrender of Its Last Vessel (New York, 1887), p. 46.

15. *ORN*, Ser. II, Vol. II, 243, Mallory-Davis, August 16, 1862.

16. Richard N. Current, "God and the Strongest Battalions" in *Why the North Won the Civil War*, ed. David Donald (New York, 1962), pp. 15–16; Current is quoting the *Lynchburg Virginian*.

17. Bulloch, *Secret Service*, I, pp. 31–32.

18. This is the opinion of Van Doren Stern in his introduction to the 1959 edition of Bulloch's *Secret Service*, p. ix.

19. In addition to the sources already mentioned, this sketch of Bulloch relies on William P. Roberts, "James Dunwoody Bulloch and the Confederate Navy," *North Carolina Historical Review*, XXIV (July, 1947), 315–66; Van Doren Stern's *When the Guns Roared* (New York, 1965), *passim,* especially pp. 149–50; and conversations of the author with the late Thomas W. Green, Southampton, England.

20. Quote appears in Bulloch, *Secret Service*, 1, 46; *ORN*, Ser. II. Vol. II, 64–65, Mallory-Bulloch, May, 9, 1861.

21. *ORN*, Ser. II, Vol. II, 69, Mallory-Conrad, May 10, 1861.

CHAPTER TWO

1. Allan Nevins, *The War for the Union*, II, *War Becomes Revolution.* (New York, 1960), p. 242. Chapter Ten, "Britain, France, and the War Issues," ought to be read carefully by all students of the war in its international dimension.

2. William L. Burn, *The Age of Equipoise: A Study of the Mid-Victorian Generation* (London, 1964).

3. The question of Britain's response to the war is most complex; it is now undergoing reexamination and an extensive body of "revisionist" historiography is developing around it. The reader may wish to sample some other sources listed in the bibliography (pp. 273–74).

4. Benjamin Moran, *The Journal of Benjamin Moran*, ed. Sarah A. Wallace and Frances E. Gillespie, 2 vols. (Chicago, 1949), II, 820; this work will hereafter be cited as Moran, *Journal.* The view above ought to be augmented by two articles: W. D. Jones, "The British Conservatives and the American Civil War," *American Historical Review*, LVIII (April, 1953)—in which the reader is warned of the difficulty that English leaders had in coming to a correct appraisal of the war and is informed that "both the extent and the intensity of Southern sympathy among the Conservatives has generally been exaggerated; and the cultural bond between the Southern planter and the British landowner was a rather slender thread" (p. 543); and Joseph M.

Hernon, "British Sympathies in the Civil War: A Reconsideration," *Journal of Southern History,* XXXIII (August, 1967). See also Martin Duberman, *Charles Francis Adams, 1807–1886* (Boston, 1961), pp. 264–65; Ephraim D. Adams, *Great Britain and the American Civil War,* 2 vols. (New York, 1925), II, 274–305.

5. London *Times,* October 15, 1861.

6. Worthington C. Ford, ed., *A Cycle of Adams Letters, 1861–1865,* 2 vols. (New York, 1920), I, 14.

7. John Morley, *The Life of William Ewart Gladstone* (New York, 1932), II, 70. Reprinted.

8. James Ford Rhodes, *History of the United States from the Compromise of 1850 to 1877,* 7 vols. (New York, 1893–1906), III, 433 for Palmerston's statement. The comment about "deep resentment" against the Morrill Tariff may be found in Van Deusen, *Seward,* pp. 276 and 293; Bright's letter is in the Charles Sumner Papers at Houghton Library, Harvard University, Bright-Sumner, September 6, 1861; Russell's remark about Northern tariff policy is in a copy of a note from Edward Everett in the William H. Seward Papers at the University of Rochester Library, Rochester, N. Y., Russell-Everett, July 12, 1861. It is worth noting also that the Confederate commissioners in Europe were instructed to stress the potentially harmful effects of Northern tariff policy in their conversations with European leaders: see, for example, *ORN,* Ser. II, Vol. III, pp. 191–95, Secretary of State Toombs to Yancey, Rost, Mann, March 16, 1861.

9. Eaton, *Southern Confederacy,* p. 68. Russell wrote Palmerston that if Britain did anything about conditions in America, "it must be on a grand scale," for it would "not do" for European powers to break the blockade merely to get cotton. Russell Papers, PRO 30/22/14, Public Record Office (London), Russell-Palmerston, October 17, 1861. Material in the Public Record Office (hereafter PRO) is used with the permission of the Controller of Her Majesty's Stationery Office.

10. Quoted in Eaton, *Southern Confederacy,* pp. 75–76; "Yancey and Rost sent a dispatch from Paris, October 5, 1861, to the Confederate government in which they reported that the distress among the laboring poor arising from the blockade of the Confederacy was greater in France than in England, that the textile manufacturers were working little more than half-time, and that the stoppage of tobacco importations had thrown many people out of employment" (p. 81). See also *ORN,* Ser. II, Vol. III, 278–80.

11. Asa Briggs, *Victorian People: A Reassessment of Persons and Themes, 1851–1867* (Chicago, 1955), p. 91.

12. G. Kitson Clark, *The Making of Victorian England,* paperback ed. (New York, 1967), p. 43; Burn, *Equipoise,* p. 304.

13. J. B. Conacher, "Party Politics in the Age of Palmerston," in *1859: Entering an Age of Crisis,* ed. Philip Appleman, William Madden, and Michael Wolff (Bloomington, Ind., 1959), p. 163. Professor Burn asserts that many ministers of the mid-nineteenth century were "like poor swimmers, content to cling to a floating plank without much attention to spare for the direction it was carrying them in." He goes on to say that the years before 1868 were marked by "a succession of weak governments or of governments which could remain in existence only by doing very little and being ready to accept all sorts of humiliations in doing that little." *Equipoise,* pp. 219–20. See also Briggs, *Victorian People,* pp. 89–90.

14. Palmerston Papers, Historical Manuscripts Commission (hereafter HMC), Chancery Lane, London, Clarendon-Palmerston, October 16, 1862. The author wishes to thank the Trustees of the Broadlands Estate for permission to consult and quote this invaluable collection.

15. Palmerston once reminded Russell, "Our House of Commons strength is great as to the ability which sits on the Treasury Bench but small as to the Balance of votes which followed us into the lobby and a small number going over or staying away might at any time leave us in a minority." Palmerston Papers, HMC, Palmerston-Russell, December 29, 1859. Some months later in a letter to the Queen he spoke of the always possible chance that "political combinations" might produce "administrative changes." Windsor Castle, Royal Archives (hereafter RA) A29/71, Palmerston-Victoria, June 18, 1861. Material from the Royal Archives is used by gracious permission of Her Majesty Queen Elizabeth II. The prime minister expressed satisfaction with "things as they are" in a letter to Gladstone. Palmerston Papers, HMC, Palmerston-Gladstone, May 21, 1864. In this period, as Professor Burn reminds us, governments were "preoccupied with the problem of remaining in power." Burn, *Equipoise,* p. 219. See also E. D. Adams, *Britain and the Civil War,* I, 76–77.

16. Brian Connell, *Regina V. Palmerston: The Correspondence Between Queen Victoria and Her Foreign and Prime Minister, 1837–1865* (London, 1962), p. 2.

17. Evan John [Simpson], *Atlantic Impact* (New York, 1952). 47, 55. "Evan John" was the author's pen name. His family name—Simpson—does not appear on the title page.

> *Hat der Teufel einen Sohn*
> *Wahrlich ist es Palmerston*

18. Burn, *Equipoise,* p. 18.

19. Walter Bagehot, *Biographical Studies,* ed. Richard H. Hutton (London, 1881), p. 341.

20. Quoted in Barbara Tuchman, *The Proud Tower: A Portrait of the World Before the War, 1890–1914* (New York, 1966), p. 123.

21. Donald Southgate, *"The Most English Minister": The Policies and Politics of Palmerston* (New York, 1966), p. xxiii. A. J. P. Taylor tells us that Palmerston was the hero of England because "he deserved to be." *The Italian Problem in European Diplomacy, 1847–1849* (Manchester, England, 1934), p. 31. Palmerston had on his side "that which is the strongest element in the mental organisation of all human society, namely the public's national prejudices." Anthony Wood, *Nineteenth Century Britain, 1815–1914* (New York, 1960), p. 229, quoting Sidney Herbert.

22. These phrases have been borrowed from Lady Violet Bonham-Carter, *Winston Churchill, An Intimate Portrait* (New York, 1965).

23. *ORN,* Ser. II, Vol. III, 716–18, Lamar-Benjamin, March 20, 1863, quote on p. 717; Russell Papers, PRO, 30/22/14, Palmerston-Russell, October 18, 1861.

24. Russell Papers, PRO 30/22/35, Lyons-Russell, April 9, 15, 1861; 30/22/21, Palmerston-Russell, September 9, 1861; Palmerston believed that "no reliance" could be placed on Lincoln and Seward from week to week. Palmerston Papers, HMC, Palmerston-Lewis, August 26, 1861; somewhat later Russell reported that Undersecretary of State Hammond was "persuaded that Seward wishes to pick a quarrel." Russell-Palmerston, September 6, 1861. In January, Lyons had informed his superiors "that Seward was a man who was wont to make political capital out of Anglo-American relations, and that he would be a dangerous foreign minister, one who would play the old game of seeking popularity at home by displaying violence toward us.' " Van Deusen, *Seward,* pp. 292–93. For added comment on British mistrust of America, see Duberman, *Charles Francis Adams,* p. 267.

25. The foregoing paragraph relies heavily on Evan John, *Atlantic Impact,* pp. 208–19; the comment about Lyon's "wisdom, etc." is from E. D. Adams, *Britain and the Civil War,* I, 67, citing a letter from Russell to Lyons, April 6, 1861 (in the Lyons Papers). The standard biography of the British minister is Thomas Newton, *Lord Lyons: A Record of British Diplomacy,* 2 vols. (London, 1913).

26. Aubrey Wyatt Tilby, *Lord John Russell* (New York, 1931), pp. 185–86.

27. Ibid., p. 186.

28. Allan Nevins, in the introduction to his new edition of James

D. Richardson's, *A Compilation of the Messages and Papers of the Confederacy, Including the Diplomatic Correspondence* (New York, 1966), p. xxvi, quotes Russell on slavery:" . . . in my opinion the men of England would have been forever infamous if, for the sake of their own interest, they had violated the law of nations, and made war, *in conjunction with these slaveholding States of America,* against the Federal States." The italics are in the Nevins quotation.

29. Palmerston Papers, HMC, Letterbook, Palmerston-John Crampton, Feb. 17, 1864. The two preceding quotations are from this source.

30. Van Doren Stern, *When Guns Roared,* pp. 19–27, quote on p. 22.

31. Ibid., p. 17; Stern is quoting Alexander H. Stephens, Confederate vice-president.

32. Tilby, *Lord John Russell,* p. 197.

33. Ibid., . 61.

34. Duberman, *Charles Francis Adams,* p. 264 and *passim.* For Russell's early career see Donald Southgate, *The Passing of the Whigs* (New York, 1962); a witty character sketch of Russell is contained in Burton J. Hendrick, *Statesmen of the Lost Cause* (Boston, 1939), especially Chapter Ten, "Queen Victoria's 'Two Bad Boys.' " Henry Adams, *The Education of Henry Adams,* paperback ed. (Boston, 1961) gives an incisive portrait of the British foreign secretary, but one which ought to be taken with a grain of salt. The acid-penned American secretary of legation is a bit harsh with Lord John. The best life of Russell is perhaps Spencer Walpole, *The Life of Lord John Russell,* 2 vols. (London, 1889). An indispensable source for the study of Russell's foreign policy is the collection of his papers at the PRO. The author would like to thank Mrs. Joan Jander for assistance with this sketch of the foreign secretary.

35. *ORN,* Ser. II, Vol. III, 191–95, R. Toombs to Yancey, Rost, and Mann, March 16, 1861.

36. Frank L. Owsley, *King Cotton Diplomacy,* 2nd ed. rev. (Chicago, 1959), p. 51.

37. Ibid.; see also pp. 52–86 for detailed treatment of the mission of Yancey, Rost, and Mann.

38. E. D. Adams, *Britain and the Civil War,* I, 67.

39. Eaton, *Southern Confederacy,* p. 71, gives a capsule description of Mason and his fitness for the London post. Perhaps the best commentary—surely one of the most succinct—on Mason is provided by Allan Nevins in his introduction to Richardson, *Messages and Papers of the Confederacy,* p. xxxviii.

40. For a somewhat kinder estimate of Mason, see Owsley, *King Cotton,* pp. 203–204.

41. Evan John, *Atlantic Impact*, p. 52. The following résumé of the career of Adams is heavily based on the following: Duberman, *Charles Francis Adams;* Henry Adams, *Education;* Charles Francis Adams, Jr., *Charles Francis Adams* (New York, 1900); Charles Francis Adams, Jr., *An Autobiography* (Cambridge, Mass., 1913); Samuel Flagg Bemis *John Quincy Adams and the Union* (New York, 1956); Jay Monaghan, *Diplomat in Carpet Slippers* (Indianapolis, 1962); and most importantly, the Diary of Charles Francis Adams (microfilm), hereafter cited as CFA, Diary.

42. Bemis, *John Quincy Adams,* p. 95.

43. Ibid., p. 480.

44. Quoted in C. F. Adams, Jr., *Charles Francis Adams,* p. 69.

45. Ibid., p. 113.

46. CFA, Diary, January 21, 1861; the comment about the political ruin of Adams and Seward is quoted in H. Adams, *Education,* p. 106. See also C. F. Adams, Jr., *Charles Francis Adams,* p. 140.

47. U. S., Congress, House, *Congressional Globe,* 36th Cong., 2nd sess., 1861, Append., pp. 124–27. For the Adams-Seward plan of mediation see CFA, Diary, *passim;* for Seward's speech see Van Deusen, *Seward,* pp. 244–46. See also Nevins, *Improvised War,* pp. 14–15 and C. F. Adams, Jr., *Charles Francis Adams,* pp. 140–46.

48. For a good account of the intra-cabinet struggle within the new administration see Nevins, *Improvised War,* pp. 37–66, Chapter Three, "Contest for Power: Seward and Lincoln." Van Deusen, *Seward,* pp. 279–84, has a good account of the controversial "Thoughts for the President's Consideration" of April 1, 1861, and that document, with Lincoln's reply, is printed in *The Collected Works of Abraham Lincoln,* ed. Roy P. Basler *et al.,* 8 vols. (New Brunswick, N. J., 1953), IV, 316–18.

49. For Lincoln's "official" explanation of his acceptance of Adams, see Basler, ed. *Collected Works of Lincoln,* IV, 292, Lincoln-Seward, March 18, 1861. The story of the appointment of Adams has been well told in Monaghan, *Diplomat in Carpet Slippers,* paperback ed. (Indianapolis, Ind., 1962), *passim.* See also C. F. Adams, Jr., *Charles Francis Adams,* pp. 140–46; Henry Adams' account of the early days of his father's mission is in *Education,* pp. 105–15 and *passim.*

50. CFA, Diary, March 8, 1861.

51. Quoted in Duberman, *Charles Francis Adams,* p. 257.

52. CFA, Diary, *passim,* and C. F. Adams, Jr., *Charles Francis Adams,* pp. 145–46.

53. James Truslow Adams, *The Adams Family* (New York, 1930), p. 255; H. Adams, *Education,* p. 114.

54. Russell Papers, PRO 30/22/21, Palmerston-Russell, December 30, 1860.

55. Palmerston Papers, HMC, Palmerston-Ellice, May 5, 1861.

56. *Hansard Parliamentary Debates,* 3rd Ser. (1830–91), CLXII, 1378–79.

57. Liverpool *Mercury,* May 4, 1861; at the other end of the country a similar view was expressed: belligerent rights were a "question of the very highest importance to the shipping and commercial interests of the kingdom." Southampton *Times,* April 20, 1861.

58. *Punch,* May 18, 1861.

59. British Foreign Office records on deposit at the Public Record Office, London, FO 414/17, Russell-Lyons, June 21, 1861.

60. *ORN,* Ser. II, Vol. III, 247–48, Russell-Yancey, Rost, Mann, August 24, 1861.

61. Sumner Papers, Bright-Sumner, May 16, 1865; the remarks of Sumner and Welles are quoted in Hamilton Cochran, *Blockade Runners of the Confederacy* (Indianapolis, 1958), p. 15. The British solicitor-general, Roundell Palmer, later noted that Americans were distressed by "recognition of the Confederates as belligerents, and complained much and often of it as an unfriendly act; though on what other footing they could have maintained a blockade of the Southern ports, visited and searched British merchant ships at sea, and seized British vessels for contraband as breach of blockade, was not explained." Quoted in Tilby, *Lord John Russell,* p. 204, note.

62. Glasgow *Herald,* July 3, 1861; much of the press stood firm against intervention, see Nevins, *War Becomes Revolution,* p. 247.

63. *Punch,* August 17, 1861 and September 28, 1861; see also Oscar Maurer, " 'Punch' on Slavery and Civil War in America, 1841–1865," *Victorian Studies,* I (September, 1957), 5–28.

64. E. D. Adams, *Britain and the Civil War,* I, 111; see also Nevins, *War Becomes Revolution,* pp. 253–54; Duberman, *Charles Francis Adams,* pp. 259–62.

65. Van Deusen, *Seward,* p. 295.

66. Duberman, *Charles Francis Adams,* p. 261.

67. Van Deusen, *Seward,* p. 295.

68. Ibid., pp. 296–99; Duberman, *Charles Francis Adams,* p. 268.

69. For a copy of Dispatch #10 see Basler, ed., *Collected Works of Lincoln,* IV, 376–80, and Allen T. Rice, "A Famous Diplomatic Dispatch," *North American Review,* CCCLIII (April, 1886), 402–10.

70. E. D. Adams, *Britain and the Civil War,* I, 127. See also Duberman, *Charles Francis Adams,* p. 268 and Van Deusen, *Seward,* p. 298.

71. Duberman, *Charles Francis Adams,* pp. 268–69, and for the "war

in five minutes" see Ford, *Cycle,* I, 16–18, Henry Adams-Charles Francis Adams, Jr., July 2, 1861; quotation is on p. 17.

72. E. D. Adams, *Britain and the Civil War,* I, 140 and *passim,* especially Chapter Five; Duberman has a good account of the negotiations in *Charles Francis Adams,* pp. 269–72.

73. Van Deusen, *Seward,* p. 295.

74. Quoted in Duberman, *Charles Francis Adams,* p. 271.

CHAPTER THREE

1. Raphael Semmes, *Memoirs of Service Afloat During the War Between the States* (Baltimore, 1869), p. 92; Edna and Frank Bradlow, *Here Comes the Alabama* (Cape Town, South Africa, 1958), pp. 19–20.

2. Charles G. Summersell, *The Cruise of C. S. S. Sumter* (Tuscaloosa, Ala., 1965), pp. 9–10. For an evaluation of Semmes' professional capabilities see Bulloch, *Secret Service,* I, 288–90.

3. Philip Van Doren Stern, *The Confederate Navy: A Pictorial History* (New York, 1962), p. 30.

4. Quoted in Summersell, *Cruise of Sumter,* pp. 50–51.

5. Ibid., pp. 52–59.

6. Ibid., pp. 60–70.

7. *ORN,* Ser. II, Vol. II, 64–65, Mallory-Bulloch, May 9, 1861.

8. Virgil Carrington Jones, *The Civil War at Sea,* 3 vols., (New York, 1960–62), I, 109–10.

9. From a speech by Charles Sumner reported in the *New York Tribune,* September 11, 1863, extract in the William L. Dayton Papers, Box 6, Princeton University Library.

10. *ORN,* Ser. II, Vol. II, 589, Bulloch-Mallory, February 18, 1864.

11. Bradlow, *Here Comes the Alabama,* p. 105. A further testimony to the effectiveness of the cruisers was furnished by the American consul at Hong Kong, who wrote to Dudley at Liverpool, telling him that the *Alabama's* presence in the Far East was making it virtually impossible to find freight for Northern vessels. Thomas H. Dudley Papers, Huntington Library (San Marino, Calif.), DU 717, Horace N. Congar-Dudley, April 19, 1864.

12. Bulloch, *Secret Service,* I, 70; *ORN,* Ser. II, Vol. II, Bulloch-Mallory, August 13, 1861, which details the opening steps of the mission. George Trenholm, of the Charleston, S.C., "home" office of this company, later became Confederate secretary of the treasury. The close business and social ties of the two branches were a considerable asset to Bulloch.

13. Van Doren Stern, *When Guns Roared,* p. 102.

14. Ibid., pp. 102–104; Moran, *Journal,* II, 832–33.

15. U.S., State Department Records, National Archives (NA), Washington, D.C., Consular Dispatches, Liverpool, XX, Dudley-Seward, December 11, 1861. Spelling and capitalization in this quotation have been slightly modified.

16. There are frequent references to Union counter efforts at Liverpool in the Dudley Papers at the Huntington Library, and Van Doren Stern has made much of this information available in his *When the Guns Roared.* See also Harriet C. Owsley, "Henry Shelton Sanford and Federal Surveillance Abroad, 1861–1865," *Mississippi Valley Historical Review,* XLVIII (September, 1961), 211–28.

17. U.S., State Department Records, NA, Consular Dispatches, Belgium, V, Sanford-Seward, July 26, August 15, 1861. According to Sanford, Bulloch was the South's "most dangerous" agent and fully qualified for his job.

18. E. D. Adams, *Britain and the Civil War,* I, 94–95; London *Times,* June 3, 1861; Foreign Office Records on deposit at Public Record Office, London, FO 5/1315 for a copy of the order of June 1, 1861, prohibiting prizes from entrance to British ports.

19. E. D. Adams, *Britain and the Civil War,* II, 149.

20. Bulloch, *Secret Service,* I, 65–66.

21. Ibid., p. 67.

22. Papers Relating to the *Alabama,* in Her Majesty's Custom and Excise Library (hereafter C & 'E Library), London, Hamel-Board of Customs, November 7, 1862.

23. Quoted in Bulloch, *Secret Service,* I, 97.

24. Ibid., pp. 67–68, 54–66.

25. For a description of Liverpool in the 1860s see *Illustrated London News,* April 20, 1865. For a colorful account of Bulloch's early days in Liverpool and of the importance of Fraser-Trenholm to his mission, see Edward Boykin, *Sea Devil of the Confederacy* (New York, 1959), pp. 80–86. The response of Liverpool and its surrounding area to the Civil War has been carefully studied in an important piece of research—Mary Louise Ellison, "The Reaction of Lancashire to the American Civil War," Ph.D. thesis, University of London, 1968. Dudley's comment about pro-South partisanship is in NA, Consular Dispatches, Liverpool, XX, Dudley-Seward, December 11, 1861.

26. Some of the more accessible sources giving information about the start of Southern activity are: Bulloch, *Secret Service,* I, 54–58; William Stanley Hoole, *Four Years in the Confederate Navy* (Athens, Ga., 1964),

pp. 24–26, 37–39. One informant told Dudley that "nothing in American waters" could catch the *Florida:* Dudley Papers, DU 1487, "Federal" Dudley, March 22, 1862.

27. For details of the early *Alabama* negotiations one may consult Bulloch, *Secret Service,* I, especially pp. 54–96; *ORN,* Ser. II, Vol. II, 440, Mallory-Bulloch, June 19, 1863. (The naval secretary insisted that the three most important requirements for a cruiser were "speed, speed, speed.") Bulloch's first major dispatch, which recounts his initial difficulties in England, may be found in *ORN,* Ser. II, Vol. II, Bulloch-Mallory, August 13, 1861, pp. 83–87. Bradlow, *Here Comes the Alabama,* p. 24 and *passim;* Kenneth Poolman, *The Alabama Incident* (London, 1958), *passim;* Van Doren Stern, ed., *Confederate Raider Alabama,* pp. 33–34; FO 5/1318-1333, "The Case of the Alabama" on deposit at the PRO, London, contains much information about this tangled affair; other aspects of the ship's career may be followed out in U.S., State Department, comp., *Correspondence Concerning Claims Against Great Britain,* 7 Vols. (Washington, 1869–71).

28. Van Doren Stern, *Confederate Navy,* pp. 36–38.

29. This contretemps, which illustrates some of the communication difficulties facing the Confederacy, may be traced in *ORN,* Ser. II, Vol. II, 98–99, 130, 176–77, 192–93, 229. Clarence Yonge, the turncoat Southerner, described North by saying ". . . his walk and everything about him indicate an indolent, rather than an energetic disposition." Dudley Papers, DU 4492, Yonge-Dudley, September [?], 1863.

30. U.S., State Department, comp., *Papers Relating to the Foreign Affairs of the United States, 1861–68,* 19 vols. (Washington, 1862–69). Hereafter this collection will be cited as *FR:year.* The information for the views of the British foreign secretary may be found in *FR: 1862,* pp. 39–40, 62–63, Russell-Adams, March 27, 1862. For North's refusal to take command of the ship see *ORN,* Ser. II, Vol. II, 141–42, Prioleau-North, February 8, 1862 and 147, North-Mallory, February 22, 1862.

31. Bulloch, *Secret Service,* I, 152–224; Hoole, *Four Years in the Confederate Navy,* pp. 23–36, especially 27–28.

32. Hoole, *Four Years in the Confederate Navy,* p. 29.

33. The PRO has a valuable collection of material on this Caribbean confrontation of Crown and cruiser in FO 5/1313 and FO 5/1314. More easily available—and based on impressive and wide-ranging sources—is Frank L. Owsley, Jr., *The C.S.S. Florida: Her Building and Operations* (Philadelphia, 1965). This may be supplemented with Hoole, *Four Years in the Confederate Navy,* pp. 31–36.

34. Bulloch, *Secret Service,* I, 165–66; Wilbur D. Jones, *The Confederate Rams at Birkenhead: A Chapter in Anglo-American Relations*

(Tuscaloosa, Ala., 1961), pp. 34–42; Hoole, *Four Years in the Confederate Navy,* pp. 33–34. The British side of the story may be found in the PRO, FO 5/1313 'and 1314.

35. FO 5/1313, Bayley-Newcastle, August 11, 1862, cited in W. D. Jones, *Confederate Rams,* pp. 41–42.

36. Van Doren Stern, *Confederate Navy,* pp. 114–16; Owsley, The *Florida,* pp. 37–42; Boykin, *Sea Devil,* 118–28; Bulloch, *Secret Service,* I, 172.

37. Owsley, *Florida,* pp. 50–55.

38. Stern, *Confederate Navy,* p. 128.

39. For details of the last days of the *Florida* see F. L. Owsley, Jr., "The Capture of the CSS Florida," *American Neptune,* XXII (January, 1962), 45–54; and the same author's, *Florida, passim.* The Glasgow *Herald* referred to the capture at Bahia as "a dastardly and cowardly act on the part of the Americans." Extracted in Greenock *Advertiser,* November 10, 1864.

CHAPTER FOUR

1. Charles Francis Adams, Jr., *Charles Francis Adams,* p. 211.

2. There is no up-to-date study of this famous incident, though Professor Gordon H. Warren is preparing a book about it. The "standard" account remains Thomas L. Harris, *The Trent Affair* (Indianapolis, Ind., 1896). Additional references to the literature on the subject are given in the bibliography (p. 266).

3. Monaghan, *Diplomat in Carpet Slippers,* p. 165, citing William Howard Russell, *My Diary North and South* (Boston, 1863), p. 237. Russell is, of course, also responsible for the cat-and-mouse comment. Recent research on the French response to the Civil War suggests that Slidell's reputation will be revised downward.

4. The statements concerning the reputation of Wilkes may be found in William Jeffries, "The Civil War Career of Charles Wilkes," *Journal of Southern History,* XI (August, 1945), 324–48 (the statement about his insubordination, impulsiveness, zeal and efficiency is on p. 324; for his self-esteem and deficiency of judgment see Nevins, *Improvised War,* p. 388).

5. Frank Moore, ed., *The Rebellion Record: A Diary of American Events, with Documents, Narratives, Illustrative Incidents, Poetry, etc.,* 12 vols. (New York, 1862–71), III, 324–25, 333–34. The sentiments of the passengers are contained in a report by Fairfax's assistant, Lt. James Greer; the incident of Miss Slidell was recounted by Commander Williams in a speech on December 12, 1861, in England.

6. Nevins, *Improvised War*, p. 390.

7. Welles' remark is quoted in Victor Cohen, "Charles Sumner and the Trent Affair," *Journal of Southern History*, XXII (May, 1956), 205–19, quotation on p. 206. U.S., Congress, House, *Congressional Globe*, 37th Cong., 2nd sess., 1861, p. 5. The views of the *N.Y. Times* and of the governor of Massachussets are quoted in Arnold Whitridge, "The Trent Affair, 1861," *History Today*, IV (June, 1954), 394–402, citations on p. 396. The sentiment of C. F. Adams, Jr., is contained in his "The Trent Affair," *Massachusetts Historical Society Proceedings*, XLV (November, 1911), 35–148, especially p. 37.

8. Quoted in Nevins, *Improvised War*, p. 388.

9. Quoted in Robin Winks, *Canada and the United States: The Civil War Years* (Baltimore, 1960), p. 96.

10. Palmerston Papers, HMC, Lewis-Palmerston, November 27, 1861.

11. Cowley Papers, PRO, FO 519/190, Hammond-Cowley, December 2, 1861.

12. RA C13/44, Victoria-Russell, November 28, 1861, and Y107/23, Victoria-Leopold, December 4, 1861.

13. Russell Papers, PRO, 30/22/21, Palmerston-Russell, November 29, 1861. Professor Duberman points out that Palmerston "apparently acted as a pacifying force in the cabinet. He objected to the original draft of Russell's note to Seward as being too strong and he supported Prince Albert's proposed alterations." See his *Charles Francis Adams*, pp. 476–77, note 74.

14. Palmerston Papers, HMC, Russell-Palmerston, December 7, 1861; on the same day the foreign secretary told his minister at Paris: "I think now the American Gvt.—under the inspiration of Seward will refuse us redress. The prospect is melancholy, but it is an obligation of honour which we cannot escape." Cowley Papers, PRO, FO 519/199, Russell-Cowley, December 7, 1861.

15. CFA, Diary, especially November 29, December 1, 2, 5, 9, 10, 1861. His son's comment is in Ford, ed., *Cycle*, I, 75–76, Henry Adams-Charles Francis Adams, Jr., November 30, 1861.

16. DU 4573, Wilding-Adams, November 27, 1861. Two days later Wilding reported to Frederick Seward that the feeling in Britain was "almost universally adverse & very bitter."

17. Seward Papers, Weed-Seward, December 2, 1961, and December 18, 1861.

18. London *Times*, November 29, 1861. *Illustrated London News*, November 30, 1861, cited in Benjamin Sacks, "Lord Palmerston's Diplomatic Partisanship in Favor of the Confederate States During the

American Civil War, April, 1861—October 24, 1862," MA thesis, 1927, McGill University.

19. Liverpool *Mercury,* November 30, 1861.

20. Southampton *Times,* November 30, 1861.

21. Glasgow *Herald,* November 28, 1861.

22. E. D. Adams, *Britain and the Civil War,* I, 212–13.

23. Van Deusen, *Seward,* pp. 306–17.

24. Bradford Perkins, review of *Britain and the Balance of Power in North America, 1815–1908* by Kenneth Bourne, *Journal of American History,* LV (June, 1968), 124–25. See also Kenneth Bourne, "British Preparations for War with the North, 1861–1862," *English Historical Review,* CCCI (October, 1961), 600–32, especially p. 629.

25. Russell Papers, PRO, 30/22/14, Victoria-Russell, October 28, 1860. The original letter is in RA C12/66; see also N23/107, Victoria-Lord Canning, August 2, 1860.

26. Palmerston Letter Book, British Museum, 48582, Palmerston-Somerset, June 23, 1861; for another expression of this view see Russell Papers, PRO, 30/22/14, Palmerston-Russell, October 27, 1863; and for still another, Palmerston Papers, HMC, Palmerston-Russell, November 7, 1861.

27. Cowley Papers, PRO, FO 519/199, Palmerston-Russell, December 30, 1861. Some months earlier, Hammond had told Cowley: "I do not believe in the honesty of the French in American matters." Cowley Papers, FO 519/190, Hammond-Cowley, September 21, 1861. When Britain saw France "cherishing, nursing and increasing her Naval Forces," Russell once told Cobden, the nation grew wary of a friendship which appeared "in so suspicious a guise." Cowley Papers, PRO, FO 519/199, Russell-Cobden, April 2, 1861 (copy). There are frequent references in the Palmerston Papers to the aggressive and threatening aspect of French naval policy.

28. Van Deusen, *Seward,* p. 313.

29. The Bright letter is quoted in E. D. Adams, *Britain and the Civil War,* I, 232; see also the accounts in Van Deusen, *Seward,* pp. 314–17 and Duberman, *Charles Francis Adams,* pp. 281–84.

30. Van Deusen, *Seward,* p. 316.

31. *ORN,* Ser. II, Vol. III, 310, Russell-Yancey, Rost, Mann, December 7, 1861.

32. London *Times,* January 11, 1862.

33. Ford, ed. *Cycle,* I, 99.

34. E. D. Adams, *Britain and the Civil War,* I, 243; see also Eaton, *History of the Confederacy,* p. 72.

35. *ORN*, Ser. II, Vol. II, 148–49, Semmes-North, February 26, 1862.

36. Ibid., p. 167, North-Mallory, March 16, 1862. Some Englishmen also noted a change in sentiment. On February 2, 1862, Bright told Sumner that the reaction against the South after the affair "has had a wonderful effect in calming men's minds." It was, he said, "difficult to find a noisy advocate of the secession theory." Sumner Papers, Bright-Sumner, February 2, 27, 1862.

37. *ORN*, Ser. II, Vol. II, 183, Bulloch-Mallory, April 11, 1862.

38. Bulloch, *Secret Service*, I, 61–62.

39. DU 4573, Dudley-Seward, May 16, 1862.

40. Bradlow, *Here Comes the Alabama*, p. 23.

41. *ORN*, Ser. II, Vol. II, 217, Mallory-Bulloch, July 12, 1862; pp. 444–45, Bulloch-Mallory, June 30, 1863.

42. Bulloch, *Secret Service*, I, 230–32.

43. NA, Consular Dispatches, Belgium, V, Sanford-Seward, September 24, 1861.

44. FO 5/1318, Customs-Treasury, July 1, 1862.

45. C & E Library, Papers Relating to the *Alabama*, Hamel-Board of Customs, June 30, 1862. On the same day, still another investigation of the request for seizure took place; the conclusion was that "at present there is not sufficient ground to warrant the detention of that vessel or any interference on the part of this department in the matter." Freemantle and Berkeley-Treasury, June 30, 1862.

46. C & E Library, Papers Relating to the *Alabama*, Hamel-Board of Customs, July 11, 1862.

47. FO 5/1318, Collier-Foreign Office, July 23, 1862. It was this opinion that moved the case into the hands of the chief law officers of the Crown, but because of Sir John Harding's illness they did not rule on the matter until July 29, when Atherton and Palmer advised the Foreign Office that "without loss of time the vessel be seized by the proper authorities." Papers Relating to the *Alabama*, C & E Library, Law Office-Foreign Office, July 29, 1862. The author would like to thank Mr. Rupert Jarvis, former Librarian of the Customs and Excise Library, for permitting me to use the papers in his care, and for taking time to discuss the ever-fascinating escape of the *Alabama* and the problems it raised for British officials. Mr. Jarvis has set forth his views on that subject in "The Alabama and the Law," *Transactions* of the Historic Society of Lancashire and Cheshire, CXI (October, 1959), 181–98.

48. Bulloch, *Secret Service*, I, 229, 238; Hoole, *Four Years in the Confederate Navy*, p. 47 and *passim*.

49. Douglas Maynard, "Union Efforts to Prevent the Escape of the 'Alabama,'" *Mississippi Valley Historical Review*, XLI (June, 1954),

41–60. See the same author's "Plotting the Escape of the Alabama," *Journal of Southern History*, XX (May, 1954), 197–209. Bulloch, *Secret Service*, I, 229; George Dalzell, *The Flight From the Flag* (Chapel Hill, N.C., 1940); Dalzell identifies the source of Bulloch's tip as "a clerk in the Foreign Office named Victor Buckley," but gives no source for the information—see especially p. 131. A man who was on friendly terms with Price Edwards (collector of customs at Liverpool) regarded him as "a very warm sympathizer with the Confederates and their cause." When this friend noted the press tendency to blame Edwards for the escape and asked about it, Edwards replied: "My dear boy how could I prevent it, for I was out of the way, at the very top of the pool, when she sailed." The friend received the very distinct impression that Edwards was "purposely out of the way" when the *Alabama* sailed. DU 3964, Deposition of W. Thitherington, January 24, 1872. Philip Van Doren Stern, *When the Guns Roared* (New York, 1965), *passim*.

50. Quoted in Hoole, *Four Years in the Confederate Navy*, p. 56.

51. Ibid., pp. 59–61; Alan R. Booth, "*Alabama* at the Cape, 1863," *American Neptune*, XXVI (April, 1966), 96–108.

52. Bulloch, *Secret Service*, I, 266; Union Admiral Farragut described his ship as "my poor little good for nothing Hatteras." Dalzell, *Flight From the Flag*, p. 144.

53. Details of the *Alabama*'s cruise and last days may be found in Van Doren Stern, *Confederate Navy*, *passim*, especially pp. 188–97; Bradlow, *Here Comes the Alabama*, pp. 98–103; Van Doren Stern, ed., *The Confederate Raider Alabama*, *passim*; there is valuable material in the Dayton Papers at Princeton, see especially Box 8; Bulloch, *Secret Service*, I, 277–94; DU 4456, Winslow-Dudley, June 24, 1864.

54. PRO, FO 83/2222, Law Office-Foreign Office, September 15, 1864. The legal advisers asserted that no "act of hostility" was involved in the *Deerhound* rescue and denied American claims that the men brought to Southampton ought to be surrendered. Such an argument, they said, was "so extravagant as to be unworthy of notice."

55. London *Times*, June 21, 1864, quoted in Van Doren Stern, *Confederate Navy*, p. 196.

CHAPTER FIVE

1. *Punch*, September 13, 1862, for an amusing statement of this view. In a cartoon entitled "Not Up To Time" (Americans might say "On The Ropes") *Punch* depicts two pugilists on the point of exhaustion and ready to throw in the towel, with a sub-caption: "Interference Would Be Very Welcome." Somewhat later in the year much of the

press still took for granted the Northern inability to conquer the South. For a fairly typical view see London *Spectator,* December 13, 1862: "We are assuming what all Englishmen now assume, that absolute subjugation of the South is a dream." Cited in Hernon, "British Sympathies in the Civil War," *Journal of Southern History,* XXXIII (August, 1967), 360. On July 3, 1861, the Glasgow *Herald* had expressed the view that "subjugation of the South by the policy of coercion appears an idle dream."

2. RA A30/94, Palmerston-Victoria, July 18, 1862.

3. *ORN,* Ser. II Vol. III, 501–503, Mason-Russell, August 1, 1862.

4. Ibid., 503–504, Russell-Mason, August 2, 1862. Russell's counter argument stated that in order for a state to merit a place among the world's independent nations, it "ought to have not only strength and resources for a time, but afford promise of stability and permanence. Should the Confederate States of America win that place among nations, other nations might justly acknowledge an independence achieved by victory and maintained by a successful resistance to all attempts to overthrow it. That time, however, has not, in the judgment of Her Majesty's Government, yet arrived." See also RA B19/132, Russell-Victoria, August 24, 1862.

5. William E. Gladstone Papers, British Museum (hereafter, BM), Add. MS 44292, CCVII, Russell-Gladstone, September 26, 1862. "It would be very awkward," the foreign secretary noted, "to have a Cabinet upon this, unless France thought the opportunity favourable, & this was previously ascertained." On September 16, Russell had written to the Queen that cabinet discussion of mediation was "probable." RA Q9/115, Russell-Victoria, September 16, 1862. See also Cowley Papers, PRO, FO 519/199, Russell-Cowley, Sept. 26, 1862: "I cannot think the South can now be conquered." Therefore, Russell thought, Britain, Russia, and France ought to join in an offer of mediation, which, if refused, might be followed by notification of an intention "to recognize the Southern States, but continue neutral in the Civil War." He also remarked that the prime minister was in substantial agreement but could not "propose it to France till we see a little more into the results of the Southern invasion of Pennsylvania." Some days later, on October 2, Palmerston told Lewis: "I am not disposed in any case to take up arms to settle the American war by force." George Peabody Gooch, ed., *The Later Correspondence of Lord John Russell, 1840–1878,* 2 vols. (London, 1925), II, 328–29.

6. Russell Papers, PRO, 30/22/14, Palmerston-Russell, September 14, 23, 1862; RA Z463/95, Palmerston-Victoria, September 14, 1862; see also RA Q9/115, 116, 117.

7. Gladstone Papers, BM, Add. MS. 44272, CLXXXVII, Palmerston-

Gladstone, September 24, 1862. In this letter the prime minister suggested that the chancellor's forthcoming speech in the North avoid mention of economy in government and reduction of taxes; there is no suggestion in this letter (or in any other that the author has seen) that the time was ripe to test public sentiment for a change of policy toward the war. An extensive search of the papers of Palmerston, Gladstone, and Russell failed to disclose any evidence that the chancellor spoke for his colleagues. On the contrary, there is ample reason to believe that Gladstone had lost touch with cabinet sentiment as it evolved from mid-September to early October. However that may be, when he spoke at Newcastle, Gladstone did not reflect the views of Palmerston. (It is necessary to note, however, that on October 12, Palmerston told Russell that Gladstone "was not far wrong in pronouncing by anticipation the National independence of the South." Quoted in Duberman, *Charles Francis Adams,* p. 481, note 128, citing Russell Papers, PRO 30/22/22.) Both Russell and Palmerston observed that Gladstone exceeded his powers as a member of the cabinet: on October 17 Palmerston told Russell that the chancellor ought to have kept clear of mentioning future actions "unless authorized by his colleagues to become . . . the organ of the Govt. for announcing Decisions come to upon suitable Deliberation." Quoted in Duberman, *Charles Francis Adams,* p. 481, note 128, citing Russell Papers, PRO 30/22/14. And on October 20, Russell told Gladstone: "Still you must allow me to say that I think you went beyond the latitude which all speakers must be allowed when you said that Jeff Davis had made a nation. Recognition would seem to follow, & for that step I think the Cabinet is not prepared." Gladstone Papers, BM, Add. MS. 44292, CCVII, Russell-Gladstone, October 20, 1862.

8. Palmerston Papers, HMC, Palmerston-Russell, October 2, 1862 and Palmerston-Granville, October 2, 1862: "In fact no offer would be accepted by the North until the South have been more decidedly successful." Future events on the battlefield, Pam said, "must determine our course."

9. Moran, *Journal,* II, 1078; CFA, Diary, October 8, 1862; Palmerston Papers, HMC, Clarendon-Palmerston, October 16, 1862; Gladstone Papers, BM, Add. MS. 44292, CCVII, Russell-Gladstone, October 20, 1862.

10. CFA, Diary, October 9, 11, 1862.

11. E. D. Adams, *Britain and the Civil War,* II, 50–51.

12. CFA, Diary, October 16, 1862.

13. Russell, "Memorandum on the American Civil War," October 13, 1862, copy in the Palmerston Papers, HMC. Though this memo is

neither pro-North nor pro-South, Russell apparently did not understand that his proposal in effect amounted to "Northern acknowledgment of defeat under foreign pressure." Nevins, *War Becomes Revolution*, p. 269.

14. Lewis, "Memorandum on the American Question," October 17, 1862, copy in the Palmerston Papers, HMC. Russell regarded Lewis' speech as "imprudent." In his view there was no necessity for a minister to make public "a line of policy not agreed upon by his colleagues." Palmerston Papers, HMC, Russell-Palmerston, October 18, 1862.

15. Palmerston Papers, HMC, Clarendon-Palmerston, October 16, 1862.

16. E. D. Adams, *Britain and the Civil War*, II, 53.

17. Palmerston Papers, HMC, Russell-Palmerston, October 16, 1862.

18. Russell Papers, PRO, 30/22/14, Palmerston-Russell, October 22, 24, 1862; also in Gooch, ed., *Later Correspondence of Russell*, II, 328.

19. CFA, Diary, October 23, 1862; Moran, *Journal*, II, 1083; see also Duberman, *Charles Francis Adams*, p. 296.

20. Russell, "Answer to Sir G. Lewis's Memorandum Re Mediation in America," October 24, 1862, copy in Palmerston Papers, HMC.

21. Gladstone, "Memorandum on the War in America," October 25, 1862, copy in the Palmerston Papers, HMC. In this, as the author admits, he was arguing in support of the Russell plan.

22. E. D. Adams, *Britain and the Civil War*, II, 57–58. Clarendon told Lewis on October 24 that Russell "always loves to do something when to do nothing is prudent, and I have no doubt that he hoped to get support in his meddling proclivities when he called a Cabinet for yesterday; but its postponement *sine die* is probably due to your memorandum. You have made so clear the idiotic position we should occupy, either in having presented our face gratuitously to the Yankee slap we should receive, or in being asked what practical solutions we had to propose after an armistice had been agreed to at our suggestion, that no discussion on the subject would have been possible, and the Foreign Secretary probably thought it would be pleasanter to draw in his horns at Woburn than in Downing Street." Quoted on p. 58. On the 23rd of the month, Russell and Palmerston had concluded that no advice could be offered to the Queen "at the present moment in relation to the Civil War in America. . . ." RA I36/38, Russell-Victoria, October 23, 1862. Soon after this decision, the French proposal gave Russell's plan a new lease on life.

23. E. D. Adams, *Britain and the Civil War*, II, 59. On November 13, Undersecretary of State A. H. Layard reported that the French did not attach much importance to the offer of mediation in America and that the emperor looked upon the proposal as discharging a duty to human-

ity. Russell Papers, PRO, 30/22/28, Layard-Russell, November 13, 1862. For the Confederate view of the plan see *ORN*, Ser. II, Vol. III, 574–78, "Memorandum of an Interview of Mr. Slidell with the Emperor at St. Cloud on Tuesday," October 28, 1862.

24. E. D. Adams, *Britain and the Civil War*, II, 61, citing a letter from Palmerston-Russell, November 2, 1862.

25. Ibid., pp. 62–63; London *Times*, November 7, 1862.

26. The reasons for rejection are set out clearly in a letter from Palmerston to Leopold of Belgium: "I can assure you that we should have been glad to have adopted the Proposal of the Emperor of the French for a joint communication to the Contending Parties in America if we had thought that such a communication as he proposed could have done any good, and was not, on the contrary, likely to do mischief. There was a time some months ago when we thought an opportunity for making some communication was approaching. The Confederates were gaining ground to the North of Washington, and events seemed to be in their favor. But the tide of war changed its course and the opportunity did not arrive.

In the present state of the war it was not likely that the Federals would agree to an armistice; and it was quite certain that they would not agree to suspend their blockade, and open the Southern ports to supplies of all sorts of things the Confederates are in want of." Palmerston Papers, HMC, Palmerston-Leopold, November 18, 1862. In a note to Russell, Palmerston had earlier said that Southern independence could only be converted into established fact by "the Course of Events alone." Russell Papers, PRO 30/22/14, Palmerston-Russell, October 26, 1862. See also E. D. Adams, *Britain and the Civil War*, II, 64 and *passim*.

27. Duberman, *Charles Francis Adams*, p. 297; for Seward's mid-August instructions to his minister see Moran, *Journal*, II, 1057. For a representative expression of the danger of truckling to Yankees see the Liverpool *Courier*, September 12, 1863: "The Government which proposed to alter the laws of England through dread of a Federal menace would merit impeachment." Palmerston, as is well known, had a keenly felt aversion to creating the slightest impression that he was subservient to any form of foreign pressure. See Duff Cooper, *Talleyrand* (reissue; Stanford, Calif. 1967), p. 328.

28. Nevins, *War Becomes Revolution*, p. 272; Duberman, *Charles Francis Adams*, p. 298; E. D. Adams, *Britain and the Civil War*, II, 72–74; Beloff, "Great Britain and the Civil War," p. 47; Cooper, *Talleyrand, passim*; Southgate, *Most English Minister*, p. xvii. Southgate reminds us of Palmerston's "high responsibility in the hour of greatest crisis," and warns of the common tendency to give it less attention

than it deserves. This chapter owes much to the editorial and stylistic assistance of Professor T. A. Wilson of the University of Kansas.

CHAPTER SIX

1. Ford, ed., *Cycle*, II, 79–89.

2. Charles Sumner Papers, Harvard University, Bright-Sumner, April 4, 1863.

3. Russell Papers, PRO, 30/22/14, Palmerston-Russell, October 2, 1862; ibid., September 14, 1863.

4. Liverpool *Mercury,* December 31, 1863. For a recent statement of the favorable economic impact of the war on one British city, see D. G. Wright, "Bradford and the American Civil War," *Journal of British Studies,* VIII (May, 1969), 69–85.

5. Southampton *Times,* September 12, 1863.

6. Liverpool *Mercury,* December 31, 1863; Russell Papers, PRO 30/22/38, Bruce-Russell, May 19, 1865.

7. Russell Papers, PRO 30/22/26, Argyll to Cabinet, March 8, 1864; ibid., PRO 30/22/96, Russell-Lyons, December 20, 1863. The foreign secretary confessed to a "grudge" against the people of Liverpool because of the *Alabama's* escape.

8. Russell Papers, PRO 30/22/21, Palmerston-Russell, December 30, 1860; ibid., 30/22/14, Palmerston-Russell, October 18, 1861.

9. Gladstone Papers, BM, Add. MS. 44273, Palmerston-Gladstone, November 7, 1864.

10. *ORN,* Ser. II, Vol. II, 191, Mallory-Bulloch, May 7, 1862. Pickett Papers, Library of Congress (hereafter LC) Mason-Benjamin, September 18, 1862. A pro-South Englishman, William S. Lindsay, apparently furnished the funds for this venture, though Mason had no authority to commit the government to the debt.

11. Bulloch, *Secret Service,* II, 272–73; FO 5/1051, Report of the collector of customs at Glasgow, October 21, 1863. Details of the transaction did not turn up until the Foreign Office conducted its investigation.

12. *North British Daily Mail,* September 12, 1864. John Carvel, *Stephen of Linthouse: A Record of Two Hundred Years of Shipbuilding, 1750–1950* (Glasgow, 1950), pp. 42–45. Alexander Stephen and Sons, Ltd., built the beautiful C.S.S. *Shenandoah,* and the manuscript diary of the founder of the firm, Alexander Stephen, is preserved in the company archives at Glasgow, Scotland. The author would like to express his appreciation to the officials of the company for allowing him this fascinating glimpse of Clydesdale shipbuilding in the 1860s.

13. FO 5/1051, for a copy of the *Canton* contract; *ORN,* Ser. II, Vol. II, 416, North-Mallory, May 6, 1863; Douglas Maynard, "The Confederacy's Super-"Alabama," *Civil War History,* V (March, 1959), 80–95.

14. For details of the *Alexandra* affair, see the following: *ORN,* Ser. II, Vol. II, 500–501, Mallory-Bulloch, September 29, 1863; p. 507, Mallory-Barron, October 17, 1863; pp. 515–16, Barron-Sinclair, November 10, 1863.

15. U. S., State Department, comp., *Claims Against Great Britain, II,* 206; NA, Consular Dispatches, Liverpool, XXII, Dudley-Seward, May 2, 1862; NA, Consular Dispatches, Glasgow, Underwood-Seward, *passim.*

16. *FR: 1863,* I, 161, Russell-Adams, March 21, 1863.

17. FO 5/1051, Adams-Russell, October 15, 1863, enclosing a report from the Glasgow consul.

18. FO 5/1051, Opinion of the Solicitor General and the Lord Advocate of Scotland.

19. FO 5/1051, Report of the Chief Constructor of the Navy, November 10, 1863; Trevor-Foreign Office, October 21, 1863; Report of Captain A. Farquhar, October 21, 1863.

20. FO 5/1051, Memorial of the Glasgow Emancipation Society dated November 4, 1863. For Northern influence in the move, see Maynard, "Confederacy's Super-'Alabama,' " p. 88.

21. FO/1051, Sinclair-Pembroke, October 21, 1863. The reader may remember that Britain had detained the famous Laird rams in September, 1863, for which see below, pp. 200–202.

22. FO 5/1051, Foreign Office-Home Office, November 13, 1863. See also Home Office records in PRO, HO 45/7261, Hammond-Waddington, November 13, 1863.

23. FO 5/1051, Foreign Office-Home Office, November 13, 1863; Home Office-Customs Office, November 13, 1863.

24. FO 5/1051, Moncrieff-Grey, November 19, 1863.

25. FO 5/1051, statement of J. Galbraith (part owner of the ship), December 3, 1863; Sinclair-Pembroke, September 24, 1863; HO 45/7261, Moncrieff-Waddington, December 1, 1863.

26. FO 5/1051, Home Office-Foreign Office, December 10, 1863; Report of the Collector of Customs, December 10, 1863.

27. FO 5/1051, Russell-Lord Advocate, March 26, 1864.

28. Brooks Adams, "The Seizure of the Laird Rams," *Massachusetts Historical Society Proceedings,* XLV (December, 1911), 243–333, quotation on 310.

29. Mountague Bernard, *A Historical Account of the Neutrality of Great Britain During the American Civil War* (London, 1870), p. 357

and *passim;* Bulloch, *Secret Service,* II, 273; HO 45/7261, Box V; Glasgow *Herald,* May 7, 1864.

30. Bulloch, *Secret Service,* II, 261–62; for details of Confederate finances abroad consult Owsley, *King Cotton,* pp. 360–93; Samuel Thompson, *Confederate Purchasing Operations Abroad* (Chapel Hill, N. C., 1935), *passim; ORN,* Ser. II, Vol. II, 295, Mallory-Maury, November 7, 1862; Van Doren Stern, *Confederate Navy,* pp. 120–21. The Matthew F. Maury Papers are in the Library of Congress.

31. FO 5/1333, Depositions of Edward Thompson and Thomas Mahon, April 15, 1863; FO 5/1317, Document Appendix, for a description of the ship. Denny and Company of Dumbarton-on-Clyde built the vessel, which was rather small for a raider, measuring 212 feet with a beam of 27 feet and a displacement of about 500 tons. Bulloch, *Secret Service,* II, 261.

32. PRO, HO 45/7261, Report of the Customs Surveyor, April 10, 1863; Bulloch, *Secret Service,* II, 261.

33. *North British Daily Mail,* April 10, 1863.

34. FO 5/1333, reports and dispatches dated April 8–11, 1863, especially a Report of the Solicitor of the Customs at New Haven and the deposition of the captain of the *Alar.*

35. FO 83/2215, Law Office Reports, April 29, May 29, 1863; FO 5/1333, Opinion of Felix Hamel, July 7, 1863.

36. Van Doren Stern, *Confederate Navy,* p. 187.

37. FO 5/1317, Customs-Treasury, May 2, 1864; Foreign Office-Treasury, May 16, 1864; Liverpool *Mercury,* May 19, 1864; HO 45/7261, Box IV.

38. FO 5/1317, Wilding-Adams, July 26, 1864, enclosed in Adams-Russell, July 27, 1864.

39. FO 5/1317, printed dispatch #66, August 11, 1864; See also London *Gazette,* September 9, 1864; FO 5/1317, Report of the Law Officers, September 1, 1864; FO 83/2222, Report of the Law Officers, September 5, 1864.

40. FO 5/1317, Bates-Foreign Office and Foreign Office-Bates, September 19, 1864; Soley, *Blockade and Cruisers,* pp. 214–15.

CHAPTER SEVEN

1. *ORN,* Ser. II, Vol. II, 69, Mallory-Conrad, May 10, 1861.

2. Ibid., pp. 456–57, Bulloch-Mallory, July 9, 1863.

3. Fox-Forbes, April 1, 1863, Box 5, Gustavus V. Fox Papers, on deposit at the New York Historical Society Library, New York, New York:

". . . if the expectations of the builders are fulfilled, they [the rams] may pay you a visit at Boston when you least expect them, or they may disperse the blockading squadron at short notice," Warren-Upton, November 3, 1862, Box 4.

4. U. S., Department of State Records, NA (Washington), Consular Dispatches, Belgium, VI, Sanford-Seward, June 9, 1863.

5. Quoted in Wilbur D. Jones, *Confederate Rams,* p. 61; see also John Bigelow, *France and the Confederate Navy* (New York, 1888), p. 194 and *passim.* For a reappraisal of the capabilities of the rams see below, pp. 213–17.

6. *ORN*, Ser. II, Vol. II, Mallory-North, May 17, 1861. With the assistance of Mr. E. K. Timings of the Public Record Office, London, the author conducted an extensive search of the Admiralty and Foreign Office correspondence for 1861–65, but was unable to find much information about this vessel. The story appears more mysterious still because, while there are index entries for the ship, the materials to which such entries refer did not appear in the designated files. Officials of John Brown and Company, Ltd. (successor to J. and G. Thomson) kindly furnished the author with material from their files on shipbuilding in the 1860s, but—sad to say—there was nothing to shed light on North's vessel or the circumstances surrounding its construction. For their expert assistance in preparation of this chapter, the author would like to thank Mr. William E. Geoghagen, Museum Specialist, Smithsonian Institution, Captain R. Steen Steenson, Royal Danish Navy, and Mr. Thomas W. Green, Southampton, England.

7. The agent left an account of the early days of his mission and of his voyage to Europe. By omission and emphasis, as much as by what it says (and it says very little), the diary is a poignant commentary on the failure of the South. See James Heywood North, Diary and Papers, in the Southern Historical Collection at the University of North Carolina, Chapel Hill.

8. *ORN*, Ser. II, Vol. II, 107, Mallory-North, June 28, 1861; for a fairly typical complaint about the lack of funds, see ibid., p. 87, North-Mallory, August 16, 1861.

9. Ibid., p. 185, North-Mallory, April 14, 1862; for a copy of the contract see ibid., pp. 193–204. Mallory had become impatient with North's lack of progress, and when Bulloch returned to Richmond in late 1861, the Navy Department added ram procurement to his other responsibilities, telling him to cooperate with North, and to get the program moving. Upon his return to Liverpool in the spring of 1862, Bulloch attempted to carry out these orders, but immediately he and North were at daggers drawn. With visions of himself in command,

North wanted a larger ship than Bulloch thought necessary. Despite inexperience in such matters, North refused to heed advice. Eventually, the program divided into two nearly independent phases, with North retaining supervision of Number 61 and Bulloch undertaking construction of the Laird rams.

10. The technical description of Number 61 was worked out by Captain Steensen and Mr. Geoghagen on the basis of information culled from *ORN* and from plans of the *Danmark* in the Danish National Archives: *Panserfregatten Danmark, Orlogsvaerftets, Construktionskontor*, July 3, 1907, #35; see also Lord Thomas Brassey, *The Navy Annual, 1887* (Portsmouth, England, 1887), p. 321 and *passim*. One may note here that *Warrior* and *La Gloire* were *not* rams, and that *Magenta* and *Solferino* (of the French fleet) were the first ironclads to be designed as rams. Information about Number 61 may be found in *ORN*: Ser. II, Vol. II, 71, 223, 461, 731, 340, 458–59, 318, 46, 240, 218–19, 222, 269, and 518. Captain Steensen and Mr. Geoghagen are long-time students of this vessel; they have in their possession a number of sketches and photos of the ship at various points in her career. In addition there is a photo of it in the Dudley Papers at the Huntington Library, San Marino, Calif., as well as a plan of her engine room profile. As late as 1962 this vessel was pictured with two turrets, and in the 1959 edition of *Secret Service*, a double turret ship is incorrectly identified as North's ironclad: photo facing I, 384.

11. *ORN*, Ser. II, Vol. II, 271, Mallory-Bulloch, September 20, 1862.

12. The correspondence of overseas agents with the Navy Department in late 1862 attests to the overextension of the program and the difficulties of meeting financial commitments. See, for example, ibid., pp. 268–69, North-Mallory, September 19, 1862—my dispatches "will tell you of the urgent necessity of sending us money out here. Payments are becoming due, with little or no money to meet [them]." See also pp. 269–71, Mallory-Bulloch, September 20, 1862 (referred to in note 11 above); pp. 291–95, Bulloch-Mallory, November 7, 1862 (More ironclads could be built in Britain, "but I cannot enter upon other contracts until the money to meet present engagements is in hand. . . ."). In this note Bulloch reported that "certain parties" were willing to advance funds for an ironclad if Fraser-Trenholm would guarantee repayment of the ship's cost. Bulloch's estimate of the money market and his willingness to allow Spence the initiative in tapping it are contained in pp. 303–305, Bulloch-North, November 26, 1862.

13. Ibid., p. 269, North-Mallory, September 19, 1862. At about this time Mason had assumed responsibility for advancing some £60,000 to Lt. Sinclair to allow him to start construction of the *Canton*; for details

of this vessel see below and Douglas Maynard, "The Confederacy's Super-"Alabama," *Civil War History,* V (March, 1959), 80–95.

14. *ORN,* Ser. II, Vol. II, 269–70, Mallory-Bulloch, September 20, 1862; pp. 287, 303–305, Bulloch-North, November 26, 1862; pp. 311–12, Bulloch-North, December 18, 1862.

15. Ibid., pp. 319, 322–23, Bulloch-North, December 23, 1862; December 28, 1862.

16. Ibid., p. 313, North-Bulloch, December 22, 1862.

17. Ibid., p. 325, Bulloch-North, December 31, 1862.

18. Ibid., p. 329, North-Bulloch, January 2, 1863.

19. Ibid., p. 337, Bulloch-North, January 9, 1863; pp. 337–38, North-Bulloch, January 12, 1863.

20. Ibid., pp. 351–52, Bulloch-Mallory, February 3, 1863. In this dispatch Bulloch again complained that fiscal affairs were in great confusion. "There seems to be much division of authority and opinion upon the subject, and there are numerous agents of different departments pressing for money, and it will be difficult to decide in what order to honor their requisitions." For a convenient summary of the disorganization in Confederate finances, see Charles S. Davis, *Colin J. McRae: Confederate Financial Agent* (Tuscaloosa, Ala., 1961), especially Chapter Four.

21. *ORN,* Ser. II, Vol. II, 366, Mason-North, February 21, 1863 (for Mason's "let them do it" remark) and pp! 366–68, Mallory-Bulloch, February 21, 1863.

22. *ORN,* Ser. II, Vol. III, 569–72, Slidell-Benjamin, October 28, 1862, for a copy of the original Erlanger proposal.

23. Ibid., pp. 654–56, Benjamin-Slidell, January 15, 1863.

24. Ibid., pp. 675–77, Mason-Benjamin, February 5, 1863 and pp. 590–93, Mason-Benjamin, November 4, 1862. In the November note, Mason reported the willingness of one British firm to purchase cotton certificates worth "from a quarter to a half million pounds sterling." Mason clearly preferred this form of financing over that proposed by Erlanger, but when asked to comment on the Slidell proposal, Mason said: "Do not understand, therefore, that the absence of my name from the paper [Slidell's proposal sent to London for his approval] imports anything more than a want of proper information." This statement, appearing on p. 592, hardly seems strong enough to support a contention that the London commissioner "must have felt that Erlanger's proposition was nothing short of a holdup." Owsley, *King Cotton,* p. 371. For the impact of the negotiations on North, see, for example, *ORN,* Ser. II, Vol. II, 329, North-Bulloch, January 2, 1863.

25. *ORN,* Ser. II, Vol. III, 730, Mason-Benjamin, March 30, 1863.

26. Ibid., pp. 735–37 and 737–38, Mason-Benjamin, April 9, 1863 and copy of the agreement to bull the market.

27. Samuel B. Thompson, *Confederate Purchasing Operations Abroad* (Chapel Hill, N.C., 1935), pp. 70–75. Thompson warns that all estimates about the proceeds of these maneuvers are little more than guesses (p. 70). It would seem, he says, the Confederates "pledged $45,000,000 worth of cotton to obtain $6,800,000 of credit in Europe for the purchasing agents" (p. 71). Owsley estimates that the total amount of cash that found its way into Confederate coffers was about $2,599,000 *(King Cotton,* p. 380). For a recent study of the affair see Richard Lester, "Confederate Finance and Purchasing in Great Britain During the American Civil War," (Ph.D. thesis, University of Manchester, England, 1962). For another account of Southern financial difficulties see James M. Callahan, *Diplomatic History of the Southern Confederacy* (Baltimore, 1901), pp. 54–65 and *passim.* There is an engaging account of the episode in Hendrick, *Statesmen of the Lost Cause,* Chapter Eight, "French Bankers Fleece the Confederacy," pp. 216–32. A concise treatment of the affair may be found in Davis, *Colin McRae,* Chapter Three.

28. *ORN,* Ser. II, Vol. II, 411–12, Hamilton-North, May 1, 1863: "Lord Palmerston's Government is opposed to the aspirations of the Southern people, and there is nothing it dares do to harm and to embarras us that it will not do." One agent confessed himself frightened by Adams' "wonderful influence over Earl Russell" p. 413, North-Slidell, May 2, 1863. Expressions of a growing anti-Southern sentiment on the part of British officials appear more frequently in the Confederate dispatches of 1863, while Northerners, in turn, were sure that Her Majesty's ministers were pro-South.

29. *ORN,* Ser. II, Vol. II, 409, Hamilton-North, April 23, 1863.

30. Ibid., pp. 415–16, 419–20, North-Mallory, May 6, 8, 1863.

31. Ibid., pp. 413–14, North-Slidell, May 2, 1863; Slidell-North, May 5, 1863. Slidell's reference was to the negotiations then underway to transfer the Laird rams to French registry.

32. Ibid., pp. 439–40, Lamar, Mason, Slidell-North, June 13, 1863.

33. Ibid., p. 440, Mason-North, June 16, 1863.

34. Ibid., pp. 476–78, Bulloch-Mallory, August 7, 1863.

35. Ibid., p. 443, North-Mason, June 26, 1863; p. 443, Mason-North, June 27, 1863; p. 443, North-Thomson, June 27, 1863.

36. Ibid., pp. 450–51, North-Mallory, July 3, 1863.

37. Ibid., pp. 471–72, Bulloch-North, July 28, 1863.

38. Ibid., Thomson-North, September 25, 1863; pp. 504–507, North-Mallory, October 16, 1863; pp. 487–89, Bulloch-Mallory, September 1, 1863; p. 502, Bulloch-Mallory, October 1, 1863.

39. Ibid., p. 527, Bulloch-Mallory, November 26, 1863; 519, North-Mason, November 21, 1863; p. 567, Barron-Mallory, December 15, 1863; p. 566, North-Mallory, December 14, 1863.

40. Ibid., pp. 326–29, Memorandum of a meeting between Messrs. Slidell, Mason, Barron, McRae, and North. This memo is followed by the articles of agreement between Thomson and the Danish agents. Further details of the transaction may be found on pp. 704, 705, 730, 735, 737.

41. Ibid., p. 785, Barron-North, January 2, 1865.

42. Ibid., p. 587, North-Mallory, February 18, 1864.

43. Ibid., p. 518, Barron-Mallory, November 10, 1863.

44. Capt. Steensen—author, various dates. Capt. Steensen cites *Marine Rundschau,* 1897, pp. 343–46, for Guyot's description, but thinks it may have been an underestimation. He suggests that the decision of the Danish naval authorities to rebuild its decks in 1876–77 is a kind of prima facie evidence of the hull's structural strength.

45. R. Steen Steensen, "Vore Panserkibe" ("Our Armorclads") in *Tidsskrift for Søvaesen* (May, 1966), pp. 233–65. Capt. Steensen kindly provided a translation from the Danish of this article for the author's use.

46. *North British Daily Mail,* February 25, 1864. This account of the launching includes a detailed description of the vessel and of the difficulty in getting it into the river. The ship, according to this paper, was "the first armour-clad vessel which has been launched with all her armour plates on."

47. Glasgow *Daily Herald,* August 27, 1864. The reporter for this paper estimated the ship's speed at about 12 knots; Capt. Steensen questions this estimate and writes that in the Danish navy its best speed was about 8.5 knots.

48. *Illustreret Tidende* (Illustrated News [Copenhagen]), October 24, 1869. Translation by Capt. Steensen.

49. When equipped by the Danes, the *Danmark* carried the following armament:

> twelve 8-inch 144 hundredweight rifled muzzle loaders
>
> twelve 6-inch 50 hundredweight rifled muzzle loaders
>
> two 18-pounder carronades
>
> eight 4-pounder howitzers

The ship continued to have a serious tactical shortcoming—no bow or stern firepower—so the Danes again rebuilt it some years later. The upper layers of the side armor aft were bent athwart-ship so that the after guns from each broadside battery could shift from their ports to new ports in the bent armor aft, permitting them to train parallel to the keel. But from dead ahead and for 65 degrees on each bow there was no arc of fire (a proposed set of nine-inch bow guns were never mounted). In the refit of 1867–68, major modifications in armament again were made, so that thereafter the ship carried:

eight 8-inch 176 hundredweight, rifled muzzle-loaders (on battery)

four 8-inch 144 hundredweight, rifled muzzle-loaders (on deck)

twelve 6-inch 50 hundredweight, rifled muzzle-loaders (on battery)

two three-inch 6 hundredweight, rifled muzzle-loaders (on deck)

CHAPTER EIGHT

1. *Illustrated London News,* November 28, 1863. The crux of the problem was the seventh section, which stated that if any person "shall equip, furnish, fit out or arm or endeavour to equip, furnish, fit out or arm, or procure to be equipped, furnished, fitted out or armed, or shall knowingly aid or assist, or be concerned in, the equipping, furnishing, fitting out or arming, of any ship or vessel with intent or in order that such ship or vessel shall be employed in the service of any Foreign prince . . . [such person shall be deemed guilty of a misdemeanor]." Cited in W. D. Jones, *Confederate Rams,* pp. 18–19, with addition from FO 5/1052 in the PRO.

2. Liverpool *Daily Courier,* November 19, 1863.

3. *FR: 1862–63,* Pt. I, 207, Russell-Adams, April 2, 1863.

4. FO 5/1048, Edwards-Goulburn, April 5, 1863.

5. *FR: 1862–63,* Pt. I, 141–42, Seward-Adams, March 9, 1863.

6. FO 5/1048, Dudley-Edwards, March 28, 1863.

7. FO 5/1048, Adams-Russell, March 30, 1863.

8. FO 5/1048, Edwards-Foreign Office, March 28, 1863; Gardner-Peel, March 30, 1863; even after the seizure, the collector of customs at Liverpool remained doubtful of the government's right to detain the vessel; Edwards-Goulburn, April 5, 1863.

9. FO 83/2217, Law Office-Foreign Office, Memorandum on the *Alexandra;* FO 5/1048, April 4, 1863.

10. FO 5/1048, Adams-Russell, April 6, 1863; *FR: 1862–63,* Pt. I, 202.

11. Russell Papers, PRO 30/22/37, Lyons-Russell, April 24, 1863; Southampton *Times,* April 11, 1863; W. D. Jones, *Confederate Rams,* pp. 44–45.

12. Liverpool *Daily Courier,* April 8, 1863.

13. Moran, *Journal,* II, 1170–71.

14. *ORN*, Ser. II, Vol. II, 433–34, North Mallory, June 6, 1863; the remark about the injurious enforcement of the Enlistment Act is in ibid., p. 423, Bulloch-Mallory, May 16, 1863; Bulloch told Mallory about the interruptions, delays, and petitions, pp. 487–89, Bulloch-Mallory, September 1, 1863.

15. Ibid., 440–42, Mallory-Bulloch, June 19, 1863, quote on 441.

16. *FR: 1862–63*, Pt. I, p. 282.

17. Ibid., p. 295. For the speech to which Cairns referred see *Hansard Parliamentary Debates*, 3rd ser., CLXX, cols. 43–59.

18. *FR: 1862–63*, Pt. I, 295.

19. Ibid., p. 299.

20. Ibid., pp. 299–300.

21. Liverpool *Mercury*, June 26, 1863.

22. Liverpool *Daily Courier*, June 26, 1863.

23. *North British Daily Mail*, June 26, 1863; comment from the *Daily News* was extracted in ibid. For a poetical commentary on the trial see Liverpool *Daily Post*, July 24, 1863:

> At Liverpool is lying now
> A certain little boat
> Which, though not finished yet
> Has caused more stir than most afloat
> We question if the Warrior
> Or any huge three-decker
> Could make one-half the noise that she
> Produced in the Exchequer

24. London *Morning Post*, August 10, 1863, quoted in C. F. Adams, Jr., *Seward and the Declaration of Paris* (Boston, 1912), p. 52

25. London *Times*, June 25, 1863. See also Horace White, *'Fossets': A Record of Two Centuries of Engineering* (Bromborough, Cheshire, England, 1958), especially Chapter Fifteen. (This is a history of Fawcett, Preston, and Company.) For the reaction of the London *Economist* see Owsley, *King Cotton*, pp. 407–408. See also *Illustrated London News*, November 28, 1863, for a fair-minded assessment of the case and its consequences.

26. Southampton *Times*, June 27, 1863.

27. Moran, *Journal*, II, 1177.

28. *FR: 1862–63*, Pt. I, 279.

29. CFA, Diary, June 24, 1863.

30. The statement about the Polish crisis is in W. D. Jones, *Confederate Rams*, p. 55; this entire book is required reading for students of the British response to the war. For Roundell Palmer's version of the

complexity of the case and the tortured evolution of legal opinion toward the war in America, see his *Memorials: Part One, Family and Personal* (London, 1896), II, 411 and *passim*. See also Owsley, *King Cotton*, pp. 403, 409, and *passim*.

31. FO 97/47, Law Office-Foreign Office, June 30, 1862, cited in Jones, *Confederate Rams*, pp. 36–37.

32. *Hansard Parliamentary Debates*, 3rd ser., CLXX, cols. 91–93. See *FR: 1863*, Pt. I, 164–82.

33. The sentence with italics is from Rupert C. Jarvis, "The Alabama and the Law," *Transactions of the Historic Society of Lancashire and Cheshire* (October, 1959), CXI, 193–94; the solicitor general's speech is in *Hansard Parliamentary Debates*, 3rd ser., CLXX, cols, 43–59.

34. Jarvis, "Alabama and the Law," *passim*.

35. *FR: 1862–63*, Pt. I, 89–91, Russell-Adams, January 24, 1863; ibid., pp. 33–37, Russell-Adams, December 19, 1862.

36. Russell-Lyons, April 7, 1863; cited in E. D. Adams, *Britain and the Civil War*, II, 135–36; W. D. Jones, *Confederate Rams*, pp. 71–72, citing Russell-Palmerston, September 3, 1863.

37. Russell Papers, PRO 30/22/22, Palmerston-Russell, August 23, 1863; *FR: 1863*, Pt. I, 182; W. D. Jones, *Confederate Rams*, pp. 49–51.

CHAPTER NINE

1. *ORN*, Ser. II, Vol. II, 131, Mallory-Bulloch, January 14, 1862.

2. Ibid., pp. 344–46, Bulloch-Mallory, January 23, 1863; see also Bulloch, *Secret Service*, I, 394–95.

3. *ORN*, Ser. II, Vol. II, 184, Bulloch-Mallory, April 11, 1862; Bulloch, *Secret Service*, I, 382–83.

4. *ORN*, Ser. II, Vol. II, 222–26, Bulloch-Mallory, July 21, 1862.

5. Ibid., pp. 51–69, Report of the [Confederate] Secretary of the Navy, April 26, 1861, especially p. 51.

6. Herbert W. Wilson, *Ironclads in Action*, 2 vols. (London, 1896), I, 220; E. D. Adams, *Britain and the Civil War*, II, 122. A sailor present at the launching of one of these vessels described its unique feature as an immensely strong "prolongation" of the ship, six or seven feet long, which would remain two or three feet below the surface when in motion. PRO, HO 45/7261, Box 2.

7. *ORN*, Ser. II, Vol. II, 222–26, Bulloch-Mallory, July 21, 1862. By concentrating his work in one yard, Bulloch hoped to save about £1,200 per ship, and by keeping his business "as little extended as possible" he hoped to decrease Union interest in his work.

8. Bulloch, *Secret Service*, I, 386. The subsequent release of the rams

to Bravay and a report from the British naval attaché at Paris suggest that the Laird firm knew of Bulloch's "official" connections: PRO 45/7261, Box 2; see also FO 5/1000, Hore-Grey, September 22, 1863.

9. Bulloch, *Secret Service*, I, 385–90 and 96–98.

10. Ibid., p. 389.

11. Ibid., II, 252; See also Van Doren Stern, *When the Guns Roared*, pp. 197–206.

12. *ORN*, Ser. II, Vol. II, 274–77, Bulloch-Mallory, September 24, 1862.

13. Liverpool *Mercury*, February 11, 1863; for conditions at Birkenhead see *Secret Service*, I, 391.

14. Details of the French naval venture may be found in: Bigelow, *France and the Confederate Navy;* Beckles Willson, *John Slidell and the Confederates in Paris* (New York, 1932); Van Doren Stern, *Confederate Navy;* Louis Sears, *John Slidell* (Durham, N. C., 1925); *ORN*, Ser. II, Vol. II, 395–96, Mallory-Slidell, March 27, 1863. For a thorough, up-to-date analysis of the French reaction to the war see Lynn M. Case and Warren F. Spencer, *The United States and France: Civil War Diplomacy* (Philadelphia, Pa., 1970); Chapter Twelve, "Confederate Naval Construction in France," is based on wide-ranging archival material, including that in the Archives de la Marine in Paris. Professor Spencer has published "Drouyn de Lhuys et les navires confédérés en France. L'Affaire des navires d' Arman," *Revue d' histoire diplomatique*, LXX (Nov.–Dec., 1963), 314–41. The author would like to thank Professors Case and Spencer for their generous cooperation in discussing the details of the French response to the war.

15. Bulloch, *Secret Service*, II, 20–25, especially p. 22; for a copy of the French proclamation see Bigelow, *France and the Confederate Navy*, pp. 20–22 (1968 edition).

16. *ORN*, Ser. II, Vol. III, 337, Slidell-Hunter, February 11, 1862.

17. Ibid., p. 347, Slidell-Hunter, February 26, 1862.

18. The letter announcing the British interpretation of the blockade —and one must stress that even though the move was largely dictated by self-interest, it was indulgent toward the North—is cited in E. D. Adams, *Britain and the Civil War*, I, 263; the Confederate announcement of the emperor's concurrence is in *ORN*, Ser. II, Vol. III, 372, Slidell-Hunter, March 26, 1862.

19. *ORN*, Ser. II, Vol. III, 372, Slidell-Hunter, March 26, 1862.

20. Ibid., pp. 393–95, Memorandum of Dispatch No. 5 (interview of W. S. Lindsay with Louis Napoleon, April 11, 1862) ; comments about the Declaration of Paris and the lack of British cooperation are on p. 393.

21. Ibid., pp. 397–98, Mason-Benjamin, April 21, 1862.

22. Ibid., pp. 395–96, Slidell-Benjamin, April 18, 1862.

23. Ibid., pp. 395–96, Slidell-Benjamin, April 18, 1862; see also E. D. Adams, *Britain and the Civil War*, I, 289–97. For the mid-summer interview with the emperor see *ORN*, Ser. II, Vol. III, 481–87, Slidell-Benjamin, July 25, 1862: "I left him with the decided impression that if England long persevered in obstinate inaction, he would take the responsibility of moving by himself" (p. 487).

24. *ORN*, Ser. II, Vol. III, 574–78, Memorandum of an Interview of Mr. Slidell with the Emperor at St. Cloud on Tuesday, October 28, 1862: Slidell said "that if the Emperor would give only some kind of verbal assurance that his police would not observe too closely when we wished to put on board guns and men we would gladly avail ourselves of it" (p. 577). Slidell reported the emperor's reluctance in his note to Benjamin, pp. 638–39, Slidell-Benjamin, January 11, 1863.

25. *ORN*, Ser. II, Vol. III, 639, Slidell-Benjamin, January 11, 1863.

26. Ibid., pp. 705–707, Slidell-Benjamin, March 4, 1863.

27. Bulloch, *Secret Service*, II, 23–39, quotations on p. 39; see also *ORN*, Ser. II, Vol. II, 524–27 (especially p. 526), Bulloch-Mallory, November 26, 1863. Notice of the signing of the preliminary contract for the corvettes is in *ORN*, Ser. II, Vol. III, 742, Slidell–Benjamin, April 20, 1863. Later, when the arrangements in France were proving something less than satisfactory, Bulloch told Mallory that the affair was one of simple deception: "I never should have entered into such large undertakings except with the assurance of success. I was, not individually, but as an agent of the Confederate States, invited to build ships of war in France, and so far at least as the corvettes are concerned received every possible assurance that they might be actually armed in the ports of construction." *ORN*, Ser. II, Vol. II, 588–90, Bulloch-Mallory, February 18, 1864. Further details of the French venture may be found on pp. 665–68, Bulloch-Mallory, June 10, 1864; pp. 689–91, Bulloch-Mallory, July 27, 1864; pp. 697–98, Bulloch-Mallory, August 5, 1864. See also *ORN*, Ser. II, Vol. III, 1028–30, Slidell-Mason, February 16, 1864; and pp. 810–14, Slidell-Benjamin, June 21, 1863; enclosing a Memorandum of an Interview with the Emperor at the Tuileries, Thursday, 18th June, 1863.

28. The attitude of Richmond officials toward the plan and the motive of the Confederate Congress are referred to in *ORN*, Ser. II, Vol. II, 416–17, Mallory-Bulloch, May 6, 1863, enclosing a copy of the act of congress. The ship's specifications may be found in the Arman-Bulloch contract, July 16, 1863, pp. 464–66.

29. *ORN*, Ser. II, Vol. II, p. 445, Bulloch-Mallory, June 30, 1863; Bulloch, *Secret Service*, I, 400 and *passim*. For a copy of the Laird-Bul-

loch-Bravay transfer, see FO 5/1000 in PRO. See also *ORN*, Ser. II, Vol. II, 375–76, Mallory-Bulloch, March 19, 1863.

30. *ORN*, Ser. II, Vol. II, 445, Bulloch-Mallory, June 30, 1863; Bulloch, *Secret Service*, I, 401.

31. *ORN*, Ser. II, Vol. II, 446, Bulloch-Mallory, June 30, 1863; Bulloch, *Secret Service*, I, 400. See also W. D. Jones, *Confederate Rams*, *passim*, especially p. 55 for comment on options open to Her Majesty's government in summer of 1863.

32. *ORN*, Ser. II, Vol. II, 507–11, Bulloch-Mallory, October 20, 1863; Bulloch, *Secret Service*, I, 417.

33. W. D. Jones, *Confederate Rams*, p. 58.

CHAPTER TEN

1. Southampton *Times*, June 27, 1863; London *Times*, August 28 and September 3, 1863; *Hansard*, 3rd ser., CLXX, Cols. 730–34; Owsley, *King Cotton*, pp. 412–14; W. D. Jones, *Confederate Rams*, pp. 54–58.

2. HO 45/7261, Dudley-Edwards, July 7, 1863.

3. Moran, *Journal*, II, 1182; CFA, Diary, July 8, 9, 10, 1863.

4. FO 5/1000, Adams-Russell, July 11, 1863; *FR: 1862–63*, Pt. I, pp. 314–15.

5. *FR: 1862–63*, Pt. I, 316, Russell-Adams, July 13, 1863.

6. FO 5/1000, Hamel-FO, July 9, 1863.

7. HO 45/7261, LO-HO, July 24, 1863.

8. The quoted portion of the statement about Adams' reluctance to see things the British way is taken from FO 5/1000, Russell-Adams, September 11, 1863; the views of Henry Adams are in Ford, ed. *Cycle*, II, 80–81, Henry Adams-Charles Francis Adams, Jr., September 16, 1863.

9. FO 5/1000, Cowley-Russell, August 24, 1863.

10. NA, Consular Dispatches, Belgium, VI, Sanford-Seward, June 23, 1863.

11. Moran, *Journal*, II, 1199.

12. *FR: 1862–63*, Pt. I, 362–63, Russell-Adams, September 1, 1863.

13. Liverpool *Mercury*, September 5, 1863; see also W. D. Jones, *Confederate Rams*, p. 69.

14. *FR: 1862–63*, Pt. I, 361, Adams-Russell, September 4, 1863; CFA, Diary, September 1–5, 1863 and *passim*. The rams, of course, had been promised for delivery in the spring, but a host of delays had impeded progress. For one thing, not all the difficulties inherent in the new techniques of naval construction had been overcome. Bending the armor plate to the curvature of the ship proved a tedious and time-consuming job. "The whole character of the work," as Bulloch informed Mallory,

was new, and builders were therefore unable to make close calculations of completion time; and riveting, "the most important part of the work," required far more time than anticipated. Other elements of delay were the political uncertainty surrounding the *Alexandra* affair and the financial messiness of the Erlanger transaction. Then, too, as Bulloch reported, the transfer to Bravay "created additional delay in finishing the ships." Under these handicaps, it was a wonder that the Laird firm finished the ships at all. See *ORN*, Ser. II, Vol. II 351–52, Bulloch-Mallory, February 3, 1863 and ibid., pp. 444–47, Bulloch-Mallory, June 30, 1863.

15. *FR: 1862–63*, Pt. I, 367–68, Adams-Russell, September 5, 1863; FO 5/1000, Adams-Russell, September 5, 1863.

16. As has been noted many times, the decision to detain the rams was carefully thought out before Adams' famous note of the fifth arrived at the Foreign Office. The PRO files show that at least three drafts of the September 1 directive to the Home Office were made. One reads: "that if any person can be found to declare that he has reason to believe that they [the rams] are intended for the Confederate States of America, Lord Russell thinks the vessels ought to be detained. . . " (HO 45/7261). In FO 5/929 there is another version of the draft with Russell's corrections inserted.

17. FO 5/1000, Russell-Layard, September 3, 1863.

18. Ibid., September 4, 1863. The quotation concerning the possibility of a "legal rebuff" is in Duberman, *Charles Francis Adams*, p. 313.

19. Palmer, *Memorials*, 11, 448. The best account of efforts to build a British case is in W. D. Jones, *Confederate Rams, passim*, especially Chapter Four.

20. Cited in W. D.. Jones, *Confederate Rams*, pp. 71–72, Russell-Palmerston, September 3, 1863. Many officials recognized that detention remained a risky business at best; few could convince themselves of the legality of the move. A larger dimension of the problem was touched on by Robert Cecil, a pro-Southern Conservative, who warned of the danger of arming the government with a new power which might be "good or bad" in itself, but which surely was an "enormous change" in the usual relation between the citizen and the executive; a change, moreover, introduced by "sheer usurpation," and which might be an illegal "breach" of the Constitution. W. D. Jones, "British Conservatives and the American Civil War," *AHR* (1953), *passim*.

21. FO 5/1000, Stuart-Russell, September 8, 1863.

22. For the views of Waddington see HO 34/17, Waddington-Layard, September 4, 1863; Palmerston's statements are in Russell Papers, PRO

30/22/22, Palmerston-Russell, September 4, 1863 and PRO 30/22/14, Palmerston-Russell, October 2, 1863. The prime minister's point was essentially the same as that made in August, 1862, at the trial of the *Florida*, and it was at the crux of the perplexing problem faced by the Crown's legal advisers. It was also the point that Americans had the most difficulty in understanding or conceding.

23. Russell Papers, PRO 30/22/26, Argyll-Russell, September 5, 1863.

24. Ibid., PRO 30/22/14, Law Office-Foreign Office, September 12, 1863. Legal advisers argued that *if* Section 150 of the Customs Act had been extended to warships, it might have provided an opportunity for avoiding some of the difficulties that arose from the "necessity of obtaining legal proof of the purpose and intent with which a vessel is equipped and fitted out."

25. FO 5/1000, Russell-Adams, September 11, 1863; *FR: 1862–63*, Pt. I, 372–74, Russell-Adams; September 11, 1863.

26. FO 5/1000, Adams-Russell, September 16, 1863; *FR: 1862–63*, Pt. I, 374–78, Adams-Russell, September 16, 1863. On September 8, Adams told Seward: ". . . it is not my disposition to say or do the least thing that may add to the difficulties inevitably growing out of it [the rams affair] between the two countries. Considering the grave nature of the issue, I have thought it wiser not to give any handle to the pretence that resort to intimidation had been attempted" (ibid., p. 367). On September 29, Adams told Russell that he (Adams) was "at a loss" to understand what parts of his correspondence could lead to Russell's charge of an intention to intimate "hostile proceedings towards Great Britain"; Adams expressed a hope that it was unnecessary to remind Russell "of the earnestness with which I have ever striven to maintain to the utmost of my power the relations of amity and good will between the two countries" (ibid., p. 385).

27. FO 5/1000, Russell-Adams, September 25, 1863. This note is marked "seen by Lord Palmerston and the Queen," and it bears a notation, possibly Victoria's: "I have read the letter of 5th with great regret."

28. Russell Papers, PRO 30/22/22, Palmerston-Russell, Sept. 22, 1863.

29. FO 5/1000, Russell Memorandum to the Cabinet on the Rams, September 12, 1863.

30. See W. D. Jones, *Confederate Rams*, p. 50, citing Russell Papers, PRO 30/22/22, Palmerston-Russell, August 23, 1863.

31. FO 5/1000, Russell Memo, September 12, 1863.

32. FO 5/1001, FO-Treasury, September 21, 1863.

33. Ibid., HO-FO, September 23, 1863; Admiralty-FO, September 19, 1863; FO-Treasury, September, 1863.

34. FO 5/1000, FO-Treasury and Admiralty-Inglefield, October 8, 1863.

35. Hamilton's statement is quoted from FO 5/1001, Treasury-FO, October 10, 1863; that of Hammond from W. D. Jones, *Confederate Rams*, pp. 92–95, quotation on p. 94. Jones is, of course, citing the Foreign Office Records in the PRO.

36. Russell Papers, PRO 30/22/26, Argyll-Russell, October 17, 1863.

37. *Ibid.*, PRO 30/22/37, Monck-Stuart, September 26, 1863.

38. CFA, Diary, September 8, 1863.

39. Ford, ed., *Cycle*, II, 79–84, Henry Adams-C. F. Adams, Jr., September 16, 1863.

40. FO 5/1000, Adams-Russell, October 12, 1863.

41. Russell Papers, PRO 30/22/37, Stuart-Russell, October 6, 1863; Lyons-Russell, October 16, 1863.

42. *ORN*, Ser. II, Vol. II 502, Bulloch-Mallory, October 1, 1863; pp. 507–11, Bulloch-Mallory, October 20, 1863, and pp. 583–86, Bulloch-Mallory, February 17, 1864.

43. FO 5/1000, FO-Treasury, October 9, 1863; Edwards-Laird, October 27, 1863; Morgan-Bravay, October 29, 1863.

44. FO 5/1002, Russell-Hammond, October 29, 1863.

45. *ORN*, Ser. II, Vol. II, 583–86, Bulloch-Mallory, February 17, 1864. Bulloch, *Secret Service*, I, 429.

46. For Napoleon's domestic troubles with Confederate shipbuilding, see H. C. Owsley, "Sanford and Federal Surveillance," *MVHR* (1961), 211–28, especially pp. 224–26.

47. Russell Papers, PRO 30/22/14, Palmerston-Russell, September 13, 1863; FO/1002, FO-Treasury, December 11, 1863.

48. FO 5/1002, Admiralty-Controller of the Navy, November 6, 1863; Liverpool *Courier*, November 9, 1863; Russell Papers, PRO 30/22/26, Somerset-Russell, February 18, 1864, and March 22, 1864. The quotation about the law suit and the valuation is taken from Bulloch, *Secret Service*, I, 440; for the statement about the fairness of the Admiralty's appraisal see p. 442. Bulloch estimated that the government paid about £ 30,000 over the original contract price; he further stated that at the time of detention (September, 1863) the Navy Department's foreign expenditures were more than £ 700,000 in excess of its resources. See pp. 442–43.

49. For a contrary view, argued with much persuasiveness, see W. D. Jones, *Confederate Rams*, pp. 96–97.

50. Bulloch, *Secret Service*, I, 432; see also *ORN*, Ser. II, Vol. II, Bulloch-Mallory, February 17, 1864.

51. Ford, ed., *Cycle*, II, 82–84, Henry Adams-C. F. Adams, Jr., September 16, 1864.

52. The quoted material in this paragraph is from W. D. Jones, *Confederate Rams*, p. 15.

53. The author would like to acknowledge that the idea for this epilogue was suggested by W. D. Jones, who appended a speculative chapter, "Had the Rams Escaped," to his study of the *Confederates Rams*. The documentary evidence for the epilogue was uncovered by the late T. W. Green of Southampton, England.

54. Van Doren Stern, *Confederate Navy*, p. 223. For an extended treatment of the *Stonewall's* story see Bulloch, *Secret Service*, II, 73–103.

55. Stern, *Confederate Navy*, p. 223.

56. Ibid., p. 246.

57. *Illustrated London News*, October 27, 1866, cited in W. D. Jones, *Confederate Rams*, p. 118.

58. Oscar Parkes, *British Battleships "Warrior" 1860 to "Vanguard" 1950: A History of Design, Construction and Armament*, rev. ed. (London, 1966), p. 80.

59. W. D. Jones, *Confederate Rams*, p. 119.

60. C. S. Williams and F. J. Merli, eds. and trans., "The Normandie Shows the Way," *Mariner's Mirror*, LIV (May, 1968), 153–62.

61. Parkes, *British Battleships*, pp. 189-90.

62. W. D. Jones, *Confederate Rams*, p. 119.

63. Thomas A. Bailey, *A Diplomatic History of the American People* (New York, 1940 *et. seq.* eds.) , pp. 372–73 (5th ed., 1955) .

64. Institution of Naval Architects [U. K.], *Transactions of the Institution of Naval Architects*, VI (London, 1865), p. 91. There is a résumé of Reed's career and professional qualifications in Parkes, *British Battleships*, pp. 82–83.

CHAPTER ELEVEN

1. Reports on the ship's condition may be found in FO 5/1052, *passim*, especially Adm-FO, October 24, 1863. The Admiralty accepted Coleman's offer in mid-September, but did not release the ship from royal service until the following month; see Adm-Superintendent Sheerness Dockyard, November 2, 1863.

2. FO 5/1052, Bernard-Treasury, December 2, 1863, forwarding the results of his investigation and the report of Coast Officer Todhunter, who had searched the ship just before its departure.

3. FO 5/1052, Adams-Russell, November 29, 1863 and December 16, 18, 1863.

4. FO 5/1052, Adm-FO, November 19, 1863; January 25, 1864.

5. Ibid., Adm-FO, February 28, 1865. For a convenient report on the Rumble trial see *FR: 1865,* Pt. I, 141–59. Other references to the legal aspects of activity at Sheerness may be found in PRO, HO 45/7261, Boxes 3 and 5.

6. The reader may remember that it was in the fall of 1863 that American representatives uncovered the connection between Arman and Bulloch and as a consequence stepped up their counter-Confederate pressure on French officials. It may also be noted that when Minister Dayton died in December, 1864, his work was continued with great skill and perseverance by John Bigelow. Bigelow's papers in the New York Public Library contain many fascinating references to this activity; in addition, he has told the story well in his own *France and the Confederate Navy,* and he has been the subject of a very fine biography, Margaret Clapp, *Forgotten First Citizen: John Bigelow* (Boston, 1947). For Seward's reaction to Confederate construction in France see, for example, *FR: 1863,* Pt. II, 734, Seward-Dayton, November 21, 1863 and *FR: 1865,* Pt. II, 230–31, Seward-Bigelow, February 21, 1865. See also Bigelow, *France and the Confederate Navy,* p. 34 and *passim.*

7. *ORN,* Ser. II, Vol. II, 517, 566–67. Barron-Mallory, November 10, December 15, 1863.

8. Ibid., pp. 583–86, Bulloch-Mallory, February 17, 1864.

9. Ibid., p. 585.'

10. Ibid., pp. 571–72, Barron-Russell, January 11, 1864.

11. *ORN,* Ser. II, Vol. III, 1037–40, especially Gosselin-Lt. W. P. A. Campbell, February 4, 10, 1864. See also FO 5/1052, Cowley-Russell, June 17, 1864.

12. *ORN,* Ser. II, Vol. III, 1037, Barron-Slidell, February 25, 1864; pp. 1037–45, *passim.*

13. Ibid., pp. 1040–42, Slidell-deLhuys, February 26, 1864; pp. 1055–56, Slidell-Mocquard, March 15, 1864.

14. FO 5/1052, Report of N. Treite, April 11, 1864.

15. *ORN,* Ser. II, Vol. II, 696–97, Barron-Mallory, August 2, 1864.

16. Ibid., p. 697 for Barron's comments about the change in attitude (which he attributed to the North's Mexican policy); Bulloch's statement may be found in pp. 697–98, Bulloch-Mallory, August 5, 1864.

17. *ORN,* Ser. II, Vol. III, 1212–15, Benjamin-Slidell, September 20, 1864. This dispatch is a bitter indictment of French policy toward the Confederacy.

18. Ibid., p. 1139, Slidell-Benjamin, June 2, 1864.

19. Benjamin's comment about Davis' indignation appears in ibid., pp. 1156–57, Benjamin-Slidell, June 23, 1864; Slidell's account of his

conversation with a French official and the "significant smile" is in pp.
1159–62, Slidell-Benjamin, June 30, 1864—another dispatch with fascinating overtones. For details of the sale and transfer of registry see
FO 5/1052, pp. 397–99, 405, 411. Slidell's caustic, concise, and correct
summary of the affair is in *ORN*, Ser. II, Vol. III, 1063–65, Slidell-
Benjamin, March 16, 1864; the quote about the series of blunders is
on p. 1065. See also *ORN*, Ser. II, Vol. II, 696–97, Barron-Mallory,
August 2, 1864 and Bulloch, *Secret Service*, II, 267–70. See also the
William Whittle Papers at the Norfolk Public Library, Norfolk, Va.,
for some additional comments by Bulloch on the affair.

20. Bulloch's account of the *Shenandoah* is in his *Secret Service*, II,
125–75. The author was privileged to see the Diary and Letterbooks of
Alexander Stephen in the company's archives in Glasgow, Scotland.
These contain many references to the ship and its career; in addition
officials of Alexander Stephen and Sons, Ltd., explained the details of
its construction, and furnished plans and photos. See also *North British
Daily Mail*, August 18, 1863 and Carvel, *Stephen of Linthouse*, pp.
45–46. For Bulloch's opinion of Carter see his *Secret Service*, II, 82–83;
Carter was "the most scrupulously loyal man" Bulloch ever knew.

21. Geneva Arbitration Tribunal, *The Case of the United States to
be laid before the Tribunal of Arbitration to be convened at Geneva
. . .* (London, 1872), pp. 416–54 and 293–96 for a summary of the U.S.
position on the *Shenandoah*. The statements of Adams and Seward are
in *FR: 1864*, Pt. II, 351–52, Adams-Russell, November 10, 1864 and p.
367, Seward-Adams, December 3, 1864. A convenient compilation of
papers on the cruiser may be found in U.S., Congress, House, 39th
Cong., 1st sess., Executive Document 36, *Message from the President of
the United States in Answer to a Resolution of the House of Representatives of the 8th Instant, Relative to the Reported Surrender of the
Rebel Pirate Shenandoah* (dated January 26, 1866 and printed as a
pamphlet). See also Moran, *Journal*, II, *passim*, especially p. 1337.

22. *ORN*, Ser. II, Vol. II, 687–88, Mallory-Bulloch, July 18, 1864;
pp. 707–708, Mallory-Bulloch, August 19, 1864; pp. 723–25, Bulloch-
Mallory, September 16, 1864; pp. 736–37, Bulloch-Mallory, October 20,
1864.

23. Details of the construction and launch of the *Sea King* are in the
Diary of Alexander Stephen. See also Carvel, *Stephen of Linthouse*, pp.
45–46 and Bulloch, *Secret Service*, II, 131–34.

24. *ORN*, Ser. II, Vol. II, 731–32, Bulloch-Whittle, October 6, 1864;
the story of the melodramatic rendezvous is repeated in William C.
Whittle, "The Cruise of the Shenandoah," *Southern Historical Society
Papers*, XXXV (1907), 235–58, especially p. 241.

25. *ORN,* Ser. II, Vol. II, 733–34, Bulloch-Ramsay, October 8, 1864 for details of the *Laurel;* the quotation about passengers and freight is from Bulloch, *Secret Service,* II, 129; details of the raider's armament are in *ORN,* Ser. II, Vol. II, 736, Bulloch-Mallory, October 20, 1864. See also Van Doren Stern, *Confederate Navy,* pp. 250–51 and Cornelius Hunt, *The Shenandoah* (New York, 1867), *passim.*

26. Nearly all who wrote of the cruise from personal recollection mentioned the difficulty of recruitment at the outset of the voyage. Hunt, for example, noted that Waddell's recruiting effort was singularly unproductive. Whittle later remembered that the total initial complement was less than fifty of the nearly 150 men needed for efficient operation and that almost one-half of the early volunteers were officers. See Hunt, *Shenandoah, passim* and Whittle, "Cruise of the Shenandoah," p. 243. Bulloch mentions the problem in *Secret Service,* II, 143–45.

27. James I. Waddell, *C.S.S. Shenandoah: The Memoirs of Lieutenant Commanding James I. Waddell,* ed., James D. Horan (New York, 1960), p. 82 for the order to damage enemy commerce as quickly as possible and *passim* for details of the voyage. It is a great pity that so valuable a source should have been published with so worthless an introduction. The origin of the plan to use this raider against the whaling fleet is uncertain, but Lt. Whittle, executive officer on the raider, gave the lion's share of credit to Bulloch's assistant, Lt. Robert Carter, as one of its earliest and most ardent advocates. On August 10, 1864, Mallory told Bulloch that the "enemy's distant whaling grounds have not been visited by us," and implied that they ought to be. Some nine days later the naval secretary acknowledged that conversations with Lt. Carter and others had "confirmed my opinions of the importance of the subject [operations against the whale trade]." See *ORN,* Ser. II, Vol. II, 701, Mallory-Bulloch, August 10, 1864 and pp. 707–708, Mallory-Bulloch, August 19, 1864.

28. Log Book of the C.S.S. *Shenandoah* on deposit at the Chicago Historical Society Library, Chicago, Illinois, various dates.

29. Van Doren Stern, *Confederate Navy,* p. 253; for variant figures, see Whittle, "Cruise of the Shenandoah," p. 257. A list of prizes captured by the cruiser may be found in Hunt, *Shenandoah,* pp. 272–73 and in Waddell, *Memoirs,* pp. 196–98.

30. After the war a number of the crew of the last cruiser published accounts of the voyage. Cornelius Hunt was one of the first to bring its story to the public. He claimed that nothing like a rebellious spirit was ever shown by any of the officers, though there apparently were some strong differences of opinion about the proper destination of the ship

after news of Appomattox reached it. Details of the cruise, from various points of view, are set out in the following: Hunt, *Shenandoah* (which, whatever its defects may be, has at least the freshness of memory to recommend it); Waddell, *Memoir*, written when its author was a very old man, many years after the war; Whittle, "Cruise of the Shenandoah"; Charles Lining, "The Cruise of the Confederate Steamship Shenandoah," *Tennessee Historical Magazine*, VII (1924), 102–11; John T. Mason, "Last of the Confederate Cruisers," *Century Magazine*, LVI (1898), 600–10; John Grimball, "Career of the Shenandoah," *Southern Historical Society Papers*, XXV (1897), 116–30.

31. PRO, HO 45/7261, Haywood-FO, November 6, 1865.

32. Ibid., Adm-HO, November 10, 1865 and Paynter-Adm, November 12, 1865. For a statement of the inconvenience of the vessel to British officialdom see Russell Papers, PRO 30/22/26, Somerset-Russell, October 13, 1865. Adams reported that the new foreign secretary, Lord Clarendon, was "incredulous" at the news of the vessel's arrival at a British port; and he also told Seward that he (Adams) was attempting to maneuver the British into declaring an official reason for detention of the ship, "without committing us to it in any manner"—or in the parlance of the present, he was trying to keep his options open. For a résumé of the early correspondence see U.S., Congress, *House Executive Document 36*, pp. 1–25.

33. Van Doren Stern, *Confederate Navy*, pp. 252–53; Hunt made some nasty charges about Waddell's honesty, but these have been questioned by Horan in his edition of Waddell's memoirs. One might mention at this point that Bulloch makes no such accusation against Waddell. See Bulloch, *Secret Service*, II, *passim;* Hunt, *Shenandoah*, especially pp. 261–63; and Waddell, *Memoirs*, p. 183.

CHAPTER TWELVE

1. *ORN*, Ser. II, Vol. II, 441, Bulloch-Mallory, June 19, 1863; for the role of Colin McRae in the formulation and execution of this plan see C. S. Davis, *Colin McRae, passim,* especially Chapter Four.

2. Thomas E. Taylor, *Running the Blockade: A Personal Narrative of Adventures, Risks, and Escapes During the American Civil War* (London, 1896). Augustus C. Hobart-Hampden, *Sketches From My Life* (New York, 1882). The Diary of Alexander Stephen contains numerous references to the beneficial economic impact of building the runners. Figures vary, but all agree that the trade was a most profitable enterprise; the above precentage is in Robert Carse, *Blockade: The Civil War at Sea* (New York, 1958), p. 44. Taylor estimated that one of the

runners on which he served made a profit of £85,000; "not," as he said, "bad work for about twenty days." Taylor, *Running the Blockade*, p. 144. For still another convenient set of figures see Van Doren Stern, *Confederate Navy*, p. 63.

3. Hamilton Cochran, *Blockade Runners of the Confederacy*, p. 13.

4. Soley, *Blockade and Cruisers*, pp. 156–57; Cochran, *Blockade Runners*, p. 61; Carse, *Blockade*, p. 168; Diary of Alexander Stephen, *passim*. For an interesting collection of photographs of the runners see the *American Neptune: Pictorial Supplement*, III, *Blockade Runners* (Salem, 1961).

5. Taylor, *Running the Blockade*, p. 67; Cochran, *Blockade Runners*, p. 50.

6. Soley, *Blockade and Cruisers*, p. 154.

7. Van Doren Stern, *Confederate Navy*, p. 63.

8. Soley, *Blockade and Cruisers*, p. 155.

9. Taylor, *Running the Blockade*, p. 144; Soley, *Blockade and Cruisers*, p. 166.

10. Cochran, *Blockade Runners*, pp. 99–121.

11. Note on a painting of the *A.D. Vance* in the Kelvin Grove Museum, Glasgow, Scotland.

12. Soley, *Blockade and Cruisers*, pp. 165–66; Van Doren Stern, *Confederate Navy*, pp. 224–31.

13. Soley, *Blockade and Cruisers*, p. 165; Marcus W. Price, "Masters and Pilots Who Tested the Blockade of the Confederate Ports, 1861–1865," *American Neptune*, XXI (April, 1961), pp. 81–106.

14. Bulloch, *Secret Service*, I, 70–80, quotation on p. 73, citing the court record in *U.S. v S.S. Bermuda and Cargo*, August, 1862.

15. Bulloch, *Secret Service*, I, 74.

16. Ibid., pp. 71–86.

17. Ibid., p. 75.

18. Ibid., p. 80; Taylor, *Running the Blockade*, p. 37.

19. Bulloch, *Secret Service*, I, 115.

20. Ibid., pp. 110–27 *(Fingal* cargo list on p. 112); Van Doren Stern, *Secret Missions of the Civil War* (New York, 1959), pp. 82–92. The "noise in the night" seems to have been a constant in the stories of the runners. See, for example, Carse, *Blockade*, pp. 256–57 and Cochran, *Blockade Runners*, p. 44.

21. Bulloch, *Secret Service*, II, 235–37.

22. Ibid., pp. 235–37; see also *ORN*, Ser. II, Vol. II, 590, Bulloch-Mallory, February 18, 1864.

23. Van Doren Stern, *Confederate Navy*, p. 225; Bulloch, *Secret Service*, II, 235–37.

24. *ORN,* Ser. II, Vol. II, 511–13, Bulloch-Mallory, October 12, 1863; C. S. Davis, *Colin McRae,* pp. 52–60; pp. 441, 574, Mallory-Bulloch, June 19, 1863 and January 16, 1864; p. 590, Bulloch-Mallory, February 18, 1864.

25. PRO, HO 45/7261, Box 1, Law Office Report, April 21, 1863 and PRO, FO 83/2217, April 21, 1863, Law Office Report: "To build ships in British ports and sell them to either belligerent, as an article of commerce, is not . . . an act which infringes the rules of international law; nor is it . . . sufficient to constitute a violation of any British law." Crown legal advisers argued that the responsibility for enforcing the blockade devolved upon the belligerents, not upon neutrals.

26. Bulloch, *Secret Service,* I, 121. While under a British flag the runners had no right to use force; "a single shot," as one of them put it, "turns the blockade-runner into a pirate." Taylor, *Running the Blockade,* p. 11. Of course, another motive for the disinclination to arm the runners was that the recoil from a heavy gun might shake them to pieces. A foreman in charge of repairing one of the vessels reported that it was "so slightly built that if a gun was fired on board . . . it would shake her from stem to stern." FO 5/1098, report of a Liverpool detective, January 21, 1863; for a similar comment see ibid., Freemantle–Treasury, May 22, 1863.

27. Taylor, *Running the Blockade,* pp. 9–10. See also *ORN,* Ser II, Vol. II, 721–22, Bulloch-Mallory, September 15, 1864.

28. Donald, ed., *Why the North Won the Civil War,* pp. 91–112, David M. Potter, "Jefferson Davis and the Political Factors in Confederate Defeat" is a provocative and carefully drawn indictment of Davis' defects as a war leader. For a more favorable estimate of Davis, see Frank Van Diver, "Jefferson Davis and the Confederate State," An Inaugural Lecture Delivered at Oxford University, February 26, 1964. (Printed as a pamphlet, Oxford, 1964.)

29. Henry Blumenthal, *A Reappraisal of Franco-American Relations, 1830–1871* (Chapel Hill, N.C., 1959), p. 159 and *passim.*

30. For the story of Spence's ambivalent relations with the Confederacy see *ORN,* Ser. II, Vol. III, 567, Hotze-Benjamin, October 24, 1862, wherein it is charged that Spence had lately "rendered the idea of ultimate emancipation unduly conspicuous." On October 31, 1863, Hotze returned to the theme of the anomoly of Spence's position—"that he assumed to occupy at one and the same time two opposite and irreconcilable positions—that of a high official of our Government owing it allegiance and that of a disinterested alien friend." Ibid., 947, Hotze-Benjamin, October 31, 1863. "You have perceived with your usual acuteness," Benjamin told Hotze on January 9, 1864, "the exact em-

barrassment under which we labor in dealing with this gentleman [Spence], whose ability and services to our cause are recognized to the fullest extent." Ibid., p. 994, Benjamin-Hotze, January 9, 1864. Benjamin told Spence on January 11, 1864, that the government in Richmond could not be expected to retain agents who were "in avowed and public opposition" to the sentiments and feelings of the Confederacy toward its peculiar institution. Letter cited in Owsley, *King Cotton*, p. 384.

31. Bulloch, *Secret Service*, II, 123–24.

32. Samuel Thompson, *Confederate Purchasing Operations Aboard* (Chapel Hill, N.C., 1935), p. 47 and *passim*.

33. Bulloch, *Secret Service*, I, 107–10; Davis, *Colin McRae*, pp. 49–60; *ORN*, Ser. II, Vol. II, 511–13, Bulloch-Mallory, October 12, 1863, for the profit motive in cotton transactions.

34. Bulloch, *Secret Service*, II, 238–50.

35. *ORN*, Ser. II, Vol. II, pp. 721–22, Bulloch-Mallory, September 15, 1864.

36. Thompson, *Confederate Purchasing*, p. 95; Bulloch, *Secret Service*, II, p. 245.

CHAPTER THIRTEEN

1. Van Doren Stern, *Confederate Navy*, p. 247.

2. Eaton, *Southern Confederacy*, p. 68. This same charge, the folly of relying upon the coercive power of cotton, is vehemently hammered home in Paul Pecquet Du Bellet, *The Diplomacy of the Confederate Cabinet of Richmond and Its Agents Abroad*, ed., Wm. Stanley Hoole (Tuscaloosa, Ala., 1963), *passim*, especially p. 98, where it is charged that the autocratic king had no power but *"to enslave Mr. Davis and Mr. Benjamin to their old and pernicious prejudices."* (italics in the original) and pp. 94–96. In the fall of 1861 Palmerston expressed some surprise at the shortsightedness of the South in foregoing the export of cotton to finance the war. Russell Papers, PRO 30/22/14, Palmerston-Russell, October 18, 1861. On October 4, 1861, Lyons had reported that the South's "principal confidence, the whole Foreign Policy of their Government, was based upon withholding cotton from Europe . . . ." Ibid, PRO 30/22/35, Lyons-Russell, October 4, 1861.

3. Eaton, *Southern Confederacy*, p. 66.

4. Emma M. Maffitt, *The Life and Services of John Newland Maffitt* (New York, 1906) , p. 379 and *passim*. The charge of neglecting the navy is echoed by DuBellet, *Diplomacy of the Confederate Cabinet*, pp. 86–87, where it is charged on the testimony of a "well informed and

trustworthy naval officer that Mr. Davis had, at the outset of the war, *opposed the building of a navy with his supreme influence"* (italics in the original). In June, 1864, Slidell told Benjamin of his growing conviction that when victory was achieved, one of the South's first objectives "should be to lay the foundation of a respectable navy." *ORN,* Ser, II, Vol. III, 1139, Slidell-Benjamin, June 2, 1864.

5. London *Times,* November 13, 1862.

6. *Punch,* October 10, 1863.

7. *Illustrated London News,* November 28, 1863.

8. G. P. Gooch, *Correspondence of Lord Russell,* II, 329.

9. London *Times,* November 13, 1862.

10. Blumenthal, *Reappraisal of Franco-American Relations,* pp. 157–59 and *passim.*

11. At one point during the war Palmerston reminded Russell that it would be illogical to recognize the Confederates while they were unsuccessful in battle, and he decried the common tendency to ignore the vital fact that between recognition of the South and breaking the blockade there was a step "as wide as the distance which separates peace from war." Pam, it should be emphasized again, had no wish to take that step. RA H 51/183, copy of a letter from Palmerston-Russell, September 16, 1863. Palmerston's sense of "high responsibility in the hour of greatest crisis" is frequently overlooked by students of the British response to the American Civil War. (I have borrowed the quoted phrase from Donald Southgate, *'The Most English Minister,'* p. xvii.)

Index

FRANK J. MERLI (1929–2000) was Professor of History at Queens College in the City University of New York. At the time of his death he was writing what amounted to a multi-volume sequel to *Great Britain and the Confederate Navy, 1861–1865*, portions of which are published under the title *The* Alabama, *British Neutrality, and the American Civil War* (Indiana University Press 2004).